THE CORRESPONDENCE OF
THOMAS STEPHENS

Revolutionising Welsh Scholarship in
the Mid-Nineteenth Century through
Knowledge Exchange

CELTIC STUDIES PUBLICATIONS
series editor: John T. Koch

THE CORRESPONDENCE OF THOMAS STEPHENS

Revolutionising Welsh Scholarship in
the Mid-Nineteenth Century through
Knowledge Exchange

Edited, Arranged, and with an
Introduction by
ADAM N. COWARD

CELTIC STUDIES PUBLICATIONS
ABERYSTWYTH
2020

Published by Celtic Studies Publications, Aberystwyth, in 2020.

CSP-Cymru Cyf.
University of Wales Centre for Advanced Welsh and Celtic Studies, National Library of Wales, Penglais, Aberystwyth, Wales, SY23 3HH

1 2 3 4 5 6 7 8 9 10

A catalogue record of this book is available from the British Library.

ISBN: 978-1-891271-30-4

Cover image: A bust of Thomas Stephens by Joseph Edwards (1814–1882), School of Art, Aberyswyth University
Cover design: John Koch

CONTENTS

ACKNOWLEDGEMENTS

THE research which informs this volume was undertaken as part of the project 'Knowledge Transfer and Social Networks: European Learning and the Revolution in Welsh Victorian Scholarship', funded by the Leverhulme Trust, at the University of Wales Centre for Advanced Welsh and Celtic Studies from 2013 to 2015. I would like to begin by thanking the the Centre for Advanced Welsh and Celtic Studies for their support and the Leverhulme Trust whose grant made this research possible.[1] Especial thanks is reserved for Dr Marion Löffler, the Principal Investigator of the 'Knowledge Transfer and Social Networks' project, who envisioned and designed the project of which this anthology of Stephen's correspondence is a product. Dr Löffler's expertise, support, and guidance has greatly informed and strengthened this volume in countless ways. Dr Löffler also offered guidance in the acquisition and transcription of several of the letters in this volume, particularly letters written in Welsh and German. I am further grateful to Dr Ceridwen Lloyd-Morgan who assisted with the transcriptions of the French letters in National Library of Wales MSS 964–5E. I am also grateful to Nely van Seventer who provided translations of several French letters, as well as guidance and corrections to the transcriptions of these letters. I would also like to thank the numerous scholars who offered questions and comments about Stephens's correspondence at conferences and workshops, especially Professor Bill Jones and Joe England, conversations with both of whom helped me to understand Stephens's community and correspondents better.

---

[1] Information about the project can be found on the website of the University of Wales Centre for Advanced Welsh and Celtic Studies, Aberystwyth, under 'Research Projects' (n.d.; accessed 6 August 2018), https://www.wales.ac.uk/en/CentreforAdvancedWelshCelticStudies/ResearchProjects/CurrentProjects/Knowledge-Transfer-and-Social-Networks/IntroductiontotheProject.aspx.

I am also grateful to the assistance of countless archivists and librarians who provided access to Thomas Stephens's correspondence, including the staff at the National Library of Ireland, Glamorgan Archives, and the Royal Irish Academy Library. I am particularly thankful to the staff at the National Library of Wales, whose expertise and patience is especially appreciated, and the Cardiff Central Library Local Studies Collection who allowed me to view items in their collection during difficult circumstances. I am further grateful to Bill Landis at Yale University Library, Gráinne Doran at Wexford County Archive, and Brian McGee at Cork City and County Archive, all of whom made special searches for letters from Thomas Stephens in their collections on my behalf. The assistance of Jane Sellwood and Sian Anthony of Merthyr Tydfil Library in accessing Thomas Stephens's personal library was also greatly appreciated, as was their cooperation throughout the 'Knowledge Transfer and Social Networks' project.

Finally, I would like to thank Professors Jane Aaron and John Koch for their editorial guidance and advice and for agreeing to publish this anthology. I would like to thank Dr Rita Singer especially for her expertise, perspective, encouragement, and, above all, patience.

INTRODUCTION

ADAM N. COWARD

THOMAS Stephens (1821–1875), best-known for his ground-breaking *The Literature of the Kymry* (1849), was a Merthyr Tydfil-based pharmacist who dedicated his limited spare time to the study of Welsh literature and history, competing in local and national eisteddfodau, and to the civic and social improvement of his community and wider Wales. In so doing, he embodied the role of the amateur Welsh scholar and involved himself within the wider scholarly discourse of nineteenth-century Europe. Stephens's writings, in which he combined native knowledge with international scholarship, subjecting accepted narratives about Welsh literature and history to critical and discerning research, earned him a reputation as an able scholar and he was often appealed to for information or opinion. These enquiries came from other Welsh scholars who wished to compare notes and from Welsh editors or publishers soliciting essays for publication, but also from scholars in other nations like Ireland, France, or Germany who were investigating wider questions of Celtic or European history or philology, or else attempting to utilise Welsh examples to further the study of their own history and culture. Stephens also reciprocated this activity, writing to scholars and librarians throughout Wales and the wider world asking for information and assistance. This resulted in a varied and voluminous correspondence—one which provides a viewpoint into nineteenth-century scholarly networks and demonstrates the processes of knowledge acquisition and intellectual development of an amateur scholar writing in a marginalised, minority nation, Arguably, Stephens was Wales's first modern, scientific, as opposed to romantic, historian.

Thomas Stephens, Knowledge Exchange, and Academic Access in Merthyr Tydfil

Stephens was an active member of the Merthyr Tydfil community in which he lived, working for social and civic improvement in the most important centre of industrial development and population growth in Wales. Much of Stephens's concern for truth, critical thought, and social improvement was prompted by his Unitarian religion, as well as by being a member of Merthyr's emergent middle class,[1] a group noted for being socially conscious, active, and sometimes radical.[2] He advocated the

---

[1] Marion Löffler, *The Literary and Historical Legacy of Iolo Morganwg, 1826–1926* (Cardiff: University of Wales Press, 2007), p. 134; Idem. 'Failed Founding Fathers and Abandoned Sources: Edward Williams, Thomas Stephens and the Young J. E. Lloyd', in Neil Evans and Huw Pryce (eds), *Writing a Small Nation's Past: Wales in Comparative Perspective, 1850–1950* (Farnham: Ashgate, 2013), pp. 67–81 (70–71). I am grateful to Dr Löffler for allowing me access to several of her unpublished papers in which she has explored the relationship between Stephens's class, religion, and scholarship further, notably 'Class, Ethnicity, and Religion: The Marginalized Welsh Amateur Scholar before 1875' presented at the international workshop organised by The University of Wales Centre for Advanced Welsh and Celtic Studies on 'The Amateur Historian and Knowledge Exchange in Nineteenth-Century Europe' at the National Library of Wales, Aberystwyth on 24 October 2015.

[2] For Merthyr politics generally, including radicalism, see Chris Evans, *'The Labyrinth of Flames': Work and Social Conflict in Early Industrial Merthyr Tydfil* (Cardiff: University of Wales Press, 1993); Ieuan Gwynedd Jones, 'The Merthyr of Henry Richards', in Glanmor Williams (ed.), *Merthyr Politics: The Making of a Working-Class Tradition* (Cardiff: University of Wales Press, 1966), pp. 28–57; Gwyn A. Williams, 'The Merthyr of Dic Penderyn', in Williams (ed), *Merthyr Politics*, pp. 9–27; Idem, *The Merthyr Rising* (Cardiff: University of Wales Press, 1988); Joe England, *Merthyr: The Crucible of Modern Wales* (Cardigan: Parthian, 2017). For the role of the middle class, see Jones 'Merthyr of Henry Richards', pp. 38–40; Joe England, 'Unitarians, Freemasons, Chartists: The Middle Classes in Victorian Merthyr', *Welsh History Review*, 23: 4 (2007), 35–58; Julie Light, 'The Middle Class as Urban Elites in Nineteenth-Century South

creation of the local health board, on which he served in 1850, and a 'non-Christian' cemetery at Cefn-coed-y-cymmer, in which he was buried. His commitment to community was demonstrated officially—in his role as High Constable in 1858—and unofficially—in his efforts on behalf of industrial workers. This included serving as a middle-man to help negotiate agreements between ironworkers and masters and, as part of his wider charitable activities, raising funds for the families of the victims of the 1862 Gethin pit no. 2 disaster.[3]

In addition to his interest in civic improvement, Stephens contributed to the scholarly life of the town. Stephens had had some formal education prior to moving, at the age of fourteen, to Merthyr from the Vale of Neath as an apprentice to the chemist David Morgan, attending Cefn Rhigos school before studying at John Davies's academy in Neath.[4] Morgan also fostered the young Stephens's academic interests. D. Rhys Phillips thought it likely Stephens 'owed some of his literary training, and the bias of his critical judgment ... to the capable scholar under whom he was

Wales', *Welsh History Review*, 24: 3 (2009), 29–55; England, *Merthyr*, pp. 240–342, esp. pp. 240–257.

[3] NLW, MS. 966C, E. J., 'A Few Notes for the Biography of Thomas Stephens', pp. 6–8, I am grateful to Dr Marion Löffler for providing me with this source; Jones, 'Merthyr of Henry Richards', 39; Margret S. Taylor, 'Thomas Stephens of Merthyr (1821–1875)', *Merthyr Historian*, 2 (1978), 135–141 (137–38); Brinley F. Roberts, 'Welsh Scholarship at Merthyr Tydfil', *Merthyr Historian*, 10 (1999), 51–62 (57–58); B. T. Williams, 'The Life of Thomas Stephens' in Thomas Stephens, *The Literature of the Kymry: Being a Critical Essay on the History of the Language and Literature of Wales During the Twelfth and Succeeding Centuries*, ed. by D. Silvan Evans, second edn (London: Longmans, Green, and Co., 1876), pp. xix–xlviii (xxi, xxxii, xl–xlii); Löffler, *The Literary and Historical Legacy of Iolo Morganwg*, p. 134; Idem. 'Failed Founding Fathers', pp. 73–74; England, *Merthyr*, p. 253.

[4] D. Rhys Phillips, *A Romantic Valley in Wales: The History of the Vale of Neath*, facsimile edn (Llandybïe: West Glamorgan County Archive Service and Neath Borough Council, 1994), p. 569; Roberts, 'Welsh Scholarship at Merthyr', 57; Taylor, 'Thomas Stephens', 135–36; Williams 'Life of Thomas Stephens', p. xx.

apprenticed'.[5] Following Morgan's death in 1841, a twenty-one-year-old Stephens took over the most prosperous pharmacy in town.[6] Stephens was an enthusiastic autodidact. B. T. Williams noted that 'if Stephens was ever missed, he was always found reading; if ever guilty of any neglect or breach of duty, it was traceable to reading.'[7] His correspondence facilitated his further learning. Stephens understood the need for guidance and was not afraid to ask for it. In 1840, he wrote to his old schoolmaster, John Davies, asking for a translation from Homer as well as advice on learning Greek.[8]

Nineteenth-century Merthyr Tydfil was a place of vibrant literary and scholarly activity.[9] Taliesin Williams (ab Iolo), son of the Welsh poet, antiquarian, and cultural inventor Edward Williams (Iolo Morganwg), established a school in Merthyr in 1816. According to the contemporary Merthyr historian, Charles Wilkins, 'as a schoolmaster, Mr. Williams earned a great repute, and from the school-room, and the influence of his teachings, went forth most of our eminent men'.[10] Ab Iolo also served as the custodian of his father's knowledge, beliefs, and manuscripts.[11]

---

5 Phillips, *Vale of Neath*, p. 569.

6 Ibid., NLW, MS. 966C, pp. 5–6; Williams, 'Life of Thomas Stephens', p. xx; ; Löffler, 'Failed Founding Fathers', p. 70.

7 Williams, 'Life of Thomas Stephens', p. xx.

8 John Davies to Thomas Stephens, Neath, 15 October 1840, NLW. MS, 965E, Letter 389 (4).

9 See Roberts, 'Welsh Scholarship at Merthyr Tydfil'. However, it should be noted, as England has argued, that Merthyr's middle class 'never had the numbers, ambition, or range of scientific interests of those who founded the Swansea Scientific Society in 1835 and gave that town an intellectual and cultural life which was at the centre of *its* urban identity'. England, *Merthyr*, p. 245.

10 Charles Wilkins, *The History of Merthyr Tydfil* (Merthyr Tydfil: Harry Wood Southey, 1867), p. 313.

11 Roberts, 'Welsh Scholarship in Merthyr Tydfil', pp. 54–56; Idem., 'Mab ei Dad Taliesin ab Iolo Morganwg', in Hywel Teifi Edwards (ed.), *Merthyr a Thaf* (Llandysul: Gwasg Gomer, 2001), pp. 57–91; Idem., '"The Age of Restitution": Taliesin ab Iolo and the Reception of Iolo Morganwg', in Geraint H. Jenkins

Jonathan Reynolds (Nathan Dyfed) was a Merthyr wheelwright and notable poet who won over 100 prizes at various eisteddfodau. His son, Llywarch Reynolds, became a Celtic scholar. Both father and son were friendly with Stephens, and Llywarch edited some of Stephens's work posthumously.[12] The clerk and later manager of the Dowlais Ironworks near Merthyr Tydfil, G. T. Clark, was also an accomplished scholar,[13] while the wife of the Dowlais Ironmaster and Merthyr MP, Lady Charlotte Guest (who would briefly take control of the ironworks after her husband's death), was the celebrated translator of the medieval Welsh tales known as the Mabinogion.[14]

The Merthyr Tydfil Cymmrodorion Society, for which Stephens served as both secretary and president,[15] promoted literature and scholarship in the town through weekly meetings and yearly eisteddfodau.[16] In addition to the notable school run by Ab Iolo, Lady Guest's schools, established for the benefit of workers' children at Dowlais, were considered the best in Wales.[17] Lady Guest's husband, ironmaster Sir John Josiah Guest,

---

(ed.) *A Rattleskull Genius: The Many Faces of Iolo Morganwg* (Cardiff: University of Wales Press, 2005), pp. 461–79; Idem., 'Taliesin ab Iolo', *Merthyr Historian*, 20 (2009), 47–59 (48–50); Löffler, *The Literary and Historical Legacy of Iolo Morganwg*, p. 81.

[12] Brynley F. Roberts noted that 'Thomas Stephens serves as a bridge between the old school—Nathan Dyfed, Taliesin ab Iolo—and the new—Llewarch Reynolds and Charles Wilkins (1831–1913).' Roberts, 'Welsh Scholarship at Merthyr Tydfil', 53.

[13] See Brian Ll. James, *G. T. Clark: Scholar Ironmaster in the Victorian Age* (Cardiff: University of Wales Press, 1998).

[14] See Revel Guest and Angela V. John, *Lady Charlotte Guest: An Extraordinary Life* (Stroud: Tempus, 2007).

[15] Thomas Stephens to Walter Davies (Gwallter Mechain), Merthyr Tydfil, 1 October 1846, 19 December 1846, 30 December 1846, 9 March 1847, 17 November 1847, NLW, MS. 1808E, Letters 1395–99; Taylor 'Thomas Stephens', 138.

[16] Wilkins, *History of Merthyr Tydfil*, p. 310.

[17] Ibid., pp. 72–75; Leslie Wynne Evans, 'Sir John and Lady Charlotte Guest's Educational Scheme at Dowlais in the Mid-Nineteenth Century', *National*

served as the chair of the board which established a public library in 1846. Stephens and Wilkins, among others, were also active on this board.[18] Stephen himself served as the library's secretary until 1870, when his failing health forced him to resign (although he remained treasurer for several more years).[19] Stephens's social efforts often focused on education and the dissemination of knowledge. Williams noted that 'Education was Stephens's idea of all reform'.[20] From the late-1840s, Stephens campaigned for state education, exchanging heated arguments with those who advocated reliance on voluntary initiatives.[21] This was part of his extensive contribution to local papers as a reporter and letter writer; he even took over the management of the *Merthyr Express* in 1864.[22]

Library of Wales Journal, 9: 3 (Summer 1956), 265–286 (265–72).

[18] Wilkins, *History of Merthyr Tydfil*, pp. 327–28; Taylor, 'Thomas Stephens', 137–38; Glanmore Williams, 'Printers Publishers and Book-Lovers in Merthyr Tydfil', *Merthyr Historian*, 11 (2000), 1–11 (9–10).

[19] 'The Merthyr Library', *The Western Mail*, 3 November 1870, 3. Stephens donated the works in his personal library to Merthyr Tydfil Library. A selection of these books have been collected and are currently housed in the Thomas Stephens Room at Dowlais Public Library. I am grateful to Merthyr Tydfil Public Libraries, particularly Sian Anthony, for her assistance in locating and collecting these books.

[20] Williams, 'The Life of Thomas Stephens', p. xxiv.

[21] Thomas Stephens, 'Education', *Monmouthshire Merlin*, 17 April 1847; Ibid., 1 May 1847; Ibid., 29 May 1847; Williams, 'Life of Thomas Stephens', pp. xxiii–xxiv; E. I. Williams, 'Thomas Stephens and Carnhuanawc on the "Blue Books" of 1847', *Bulletin of the Board of Celtic Studies*, 9: 3 (November 1938), 271–274.

[22] Williams, 'The Life of Thomas Stephens', p. xliii; England, *Merthyr*, 253.

THOMAS STEPHENS AND THE WELSH REPUBLIC OF LETTERS

Such local developments were crucial as Wales continued to lack a national university, library, or museum for much of the period.[23] Alternative avenues to Welsh scholarship included educational institutions such as St Davids College in Lampeter (founded 1822), but much native scholarship was undertaken by amateur scholars—clergy, schoolteachers, or gentry, or craftsmen and tradesmen striving for self-improvement and social and intellectual distinction—like Stephens. Societies with an interest in Welsh antiquities, patronising their study and publication, had emerged in the late-eighteenth century, notably the Cymmrodorion (1751, re-established 1820, 1873) and Gwyneddigion (1770) Societies, both based in London.[24] The latter was largely responsible for the re-emergence of the eisteddfod movement in the late-eighteenth and early-nineteenth centuries, which provided not only a platform for the celebration of Welsh culture, music, poetry, and scholarship, but financial incentive for literary and scholarly activity by offering prizes.[25] Indeed, Hywel Teifi Edwards described the essay competitions at nineteenth-century eisteddfodau as seeking 'to make good the want of that scholarly,

---

[23] See J. Gwynn Williams, *The University of Wales 1839–1939* (Cardiff: University of Wale Press, 1997); Prys Morgan, 'The Creation of the National Museum and National Library' in John Osmond (ed.), *Myths, Museums and Futures: The National Library and National Museum in the Story of Wales* (Cardiff: Institute of Welsh Affairs, 2007), pp. 13–22; Rhiannon Mason, *Museums, Nations, Identities: Wales and its National Museums* (Cardiff: University of Wales Press, 2007), esp. pp. 107–147.

[24] See R. T. Jenkins and Helen Myfanwy Ramage, *A History of the Honourable Society of Cymmrodorion and of the Gwyneddigion and Cymreigyddion Societies* (London: Honourable Cymmrodorion, 1951).

[25] Neil Evans and Huw Pryce, 'Writing a Small Nation's Past: States, Race and Historical Culture', in Evans and Pryce (eds), *Writing a Small Nation's Past*, pp. 3–30 (p. 21); Marion Löffler, 'Failed Founding Fathers and Abandoned Sources', p.71.

disciplined investigation of their cultures enjoyed by countries that could boast a national university.'[26] Moreover, mirroring academic developments across Europe, societies devoted to the advancement of knowledge soon emerged within Wales such as the Welsh Manuscripts Society (1837), Cambrian Archaeological Association (1846), and the Cambrian Institute (1855), holding meetings and publishing journals.

While access to manuscript materials improved across the nineteenth century, research remained onerous. Manuscripts continued to be consolidated in private hands, albeit with the aim of making them accessible, notably the Hengwrt Manuscripts held by William W. E. Wynne at Peniarth and the manuscripts of Iolo Morganwg held at Llanover Court. Others manuscripts remained in libraries in Oxford or London.[27] Access depended upon having the ability to travel and the availability and permission of the manuscripts' owners. Evidence of these issues are shown in Stephens's letters. On one occasion he made a fruitless visit to Peniarth because Wynne was not at home when he called.[28] Another time, he requested Thomas Wakeman to copy a manuscript for him at Llanover as Lady Hall had 'a pique' against him.[29] Problems of accessibility were partially relieved as

---

[26] Hywel Teifi Edwards, *The Eisteddfod* (Cardiff: University of Wales Press, 2016), p. 18.

[27] See Lemuel J. H. James, 'The Llanover Manuscripts', *The Journal of the Welsh Bibliographical Society*, 1: 6 (February 1914), 180–183; E. D. Jones, 'Deposited Collections: 3. The Wynnstay Manuscripts and Documents', *The National Library of Wales Journal*, 2: 1 (Summer 1941), 26–32; Maxwell Fraser, 'Sir Benjamin and Lady Hall in the 1840's (Part II: 1846–1849)', *National Library of Wales Journal*, 14: 2 (Winter 1965), 194–213 (196); Idem, 'Lady Llanover and her Circle', *Transactions of the Honourable Society of Cymmrodorion*, 1968, part 2, 170–96 (190).

[28] See William W. E. Wynne to Thomas Stephens, Peniarth, [25 August 1863], NLW, MS. 965E, Letter 372a; William W. E. Wynne to Thomas Stephens, Peniarth, 25 October [1864], NLW, MS. 965E, Letter 373a. See pp. 66–67 below.

[29] Thomas Stephens to Thomas Wakeman, Merthyr Tydfil, 8 December 1856, NLW, Tredegar MS. Letter 1309. See pp. 53–54 below.

Wales, like other nations,[30] sought to publish its ancient manuscripts.[31] Still, while these sources, along with books and periodicals devoted to their study, were increasingly printed, the accessibility of these publications still depended on local availability and cost. This was particularly the case for works published abroad, and Stephens's correspondence contains many appeals for information or volumes, sometimes offering books in trade.

Overcoming these difficulties, Stephens achieved success at eisteddfodau at the young age of nineteen, winning a prize at the 1840 Liverpool eisteddfod for his essay on 'The Life and Times of Ieustan ap Gwrgant, the last native Lord of Glamorgan'.[32] Thereafter, he won regularly at eisteddfodau throughout Wales, sometimes competing at multiple eisteddfodau per year and winning multiple prizes at individual eisteddfodau. His most notable essays were undertaken a decade apart. In 1848 he competed for a prize sponsored by the Prince of Wales for the best critical essay on the 'History of the Language and Literature of Wales, from the time of Gruffydd ap Cynan, and Merlin, to that of Syr Gruffydd Llwyd and Gwilym Ddu.' He was successful and there were immediate calls for publication, with John Josiah Guest offering his patronage. Lady Guest, who had recently published her *Mabinogion*, advised Stephens on publishing and dedicating the work to the Prince of Wales.[33] This support was welcomed,

---

[30] See Dirk Van Hulle and Joep Leerssen (eds), *Editing the Nation's Memory: Textual Scholarship and Nation-Building in Nineteenth-Century Europe* (Amsterdam: Rodopi, 2008); Mary-Ann Constantine, 'Welsh Literary History and the Making of "The Myvyrian Archaiology of Wales"', *European Studies*, 26 (2006), 109–28.

[31] The Welsh MSS. Society included a statement of its aims, organisation, progress, and membership at the beginning of each volume it printed, outlining the need for the 'Bardic and Historical Remains of Wales' to be printed.

[32] Taylor, 'Thomas Stephens of Merthyr', 136; Wilkins, *History of Merthyr Tydfil*, p. 258; Williams 'Life of Thomas Stephens', p. xxii.

[33] Lady Charlotte Guest to Thomas Stephens, 10 November 1848 to 18 August

and in 1849 Stephens's magnum opus, *The Literature of the Kymry*, appeared.[34]

The Literature of the Kymry brought Stephens national and international renown. This was compounded in 1858 by another essay, albeit one which was unsuccessful. A prize was offered at the first 'national' eisteddfod in Llangollen for the 'best essay on the Discovery of America in the Twelfth Century by Prince Madoc ap Owen Gwynedd.' In his essay, Stephens authoritatively demonstrated that a medieval Welsh prince did not discover America. The adjudicators, D. Silvan Evans, Thomas James (Llallawg), and Evan Davies (Myfyr Morganwg), disagreed over whether the essay was even eligible for consideration—Evans declared it the clear winner, Myfyr decided it was off-topic, and Llallawg resigned. In the end, the eisteddfod organisers stepped in and denied Stephens the victory.[35] The controversy continued, symbolising the break between the 'scientific' and 'romantic' strands of nineteenth-century Welsh historiography.[36] Although Stephens published a summary of the essay's argument in *Y Brython* in 1859,[37] Madoc's supposed discovery of the New World

---

1849 and William Rees to Thomas Stephens, 2 August 1849, NLW, MS. 964E, Letters 101a–e.

[34] Löffler, 'Failed Founding Fathers', p. 71; Roberts, 'Welsh Scholarship at Merthyr', 59; Taylor, 'Thomas Stephens of Merthyr', 136; Williams, 'Life of Thomas Stephens', pp. xxii, xxv, xxx.

[35] Edwards, *Eisteddfod*, pp. 20–1; Llywarch Reynolds, 'Editor's Preface', in Thomas Stephens, *Madoc: An Essay on the Discovery of America by Madoc ap Owen Gwynedd in the Twelfth Century*, ed. by Llywarch Reynolds (London: Longmans, Green, and Co., 1893), pp. v–xv (pp. iv–viii); Roberts, 'Welsh Scholarship at Merthyr', pp. 60–61; Taylor, 'Thomas Stephens', 139–40; Gwyn A. Williams, *Madoc: The Making of a Myth* (London: Eyre Methuen, 1979), pp. 199–202.

[36] See Löffler, 'Failed Founding Fathers'; Roberts, 'Welsh Scholarship at Merthyr', 56–57; Ben Bowen Thomas, 'The Cambrians and the Nineteenth-Century Crisis in Welsh Studies, 1847–1870', *Archaeologia Cambrensis*, 127 (1978), 1–15.

[37] Thomas Stephens, 'Y Madogwys', *Y Brython*, 2 (1859), 65–67, 81–2, 100-101.

occupied his attention for the rest of his life. The full essay was, eventually, expanded by Stephens and edited and published posthumously by Llewarch Reynolds in 1893.

THOMAS STEPHENS: REVOLUTIONISING WELSH SCHOLARSHIP

Stephens's Madoc essay followed an escalation of critical historical iconoclasm in which he scrutinised several historical legends cherished by many Welsh cultural leaders. In 1885, the romantically-inclined critic of Stephens, James Harris, even went so far as to describe his approach as 'Here is a popular tradition coming, let us go and kill it'.[38] This climaxed in two series of articles — 'Studies in British Biography' in the *Cambrian Journal* (1854–57) and 'Sefyllfa Wareiddiol y Cymry' in *Y Traethodydd* (1857), both of which scrutinised and ultimately dismissed historical events, characters, and documents which the following generation of professional historians would determine to have been based on the forgeries of Iolo Morganwg.[39]

These forgeries and invented histories were supposed to have passed orally in an unbroken line from time immemorial to Iolo himself. Iolo also invented or elaborated historical figures and founding fathers for the Welsh nation, many of whom appeared in the second volume of the *Myvyrian Archaiology of Wales* (1801).[40] As Marion Löffler has shown, Iolo's ideas had increasing

---

[38] James Harris, 'The Massacre of the Welsh Bards: An Examination of a Passage in Stephens' *Literature of the Kymry*', *Red Dragon: The National Magazine of Wales*, 7 (1885), 534–41 (536).

[39] Löffler, 'Failed Founding Fathers', p. 74.

[40] Rachel Bromwich, *'Trioedd Ynys Prydain'*, in *Welsh Literature and Scholarship* (Cardiff: University of Wales Press, 1969). Adam Coward, 'Exiled Trojans or the Sons of Gomer: Wales's Origins in the long Eighteenth Century', in Lotte Jensen (ed.), *The Roots of Nationalism: National Identity Formation in Early Modern Europe, 1600–1815* (Amsterdam: Amsterdam University Press,

influence on Welsh culture and historiography across the latter half of the nineteenth century, particularly in connection with the eisteddfod movement and a small group of influential cultural figures, such as Ab Ithel and Myfyr Morganwg.[41] His importance increased with the publication of the *Iolo Manuscripts* (1848), and *Barddas* (1862–1874), both edited by Ab Ithel and published by the Welsh Manuscripts Society, and the availability of Iolo's manuscripts at Llanover.[42] Not everyone was impressed with the authenticity of Iolo's vision of history. The two men who began the *Archaeologia Cambrensis*, the organ of the Cambrian Archaeological Association, in 1846, Ab Ithel and Harry Longueville Jones, were on opposite sides of the question. The differences between Ab Ithel and other members of the Association, including Longueville Jones and W. Basil Jones, with whom he co-edited *Archaeologia Cambrensis*, came to a head in 1853 and Ab Ithel left to start his own periodical, the pro-Iolo *Cambrian Journal*.[43]

It was in the first volume of the *Cambrian Journal* that Stephens published his controversial 'Studies in British Biography'. Printed in three instalments examining the supposed founder of Wales's legal traditions, Dyfnwal Moelmud,[44] his laws,[45] and one of the alleged founders of Britain, Prydain ap Aedd Mawr,[46] this series showed all three to be largely fictitious. These ideas were not well received by the *Cambrian Journal*'s readership, eliciting immediate responses in the journal's correspondence pages. Ab Ithel himself inserted an editorial after the second instalment in which he registered 'a distinct record of

---

2016), pp. 167–81 (pp. 172–74).

[41] Löffler, *The Literary and Historical Legacy of Iolo Morganwg*.

[42] Fraser, 'Lady Llanover and her Circle', 190.

[43] Thomas, 'Nineteenth-Century Crisis in Welsh Studies', 2–9.

[44] Thomas Stephens, 'Studies in British Biography I: Dyvynwal Moelmud', *Cambrian Journal*, 1 (Alban Hevin 1854), 160–72.

[45] Thomas Stephens, 'Studies in British Biography II: The Laws of Dyvynwal Moelmud', *Cambrian Journal*, 2 (February 1855), 33–59.

[46] Thomas Stephens, 'Studies in British Biography III: Prydain ab Aedd Mawr', *Cambrian Journal*, 4 (Alban Arthan 1857), 241–67.

his protest against the historical assertions which it contains'. The journal had 'received several remonstrances against the insertion of the former portion of the article' and Ab Ithel directed readers 'to the letter signed "Caradoc ap Bran" ... for an elaborate and complete refutation'.[47] Despite his apologies to readers 'for the introduction of controversy' into the journal,[48] Ab Ithel chose to publish the third instalment without editorial comment, even as Stephens's name continued to be lambasted a few pages later.

MERTHYR TYDFIL, WALES, AND THE WORLD: THOMAS STEPHENS AND INTERNATIONAL SCHOLARSHIP

Stephens's critical approach to Welsh history also attracted the notice of scholars abroad.[49] Nineteenth-century Wales was well-connected with wider European learning. The Abergavenny Cymreigyddion Society, for whose 1848 eisteddfod Stephens wrote *Literature of the Kymry*, and the associated 'Llanover Circle' of scholars and cultural patrons is an exemplar of this.[50] At

---

[47] John Williams ab Ithel, 'Editorial Note', *Cambrian Journal*, 2 (February, 1855), 59. See 'Caradoc Ap Bran', 'Dyvynwal Moelmud', *Cambrian Journal*, 1 (Alban Elved 1854), 269–71 (271). Also Idem, 'Dyvynwal Moelmud', *Cambrian Journal*, 2 (Alban Hevin 1855), 141–143.

[48] Ab Ithel, 'Editorial Note', 59.

[49] Löffler, 'Failed Founding Fathers', p. 72; Williams, 'Life of Thomas Stephens', pp. xxv, xxvii, xxxiii.

[50] See Fraser, 'Lady Llanover and her Circle'; Idem, 'Sir Benjamin and Lady Hall in the 1840's (Part I)' *National Library of Wales Journal*, 14: 1 (Summer 1965), 35–52; Mair Gregory, 'Cymdeithas Cymreigyddion y Fenni' *Llên Cymru* 1: 1 (Ionawr 1950), 97–112 and 3: 1 (Ionawr 1954), 32–42; Prys Morgan, 'Lady Llanover (1802–1896), "Gwenynen Gwent"', *Transactions of the Honourable Society of Cymmrodorion*, New Series: 13 (2007), 94–106; Mair Elvet Thomas, *The Welsh Spirit of Gwent* (Cardiff: University of Wales Press, 1988), pp. 8–9.

their heart was the notable Welsh cultural patron and inventor of the Welsh costume Lady Augusta Hall of Llanover. Lady Hall was the sister-in-law of the Prussian diplomat and scholar Baron Christian Charles Josias von Bunsen who attended a Cymreigyddion eisteddfod in 1838, meeting Welsh scholars and writers including Thomas Price (Carnhuanawc), John Jones (Tegid), and William Williams of Aberpergwm. Coincidentally, a Breton delegation, including the antiquarian and folklorist Viscount Theodore Hersart de la Villemarqué, was also in attendance, and it was at this eisteddfod that La Villemarqué was inducted into the Gorsedd of the Bards.[51]

Bunsen was well-connected in German scholarly circles and encouraged the Society to set topics which would appeal to Continental writers. In 1840, he adjudicated a prize for the best essay on 'The Effect which Welsh Traditions have had on the Literature of Germany, France and Scandinavia', won by the German Arthurian scholar Albert Schulz (San Marte). Two years later, Bunsen was the prime motivator behind a prize for the best essay on 'the place which the Welsh Language occupies among the Languages of the Celtic family; and together with the other branches of the same, among the Languages of the Indo-European race', adjudicated by James Cowles Prichard, author of *Eastern Origins of the Celtic Languages* (1831), and won by the German scholar, Carl Meyer.[52] Bunsen's design of the question came from a desire to attract the notice of European scholarship and draw Welsh scholars into greater contact with European comparative philology.[53] Meyer remained in Wales after the

---

[51] Mary-Ann Constantine, '"Impertinent Structures": a Breton's adventures in neo-Gothic Wales', *Studies in Travel Writing*, 18: 2 (2014), 134–147 (135).

[52] Carl Meyer, 'An Essay on the Celtic Languages, in which They are Compared with Each Other, and Considered in their Connection with the Sanscrit [sic], and the Other Caucasian Languages', trans. by Jane Williams (Ysgafell), *Cambrian Journal*, 1 (Alban Eilir 1854), 1–33.

[53] See, David Thorne, 'Cymreigyddion Y Fenni a Dechreuadau Ietheg Cymharol yng Nghymru', *National Library of Wales Journal*, 27: 1 (Summer 1991), 97–107.

eisteddfod in order to visit Welsh scholars, learn the Welsh language, and study Welsh literature and culture before becoming librarian to Prince Albert.[54] All three of these Germans—Bunsen, Schulz, and Meyer—went on to have some connection with Stephens. Bunsen adjudicated at a Cymreigyddion eisteddfod in 1853 where he enthusiastically praised Stephens's essay on the history of trial by jury in Wales.[55] Meyer, in his role as royal librarian, had the privilege of receiving Stephens's *Literature of the Kymry* on behalf of the Royal Family.[56] Schulz published a German translation of Stephens's *Literature of the Kymry* in 1862. La Villemarqué also became one of Stephens's regular correspondents and provided an introduction to the French historian Henri Martin, with whom Stephens also corresponded.

Reputation, introductions, and the recommendations of others were important aspects of the operation of Stephens's correspondence and the letters exchanged between Stephens and members of the Royal Irish Academy illustrate how far these introductions could go: Stephens was 'introduced' to Eugene O'Curry and John O'Donovan, by William Wilde,[57] who had been 'introduced' to him by James Henthorn Todd,[58] who had been 'introduced' to him by the Welshman J. Bruce Pryce who asked Stephens to assist in a dispute between Todd and members of the Cambrian Archaeological Association.[59] Importantly, Stephens

---

[54] Gregory, 'Cymdeithas Cymreigyddion y Fenni', 33–6; Thomas, *Welsh Spirit of Gwent*, pp. 8–9; Thorne, 'Cymreigyddion y Fenni a Dechreuadau Ieitheg Cymharol yng Nghymru', 97–107; Marion Löffler, 'Bunsen, Müller a Meyer: Tri Almaenwr, y Gymraeg, y Frenhines a'r Ymerodraeth', *Y Traethodydd* (Ionawr 2018), 19–32 (21–23).

[55] Williams, 'Life of Thomas Stephens', pp. xxx–xxxi.

[56] Carl Meyer to Thomas Stephens, Windsor Castle, 1 November 1849, NLW, MS. 965 E, Letter 201.

[57] William Wilde to Thomas Stephens, Dublin, Postmarked 29 July 1855, NLW, MS. 965E, Letter 327. See p. 88 below.

[58] William Wilde to Thomas Stephens, Dublin, 23 June 1854, NLW, MS. 965E, Letter 332a. See p. 82 below.

[59] J. Bruce Pryce to Thomas Stephens, Cardiff, 24 September 1849, NLW, MS.

had only met the last of these men in person before exchanging letters. In these cases it was thought necessary for a common correspondent to recommend the letter-writer, or else the letter was prefaced with an apology and explanation of how the parties were 'known' to each other through reading or a mutual acquaintance. An exception which reinforces the rule is provided by W. Basil Jones who wrote to Stephens concerning place names, remarking, 'I will not apologize for troubling you with this letter, as I consider myself officially entitled to correspond with all the antiquarians of Wales.'[60]

In addition to these introductions, Stephens's correspondents often discussed third parties, further illustrating the scholarly networks which stretched across Europe. This often took the form of criticising the antagonists in Stephens's many controversies. Correspondents also discussed the merits of other scholars' works or else asked for Stephens's opinion regarding them. In 1854, Stephens discussed the work of the German Celticist and philologist Johan Kaspar Zeuss with Wakeman.[61] The Irish scholar William Rushton wrote in 1861 recommending Ferdinand Walter's *Das Alte Wales* (1859),[62] and later enquired about Schulz's works.[63] Stephens's correspondents also discussed his scholarship with other major European figures. La Villemarque debated some of the same issues with both Stephens and Jakob Grimm.[64] In 1853, William Owen proposed sending a copy of Bunsen's adjudication of Stephens's 'History of Trial by

---

965E, Letter 241a. See p. 71 below.

[60] W. Basil Jones to Thomas Stephens, Gwynfryn, Machynlleth, 10 August 1857, NLW, MS. 954E, Letter 167.

[61] Thomas Wakeman to Thomas Stephens, Graig, 4 December 1854, NLW, MS. 965E, Letter 311. See p. 49 below.

[62] William Rushton to Thomas Stephens, Ruthin, 8 July 1861, NLW, MS. 965E, Letter 274. See p. 96 below.

[63] William Rushton to Thomas Stephens, London, 17 May 1864, NLW, MS. 965E, Letter 277.

[64] Théodore Hersart de la Villemarqué to Thomas Stephens, Kemperlé, 14 July 1856, NLW, MS. 965E, Letter 306a. See pp. 122, 125 below.

Jury in Wales' to his 'valued friend' Leopold Von Ranke.[65] This was more than mere 'name-dropping', as Stephens's ideas were circulating in a vast network of nineteenth-century European knowledge exchange.

Stephens's scholarly reputation travelled not only across the English Channel and Irish Sea, but across the Atlantic and Indian Oceans, where Welsh emigrants contributed to its wider transmission. In 1861, Stephens received letters from two Welsh expatriots, B. G. Davies and John D. Jones. Davies had emigrated from Merthyr Tydfil to Australia in 1857.[66] In his letter, he remarked on Welsh-Australian scholarship, including the reception of *Literature of the Kymry* there. He also discussed the state of local Australian politics and demonstrated the strength of his continued connection with Merthyr by sending zoological specimens, including an iguana and a platypus, for the museum of the Merthyr Tydfil library.[67] Jones, then teaching at Yale, wrote to Stephens in the same year, praising Stephens's reputation, which was 'not altogether unfamiliar to American Scholars on this side of the Atlantic', requesting Stephens's opinions on an essay and asking for 'a copy of Dafydd Ap Gwilym's poems together with Revd Thos Rowland's Grammar of the Welsh Language, for James Hadley, a professor of Greek at the College'.[68] Stephens provided the books and in 1865 was in correspondence with Hadley, and

---

[65] William Owen to Thomas Stephens, St Asaph, 29 October 1853, NLW, MS. 965E, Letter 227a. See p. 112 below.

[66] 'Presentation Dinner to Mr. B. G. Davies, on his Departure for Australia', *The Merthyr Telegraph and General Advertiser for the Iron Districts of South Wales*, 18 July 1857, accessed via *Welsh Newspapers Online*. I am grateful to Prof Bill Jones for providing me with information about, and sources regarding, B. G. Davies.

[67] B. G. Davies to Thomas Stephens, Tarnagulla, Victoria, Australia, 23 January 1861, NLW, MS. 964E, Letter 31.

[68] John D. Jones to Thomas Stephens, New Haven, Connecticut, USA, 30 November 1861, NLW MS. 964E, Letter 159.

through Hadley with the American scholar John Russel Bartlett, on the Madoc question.[69]

THE LETTERS

Writing in 1876, B. T. Williams noted that 'The publication of [Stephens's] correspondence, if it could be got together … would be welcomed by all Celtic Scholars.'[70] Many of the letters were 'got together' and are currently housed at the National Library of Wales. Four manuscript volumes,[71] a smaller volume containing forty-eight letters,[72] and several smaller collections of letters on dedicated subjects comprise the bulk of the extant letters sent to Stephens. Stephens's manuscripts were deposited in the National Library in the early twentieth century (1916, 1921) by Stephens's brother-in-law, Richard Rhys Davis, who also took over his pharmacy after his death:[73] a schedule placed at the end of the final major volume of letters notes that he and Mary Williams Davis of 40 High Street, Merthyr Tydfil presented the main collection of letters to the National Library on 20 March 1917.[74] Additional manuscripts were donated after Davis's death in 1939.[75] Letters by Stephens appear in many of the collected correspondences of nineteenth-century Welshmen at the National Library and others have been found in Cardiff Central Library, the National Library of Ireland, the Library of the Royal Irish Academy, and the National Library of Switzerland. Over 620 in

---

[69] James Hadley to Thomas Stephens, New Haven, Connecticut, USA, 4 October 1865, NLW, MS. 963C, Letter 59. See pp. 218–222 below.

[70] Williams, 'Life of Thomas Stephens', p. xxvii.

[71] NLW, MS. 964–5 E.

[72] NLW, MS. 942 C.

[73] England, *Merthyr*, p. 254.

[74] NLW, MS. 965 E, unnumbered.

[75] W. Ll. Davies, 'The Thomas Stephens Manuscripts', *National Library of Wales Journal*, 1: 2 (Summer 1939), 96.

total, the letters in Stephens's correspondence were sent from Wales, England, Scotland, Ireland, France, Germany, Belgium, Switzerland, Australia, and the United States, written in Welsh, English, German, and French, with passages in Gaelic, Breton, Latin, and Greek and individual words in languages from middle Cornish to Sanskrit.

It is clear that the letters collected together and preserved in the National Library have been selected and arranged. There is a conspicuous lack of friendly or familial letters; the focus, rather on scholarship and social reform, although the latter forms a much smaller category. The arrangement of some letters bear witness to their use beyond communication. Several letters from Ebenezer Thomas (Eben Fardd) on place names in north Wales were collected together with notes compiled for the purpose of revising *Literature of the Kymry*.[76] Two further volumes of letters bear testimony to Stephens's continued interest in the Madoc question. The first collection, containing letters from the adjudicators and supporters and press-cuttings about the Madoc incident, chronicles the controversy which followed in the Llangollen Eisteddfod's wake.[77] The second volume collects letters containing information about materials related to the Madoc question.[78] These are arranged like notes and can be read alongside Stephens's heavily amended essay and Reynolds's published edition as an archaeology of Stephens's thought.

There are occasional glimpses of personal conversations and social interactions in the letters Stephens received. In investigating the supposed settlements of Welsh Native American tribes, Stephens wrote to several Neath Quakers who he knew from childhood, asking for information related to the Quaker settlement in Pennsylvania: their replies mixed scholarly information and personal messages. The frustration which arises from the piecemeal nature of these letters' preservation is illustrated in an undated letter from Fredric R. Evans. Advising

---

[76] NLW, MS. Minor Deposit 151 A. See pp. 44–45 below.

[77] NLW, MS. 962C.

[78] NLW, MS. 963C.

Stephens on his handling of a public controversy, he alludes to Stephens's 'stray sheep' and a 'lamb' which 'may have strayed as far as Aberdare' before cautioning Stephens to 'take some Blue pill ere I come down else the consequences may be fatal'.[79] The discussion of 'sheep', 'lamb' and 'Blue pill' were obviously meaningful to these men, an 'inside' joke which has lost its context, both by the selectivity of the letters' survival and its own lack of date. This letter's lack of context therefore merely serves to hint at wider, lost conversations.

Social issues of importance to Stephens also appear in his letters. The vast majority involved the setting up of local institutions, particularly the Merthyr Tydfil Library, and national education efforts. Stephens was supportive of Henry Austin Bruce, Member of Parliament for Merthyr Tydfil 1851–1868. Importantly, his opinions of Bruce were backed by research: utilising methods similar to his scholarly research, he wrote to many MPs enquiring after Bruce's conduct in office.[80] As a member of the emergent middle classes, Stephens also negotiated between the iron masters and aristocracy on the one hand, and the labouring and lower classes on the other. During the ironworkers' strike of 1853, for instance, Stephens served as chairman of a public meeting held to discuss the issue, writing to the ironmasters of the labourers' conclusions, offers, and demands.[81]

---

[79] Frederic R. Evans to Thomas Stephens, undated ('Monday Evening'), NLW, MS. 965E, Letter 389 (3).

[80] Edward James to Thomas Stephens, Leeds, 29 September 1868, NLW, MS. 964E, Letter 2; Jacob Bright to Thomas Stephens, Manchester, 17 October 1868, Ibid., Letter 18; George Hadfield to Thomas Stephens, Isle of Wight, 30 September 1868, Ibid., Letter 109; S. Morley to Thomas Stephens, London, 28 September 1868, NLW, MS. 965E, Letter 208; Hugh Owen to Thomas Stephens, Pwllheli, 3 September 1868, Ibid., Letter 223a; Hugh Owen to Thomas Stephens, Chester, 4 September 1868, Ibid., Letter 223c; Robert N. Philips to Thomas Stephens, Manchester, 7 October 1868, Ibid., Letter 231; Bannar B. Polter, Ballinluig, 27 September 1868, Ibid., Letter 236.

[81] Jones, 'The Merthyr of Henry Richards', p. 39; Thomas Stephens to 'The

The largest portion of Stephens's letters, and the focus of this collection, concern scholarly activities and knowledge exchange. The dating of the letters reflects this, with the majority sent between the late 1840s and early 1860s—clustering around 1848 and 1858. Those letters which comment on Stephens's scholarship are surprisingly positive, considering the controversy he aroused. Löffler has noted the decline in patronage of Stephens, as his historiography became more critical and iconoclastic.[82] While the decline in letters offering patronage reflect this trend, letters of support and praise continued to arrive, demonstrating his growing reputation and involvement in heated controversies. Conversely, there are few letters from the figures with whom he openly debated in the press such as Ab Iolo, Ab Ithel, or Myfyr Morganwg, and where these letters are extant, they are on relatively undisputed topics.[83] It may be the case that acerbic debates between opposing scholars were preserved for a public sphere, where they were relegated by public discourse and the rules of open debate,[84] but the absence of controversial material may also be related to selective retention.

Knowledge transfer and collaboration, rather than flattery, was the purpose of most of Stephens's extant correspondence. Occasionally, and particularly with international correspondents, this involved sending books or journals which were unknown or inaccessible to him. However, Stephens's correspondents most often asked or answered questions, as each new publication or

---

Masters of Merthyr District' (Charlotte Guest), Public Meeting held at the Market Square, 18 August 1853, Glamorgan Archives DG/A/1/283/697; Charlotte Guest to Thomas Stephens, Cranford Manor, 22 August 1853, NLW, MS. 964E, Letter 103.

[82] Löffler, 'Failed Founding Fathers', pp. 73–76, esp. pp. 73–74.

[83] For instance, in John Williams ab Ithel to Thomas Stephens, Llanymarwddwy, 9 January 1852, NLW, MS. 965E, Letter 344, although the two men's difference of opinion over the medieval poem 'Y Gododdin' is mentioned, the tone of the letter was civil.

[84] See Thomas Price (Carnhuanawc) to Thomas Stephens, Cwmdû, 27 October 1845, NLW, MS. 965E, Letter 237, pp. 6–10 below.

eisteddfod essay brought further solicitations of his opinions and requests for further information. This knowledge exchange was not one-sided, and a system of reciprocity was usually implied by the asking of questions, inviting the questioned to become a questioner at a later date if necessary.

*   *   *

Despite its selective nature, this correspondence offers much insight into the nature and operations of nineteenth-century scholarly networks of knowledge exchange and transfer. Stephens's letters, spanning ten nations and three continents, show the extent to which the nineteenth-century 'republic of letters' was able to transcend national and linguistic boundaries. It also traversed boundaries between 'amateur' and 'professional' scholars and is highly interdisciplinary, incorporating literary history, folklore, history, archaeology, linguistics, and comparative philology. There are even letters about scientific knowledge, particularly chemistry—reflective of Stephens's profession.[85] The varied nature of this correspondence illustrates Stephens's eclectic intellectual and social passions, his valuable contributions to the history of Welsh and Celtic languages, literature and history, and his role within the social and institutional development of Merthyr Tydfil. Read alongside his published writings in periodicals, *Literature of the Kymry* and posthumously published works, Stephens's collected letters reveal the evolution of his thought as well as the nature and process of acquiring information in the period. The letters' contents, therefore, richly contribute to knowledge of nineteenth-century intellectual cultures and discourses particularly those in marginalised or minority nations, and they are vital to understanding the life and thought of Thomas Stephens, one of the most important intellectual figures of nineteenth-century Wales.

---

[85] For instance, Thomas Stephens to Unknown, Merthyr Tydfil, 16 October 1847, NLW, MS. 965 E, Letter 376 contains a soil analysis. See also Williams, 'Life of Thomas Stephens', p. xx.

NOTE ON THE TEXT

THE aim of this volume is to collect together a selection of Thomas Stephens's scholarly correspondence related to several major themes so that it may be read as a coherent account of his thought and participation in the wider development of Welsh studies both inside Wales and internationally. The letters as they exist in manuscript collections can be difficult to read in this way. The four large volumes of National Library of Wales MSS 964–5E, the bulk of the letters received by Stephens, have been arranged alphabetically by senders' surname and then chronologically. This organization is even maintained where a person's surname changed, as it did with Lady Charlotte Guest who remarried, becoming Charlotte Schreiber (Guest is under 'G', Schreiber under 'S'). Within this, letters related to the Madoc controversy, for instance, have been separated out from the whole, likely by Stephens himself. In the cases of letters sent to Stephens by D. Silvan Evans and W. Walker Wilkins, the separation of letters containing information on Madoc has broken up the conversations badly, so that various comments, questions, passages, and allusions contained in the letters of one collection can only be fully understood with reference to those in another collection. In this same vein, letters sent by Stephens are largely absent, the conversations remaining one-sided. The organisation of the present volume, therefore, attempts to reconstruct conversations where possible and to order Stephens's correspondence in a way which allows the reader to see how the letters interact, correspond to or even inspire one another.

In transcribing the letters, fidelity to the original has been paramount. This includes, where legible, passages which have been crossed out in the original as well as later additions, which are denoted as follows: '^ ... ^'. Words which have been underlined in the original have been italicised in the transcriptions; double underlines are both italicised and underlined. In the few instances where something has been glossed by the editor, the editor's additions are surrounded by square brackets. Unconventional spelling and grammar has not been glossed with 'sic'. However, the Welsh 'dd', which was often written as 'ᵭ' has been represented as a 'dd' in order to ensure readability. The letters are transcribed in the language in which they were written, with translations of Welsh words, passages, and a single letter provided. Translations have also been provided for letters written in French and German. Many of these letters were translated by or for Stephens, and where possible, contemporary translations have been provided. However, as these contemporary translations were intended only for Stephens's private use, they often contain multiple corrections, additions, alternative texts, or omissions. For this volume, they have therefore been edited for readability, rather than to ensure, as in the case of the original letters, a faithful transcription of the manuscript. Modern translations have been provided for those letters or parts of letters for which no contemporary translation is extant. These modern translations are identified in the text and their translator named.

THE CORRESPONDENCE OF
THOMAS STEPHENS

1

'MY AMBITION IS TO BE THE HISTORIAN OF MY COUNTRY'S LITERATURE': THE EARLY SCHOLARLY CORRESPONDENCE

BY HIS early twenties, Thomas Stephens had already found some measure of success in both his amateur and professional lives, winning his first prize at an eisteddfod at nineteen,[1] and taking over the chemist's shop in which he worked at twenty-one.[2] As the letters in this section show, the high calibre of his work was widely recognised almost immediately in Welsh scholarly circles, particularly his impressive knowledge of Welsh literature and critical use of sources. He was already noted too, however, for his willingness to argue unorthodox opinions and an occasionally bellicose debating style, most notably in a series of letters exchanged in the pages of the *Cambrian* between November 1842 and March 1843. As Marion Löffler and Hywel Gethin Rhys have noted, 'The missives exhibited a wide range of scholarly learning and revealed an analytic mind of a scientific bent; but they also showed a tendency to savagely and, at times, unfairly criticize and berate acknowledged cultural leaders and their deeds.'[3] In these public letters, Stephens reproached the old guard of Welsh cultural and intellectual circles, but as the letters here show, he

---

[1] Taylor, 'Thomas Stephens of Merthyr', 136; Wilkins, *History of Merthyr Tydfil*, p. 258; Williams 'Life of Thomas Stephens', p. xxii.

[2] Phillips, *History of the Vale of Neath*, p. 569; NLW, MS. 996C, pp. 5–6; Taylor, 'Thomas Stephens of Merthyr', 135–6, Williams, 'Life of Thomas Stephens', p. xx.

[3] Marion Löffler and Hywl Gethin Rhys, 'Thomas Stephens and the Abergavenny Cymreigyddion: Letters from the *Cambrian* 1842–43', *National Library of Wales Journal*, 4 (2009), 399–451 (quote on p. 400).

[3]

also received advice and encouragement from established and respected authorities. The difference between the letters printed in the *Cambrian* and those transcribed here are striking, both in their content and tone. As was discussed in the 'Introduction', it is evident that Stephens's extant letters have been carefully selected and arranged for preservation. While many letters do discuss controversies in which Stephens was involved, they are largely sympathetic, rather than condemnatory or argumentative. Even the disapproval offered in the first letter printed here is softened by both the friendly sentiments at the end of the letter and because the advice came from the great Welsh historian and scholar, Thomas Price (Carnhuanawc). Carnhuanawc even alludes to the different approaches taken in public and private letters, as he discusses his preference for a civil discussion behind closed doors over 'a wager of battle in a newspaper, which generally terminates in something like a pelting of mud in the street'.[4]

The letters in this section also show that while Stephens could criticise the old guard of prominent Welsh scholars, he was also prepared to learn from them and sought their validation. Stephens came of age intellectually at the end of the first half of the nineteenth century, a period which was referred to by Bedwyr Lewis Jones as the 'golden age' of 'yr hen bersoniaid llengar' [the learned clergy], officials in the Anglican Church who helped to revolutionise Welsh literature, history, and culture across the nineteenth century.[5] One of the most prominent of these men was the poet, historian, and antiquarian, Walter Davies (Gwallter Mechain), with whom Stephens corresponded until Gwallter Mechain's death in 1849. This correspondence, which is significant for its convivial tone and glimpse into Stephens's personal character, runs through this section. In it

---

[4] Thomas Price (Carnhuanawc) to Thomas Stephens, Cwmdu, 22 October 1845, NLW, MS. 965E, Letter 237. See pp. 6–10 below.

[5] 'Hanner cyntaf y ganrif diwethaf yw eu hoes aur'. Bedwyr Lewis Jones, *'Yr Hen Bersoniaid Llengar'*, (Penarth: Gwasg yr Eglwys yng Nghymru, 1963), p. 6.

Stephens, the young, Unitarian, social reformer and passionate challenger to established historiography continually seeks the opinion and approval of Gwallter Mechain, the elderly, established, Anglican authority. Approval of Stephens's intellectual and critical abilities is the theme of the majority of letters in this section. Much of this praise followed his successful 1848 Abergavenny eisteddfod essay and the publication of his groundbreaking *Literature of the Kymry*, a period which Löffler has identified as the height of Stephens's popularity amongst the patrons of Welsh literature and culture.[6] This patronage is also evident in these letters, which include the acceptance of his work on behalf of the royal library by Carl Meyer and Lady Guest's advice on publication. Although *Literature of the Kymry* was far from uncritical of Welsh literary history, and praise of Stephens's academic ability continued across his career (and in the subsequent sections of this volume), the period covered in the following letters, late 1840s and early 1850s, marked the high point of Stephens's popularity among Welsh cultural and literary elites.

* * * *

[6] Löffler, 'Failed Founding Fathers', pp. 71–72.

NLW, MS. 965E, 237
Thomas Price (Carnhuanawc) to Thomas Stephens

[In 1844, the Cheltenham solicitor and co-founder of Sherborne Spa, Thomas Henney, offered a prize at an Abergavenny Cymreigyddion Society eisteddfod for the best essay on 'the evils arising from the destruction of salmon when full of spawn'. In their contributions, essayists were expected to argue that the taking of unseasonable fish was unlawful, unhealthy, immoral, and a hindrance to the economy. Thomas Stephens was one of the two competitors for the prize. Contrary to Henney's advertisement, he argued forcefully against the utility of fishing seasons for preserving fish before proceeding to an impassioned discussion of socio-economic inequality which criticised laws which preserved recreational fishing rights at the expense of poor Welshmen. As can be seen by this letter, his contribution was not well-received by the adjudicator Thomas Price, Carnhuanawc, who counselled a young Stephens about the tone as well as the content of his arguments.][7]

Cwmdû, Oct. 22, 1845,

Dear Sir
　　Your letter arrived just in time to prevent the Essay being sent to Mr. Henney. I will forward it to you without delay. In the mean time allow me to ask what advantage you contemplate in its publication? If you give it as the Essay sent in by you, you must print it *verbatim & literatim*, and either add my reasons for rejecting it or call upon me to do so myself, and in order to enable you to judge of the expediency or inexpediency of such a step I send you the following as amongst my chief reasons.
　　　　1.　A misconstruction of the Law.
　　　　2.　An acrimony of style scarcely consistent

---

[7] NLW, MS. 916E, Thomas Stephens, 'The Evils Arising from Killing Salmon, out of Season, and, when full of Spawn'. See also Adam N. Coward 'English Anglers, Welsh Salmon and Social Justice: The Politics of Conservation in mid-nineteenth-century Wales', *Welsh History Review*, 27: 4 (2015), 730–54.

with the conventionalities of life, and certainly not admissible in a work sanctioned by a society such as the Cymreigyddion.

3. A somewhat uncalled for harshness in the treatment of Mr. Henney, who is I understand a very worthy man, and his only fault in this matter appears to be a misapprehension of the scope of his subject, whereas you lash him with the severity of a person punishing a criminal.

This alone would be sufficient to decide me in my judgment and I think to justify me in it

4. An avowed determination on your part to publish the essay whether successful or not, in defiance of the condition, prefixed by yourself, that the successful composition was to be the property of the Donor of the Prize. *How could I give Mr. Henney's money for the copyright of a work that was immediately to be pirated*?

5. An attack upon the Magistracy, which if justifiable in principle, is in my opinion too acrimonious in style—but which if not justifiable is I am convinced actually *libellous* if not *seditious*.

This argument I do not urge, and I think Mr. Henney has laid too much stress upon the rights of the poor as well as yourself.

6. A fallacious idea of the right of the poor to fish. The *poor* strictly speaking can have no right of the kind. *Poverty* implies an absence of property and a right of fishery is a property. Indeed it does not appear that any man has a right to fish except on his own property as a land-owner or by charter &c. So that I take it that every portion of a River (the Usk, for instance) from the source to the mouth is the property of some one or other. And the absolutely *Poor man* has no right to touch a drop of it, or even to approach it,

excepting he wades through it at a ford.
He can only fish by permission.

These are my principal reasons for wishing to dissuade you from printing the Essay without subjecting it to a rigid examination and revision. And I think you will admit the force of some of my arguments. As to the 1st. Should you still continue to doubt it, there is no way of settling the question but by Counsel's opinion, and that I do not think in the present state of the matter either you or I would be at the trouble and expense of procuring and until some such authority can be produced, any appeal to the public would be worse than useless. I will adopt your suggestion of writing to Mr. Henney on the subject, and referring him to you. And will recommend the Cymreigyddion and Mr. Henney to place the matter in your hands, that you may so remodel your Essay as to make it useful to carry out the intention the prize, which is the preservation of salmon, and the prevention of their illegal capture, as I imagine, that is Mr. Henney's object. And I think ^it^ will be a much more rational mode of dealing with the matter than a wager of battle in a newspaper, which generally terminates in something like a pelting of mud in the street, where the combatants bespatter each other for the amusement of lookers on.[8]

And now I will take the liberty of continuing some of the remarks which you gave me permission to make, when I had the pleasure of seeing you at the Eisteddfod. In the first place, with regard to your style of writing, I perceive a great difference betwixt the tone of the Salmon Essay and that of the Heraldic Poetry.[9] In the last there is nothing whatever of acerbity of

---

[8] This may be a reference to Thomas Stephens's vocal and public criticism of past Abergavenny Cymreigyddion Society eisteddfodau in the pages of the *Cambrian* in 1842–3. See Löffler and Rhys, 'Thomas Stephens and the Abergavenny Cymreigyddion'; eadem, 'Thomas Stephens a llythyru cyhoeddus yng Nghymru Oes Victoria', *Y Traethodydd* (Ionawr 2010), 35–49.

[9] At the same eisteddfod, Stephens won a prize of five guineas for the best essay on 'The Heraldic Poetry of Wales'. 'The Eisteddfod', *Cardiff and Merthyr Guardian, Glamorgan, Monmouth, and Brecon Gazette*, 1 November 1845,

expression, and I thought you left off much too soon, whereas in the other I wished every sentence to be the last, and never turned a leaf without dreading to meet in the next page some explosion of angry feeling against some unoffending object or other, every one of which was adding to the impossibility of my awarding the prize to a composition which evidenced the existence of abilities of the highest order. All this has worked on my mind the conviction that you are in a degree of which you are not aware, the *creature of impulse*. And you will allow that impulses even though rightly directed yet may sometimes act with an undue impetuosity. I have heard a very observant person say that if however excited by anger a ^man^ may be, yet if he at the moment, speak in a low or deep tone of voice, he shall not commit ~~themselfe~~ himself by a hasty or intemperate expression. How far this is true I cannot say but I am inclined to think there is a great deal of truth in it, and when I am next tempted to scold I will endeavour to practice ~~it~~. Now I feel disposed to believe that such a lowering of our mental utterance may also be put in practice. Such an under tone as may save us from the extreme *alto* pitch of remonstrance. Indeed I am satisfied such an exercise of patience and mental revision is very practicable, and I would (under the same licence of speaking my mind on this subject that you allowed me) submit to you whether it would not greatly aid in directing and moderating the impetuosity of your own mind, were you to have recourse to some such expedient.

I am sure of this, that the absence of such moderation will always act to the disadvantage of any writing whatever and that in such a manner as to neutralize all its merits be they what they may. It is offering violence to the received and conventional rules of literature and however some may be amused or even satisfied with the cleverness with which such shafts are discharged and the sharpness of their point, yet you will find that in the end those whose good opinions you would value will rather get out of the way of such dangerous missiles, and in this as in every thing else public opinion will declare against the practicer of such archery.

---

accessed via *Welsh Newspapers Online*.

Hoping that you will give me credit for writing these remarks with the same friendly disposition that our conversation was carried on at Abergavenny.

I am
Yours very truly
T Price

The Heraldic Essay is the property of the Cymreigyddion, but I have no doubt they will let you have it on applying to the secretary.

*   *   *   *

NLW, MS. 964E, 200
Carl Meyer to Thomas Stephens

Dear Sir

I have the great pleasure of hereby transmitting to you, in the name of His Royal Highness Prince Albert, a check for the amount of the Prize proposed by His Royal Highness the Prince of Wales, for which you were the successful competitor.[10] Allow me to profit of this opportunity to congratulate you upon your success and to tell you how anxious I am to read your Essay as soon as it will be published.

Believe me, dear Sir,
Yours faithfully
C Meyer

Windsor Castle 24/10/48

Thomas Stephens Esq.

*   *   *   *

---

[10] This prize worth £25, the first eisteddfodic prize to be patronized by the Prince of Wales, was awarded for Stephens's essay on the 'Literature of Wales During the Twelfth and Succeeding Centuries' at the 1848 Abergavenny Cymreigyddion Society eisteddfod. This essay was the basis for his *Literature of the Kymry*. Williams, 'Life of Thomas Stephens', pp. xxiv–xxv.

NLW, MS. 964E, 42
Walter Davies (Gwallter Mechain) to Thomas Stephens

Llanrhaiadr
Oswestry
Novr 7th 1848

My dear Sir/

What shall I say first upon this important occasion? *Shall I say I wish you Joy*? Let it be so: and I do it with my whole heart. Lady Hall of Llanofer soon after the late Jubilee, sent me a Hereford Times, which gave me the very grateful information that you had carried away the Prince of Wales's *plume* in triumph.[11] I must again wish you joy. But let me tell you, that I was not at all *surprised* at the intelligence, for I had been well satisfied a long time previously of the powers of the Candidate who signed *Gwyddon Canhebon* to his Essay. The last Letter I received from you and which I am grieved to own I never answered—I endorsed this Letter *"Preserve this—for it contains much excellent Criticisms."* and I consented to their propriety I believe in every particular. Had I been 20 or 30 years younger at that time, I would not have dropped the correspondence with Gwyddon so abruptly as I did at that time. *Henaint a'i Gydymaith ^Clefni^*[12] were the only occasions of my indifferences. I considered myself as they say *"ac un troed yn y bedd a'r llall allan"*[13]. I am so still. Amynedd a diwedd da im'.[14] I beg leave to apologize for not congratulating *Gwyddon Canhebon* sooner, but may it be accepted though late.

I expect that the loud *Gong* of the Venni[15] Eisteddfod this year will have the effect of putting to silence the puny flutes and flageolets of the minor Eisteddfodau at Merthyr, Coed y Cymmer—Pont y pridd &c and we shall hear no more of them for some years to come—At least, for my part, I am resolved *not* to

---

[11] See NLW, MS. 964E, Letter 200, pp. 10 above.

[12] 'Old age and its companion illness'.

[13] 'One foot in the grave and the other out'.

[14] 'Patience and a good end for me'.

[15] Y Fenni is Welsh for Abergavenny.

have any more to do with *adjudications*,[16] if such they may be called. A committee may be formed *in each Society*—quite capable of such decision. I want to rest, being on the verge of 88.

First and last—I wish you joy Who am My dear Sir
    Your very obdt Servt
        Walter Davies
Mr Thos Stephens.

*   *   *   *

NLW, MS. 1808E, 1401
Thomas Stephens to Walter Davies (Gwallter Mechain)

Merthyr Tydfil
Nov 11th 1848

Dear Sir/

Having gone to Lady Charlotte Guest to make some arrangements as to the type, and number of copies to be printed, of my Llyfr,[17] I found on my return two letters from your locality. One bearing on the back the wellknown and much reputed characters of Hen Fardd Manafon, and containing inside a Jeremiad on his old age, with a Congratulation on my running away with the Prince's Plume.[18] Well so be it. I have been shaken by the hand by the Chevalier Bunsen,[19] flattered by the Colonel in

---

[16] Walter Davies was a frequent adjudicator at a variety of local eisteddfodau, including the Merthyr Tydfil Cymreigyddion Society Eisteddfod, held on Christmas Day 1846 at the White Lion. Owing to confusion over dates and addresses and the late arrival of the adjudications from Davies, the eisteddfod was postponed until St David's Day 1847. It was in communication about this eisteddfod that Stephens began his correspondence with Davies. Thomas Stephens to Walter Davies, Merthyr Tydfil, 1 October 1846, NLW, MS. 1808E, Letter 1395.

[17] 'Book'. Lady Guest was assisting Stephens with the publication of *Literature of the Kymry* and its preparation for presentation to the Queen.

[18] See NLW, MS. 964E, Letter 42, p. 11 above.

[19] Christian Carl Josias von Bunsen (1791–1860).

the Chair, and handsomely complimented by the Marquis of Northampton &c &c; and yet "mewn gair a gwirionedd"[20] there are two little incidents which I shall remember when these are forgotten—the first ~~of~~ was the blush deep and joyful which suffused the cheek of one of the Misses Williams of Aber-pergwm[21] at the success of the little boy from Glynnedd,[22] and the other, the hearty greeting of Gwallter Mechain. The praise of others was but the cuckoo note, which coming from high quarters finds echoes in lots of sycophant bosoms; but you my old friend knew what you said, and therefore do I thank you most sincerely.

When you see the Essay which will be out I trust in two or three months, you will I feel assured, be convinced that some at least of Archdeacon Williams' praise is deserved. The novelties of the Essay are a dissertation on the introduction of the Bagpipes by G ap Cynan,[23] an attempt to show that "Hud a lledrith a phob arddangos"[24] at the Eisteddfod of Gruffydd ab Rhys in 1136 were ~~mo~~ an incipient *drama* like the masks and Mysteries of other countries;[25] a long dissertation of the Bard his social position, sycophancy, learning, distinctions, &c &c;[26] an attempt to fix the mythological poems in the 13th and 14th century;[27] a critical

---

[20] 'In word and truth'.

[21] Maria Jane Williams (Llinos) (*c.*1795–1873) or her sister Ann Williams, both of Aberpergwm in the Vale of Neath, who lived together at Ynys-las Cottage nearby and were involved with the Abergavenny Cymreigyddion Society.

[22] Thomas Stephens was originally from Pontneddfechan which, like Aberpergwm house, is located near Glynneath (Welsh, Glyn-nedd).

[23] Gruffydd ab Cynan. See Thomas Stephens, *Literature of the Kymry; Being a Critical Essay on the History of the Language and Literature of Wales* (Llandovery: William Rees, 1849), pp. 64–79.

[24] 'Magic and fantasy and every exhibition'. In the *Literature of the Kymry*, the phrase 'A chynnal pob chwareuon Hud a Llendrith, a phob arddangos,' is translated as 'And there were performed all sorts of plays of illusion and phantasm, and every kind of exhibition.' Stephens, *Literature of the Kymry*, p. 79.

[25] See ibid., pp. 79–93.

[26] See ibid., pp. 94–128.

[27] See ibid., pp. 176–206.

dissertation on the Hoianau and Afallaneu of Merddin fixing them in the reign of Llywelyn ab Iorwerth;[28] a disproof of the Massacre of the Bards;[29] and an identification of the Ysgolan of the Twr Gwynn with St Columbia—exploding the old story about the burning of the books.[30] Our writers have done the literature of Wales a great deal of harm by their indiscriminate zeal and want of critical sagacity. I am dreaming of setting seriously to work on "a History of the Literature of Wales"; what think ^you^ of the project? I am young (~~only~~ not 28), and hope yet to do my country some little service in that way.

I wish you were near me to assist in getting out the book, as I find it difficult to give explanatory notes to the specimens which have been translated. In Cynddelw's Marwnad to Owen Gwynedd he speaks of Eiof, Dillus ab Erfai, Greidwyr, Cywyr, who were they? Hywel ab Owain Gwynedd speaks of going from Ceri to Caerlliwelydd. Where is Caerlliwelydd? Evan Evans (dissertatio de Bardis)[31] says it is Carlisle; but unless there be a Carlisle in North Wales, it cannot be the one in Cumberland. Rheged, and Tegengl are in the same neighbourhood. Tegengl I know is in Flint; Rheged must be within a night's ride of Maelienydd in Radnorshire (as Hywel says he accomplished the distances; and Caerlliwelydd must be somewhere in Montgomery, Denbigh or Flintshires

Etto[32]—Where is Llan Egwest? It was somewhere in Powys, and apparently from the 1st poem of Einion Waun within the Lordship of Maelor. Pa le mae Hirvryn?[33]

My pen has run away with me. I spoke of having received *two* letters; but I had nearly forgotten the other. I had occasion to

---

[28] See ibid., pp. 217–81.

[29] See ibid., pp. 343–5.

[30] See ibid., pp. 345–54.

[31] Evan Evans, *Some Specimens of the Poetry of the Ancient Welsh Bards* (London: J. Dodsley, 1764), pp. 63–93.

[32] 'Once more'.

[33] 'Where is Hirvryn?'

write to Mr Robert Williams of Llangadwaladr,[34] and desired him to present my best respects to you; and so you see that if my modesty prevented my sending you a paper you were not forgotten. Your neighbour replies, "Walter Davies lives about nine miles off. I have not seen him for some time, he is however hale and healthy" *er ei fod yn 88 oed*.[35]

I sent you yesterday the *Guardian* containing a notice of the sudden death of Carnhuanawc; it was told me at Abergavenny that *he* was a competitor for the Royal prize. Be that as it may, I deplore his death. He has done much for the literature of Wales; and cannot even now be well spared. He looked very unwell at the Eisteddfod; but I did not anticipate so speedy a demise.

You say "Amynedd a diwedd da im".[36] I know of no man who ought to have more amynedd[37] than yourself, being in the possession of ^the good opinion^ of every man with whom I have ever spoken of you. Next door to me there lives a brother of Gwilym Mai[38] of Carmarthen, who is never tired of praising you. He begins with your appearance at Carmarthen in 1819 or 1820, always relates an anecdote that on some occasion when you and others were judges—you said to your fellow judge "paid a *bod yn galed*, y mae'r ffordd yn gul iawn",[39] and finishes with an exclamation, "Kind old man!" Now mark me this man is disinterested, and quite sincere; indeed he has more cause to quarrel with you than to sing your praise. You may possibly not have forgotten, having to decide between two translations of some Oddfellow's Rules—he was the defeated candidate, and I believe owning the justice of the decision kissed the rod, and went on praising you as lustily as ever. Knowing his regard for you, I in the exuberance of my delight showed him your last letter. A dozen times in reading it he exclaimed "poor old fellow", and

---

[34] Robert Williams (1810–1881).

[35] 'Although he is 88 years old'.

[36] 'Patience and a good end for me'.

[37] 'Patience'.

[38] William Thomas (Gwilym Mai) (1807–1872).

[39] 'Do not be *hard*, the road is very narrow'.

finished by gravely exhorting me to, "write a good letter to the old man—mind a good letter." Now if that does not give you ~~pleasant~~ "rosy dreams and slumbers light"[40] for one night at least I know not what will. Now at parting—I intend to make the tour of North Wales next summer starting from Oswestry, when I shall call upon you and claim "bara haidd a maidd glas"[41]

Dear Sir

My paper is ended, by trust never to cease being—Walter Davies' Sincere admirer

Thomas Stephens

I thought to have finished, but here I am at [damaged] I have a section showing how many of the metres were [damaged] use during the period of which I treat, though not being one of the *prydyddion*[42] my knowledge is limited, perhaps deficient. Much valuable assistance was derived from your very lucid Essay, but I want *English* specimens of the~~se~~ Welsh metres. I think the following will do for the Old Huppynt[43] (y ffordd hwyaf)[44]

Be violets in their secret mews
The flowers the wanton Zephyrs choose;
Proud be the rose, with rains and dews
 Her head impearling;
Thou liv'st with less ambitious aim,
Yet hast not gone without thy fame;
Thou art indeed by many a claim
 The Poet's darling.
  Wordsworth, to the Daisy.[45]

---

40 This appears to be a common mis-quote of the final lines of Walter Scott, *Marmion; A Tale of Flodden Field*, second edn (Edinburgh: J. Ballantyne and Co., 1808), p. 377. The original reads, 'To all, to each, a fair good night, / And pleasing dreams, and slumbers light!'.

41 'Barley bread and milky whey'.

42 'Poets'.

43 A metre of poetry

44 'The longest way'.

45 Wordsworth's poem 'To the Daisy' was used as an example of huppynt in the *Literature of the Kymry* as well as in a later letter to *Archaeologia*

Of Proest Cadwynawdl[46] there are plenty of English specimens;
there are several (rather poor) Englynion[47] "yn iaith y Sais";[48] you
give an English Fachawdl;[49] and I have translated the Welsh
specimen given of Dyri[50] in your Essay, thus,

> While on the hill lies thick the snow,
> Shorn trees and icebound brooks below,
> Without a fear my sons I fame,—
> A daring bard by household flame;
> My mind's at ease, and to my cot,
> (Where I'm asking) grim care comes not.

All the others I want, and should you in your reading have met
English specimens of them, you would do me a great favour to
point them out. Do you consider the poems of the
"gogynveirdd"[51] to be *cynghaneddol*?[52]

TS

*   *   *   *

Cambrensis on 'Llywarch Hen and Uriconium'. Stephens, *Literature of the
Kymry*, p. 508; Idem., 'Llewarch Hen and Uriconium', *Archaeologia Cambrensis*,
Third Series, 37 (January 1864), 62–74 (66).

[46] A metre of poetry.

[47] A metre of poetry.

[48] 'In the language of the Englishman'.

[49] A metre of poetry.

[50] A metre of poetry

[51] A term for the bards who lived and composed between the first half of the
twelfth century and the second half of the fourteenth century. It is more or
less synonymous with the *Beirdd y Tywysogion* (The Poets of the Princes).
Meic Stephens (ed.) *The New Companion to the Literature of Wales* (Cardiff:
University of Wales Press, 1998), s.v. 'Gogynfeirdd, Y'.

[52] A metre of poetry (cynghanedd) made into an adjective.

NLW, MS. 964E, 64
D. Silvan Evans to Thomas Stephens

Llandegwning Pwllheli
Aug. 27, 1849
Sir
   Your "Literature of the Kymry" has just reached me; and
although I have had time only to glance very curiously over its
contents, I do not hesitate to pronounce it a most masterly production, reflecting the highest credit on yourself and conferring a
boon of infinite worth upon the Literature of the Principality.
   What you have done you have done admirably well; but all has
not yet been achieved, and the literary history of ~~Welsh~~ Wales is
not yet complete. We want a continuation of your work down to
the present times—and you are the very person to undertake it.
Let therefore a stranger whose name has probably never reached
your ears prevail upon you to write a History of Welsh Literature
from the time at which your present volume leaves off to the
middle of the nineteenth century
      I remain, Sir
         Yours respectfully
            D. Silvan Evans
(Curate of Llandegwning, Carnarvonshire, and late Welsh
Lecturer at St. David's College Lampeter)

Th. Stephens, Esq.

*   *   *   *

NLW, MS. 964E, 183
Mary Pendrill Llewelyn to Thomas Stephens

3 Septr 1849
Dear Sir
   I ought before to have acknowledged your laborious Book The
Literature of the Kymry—it is indeed most ably written & beauti-
fully got up. I wish we had more like yourself capable & willing to

open the portals of our native literature and display them to the world—I have known many patriotic Welsh men well able to serve Wales by revealing the intellectual stores in her possession but alas! so few possess the persevering industry that you display throughout—"Good luck have thou with these honors"[53]

Mr Ll[54] is delighted with it & as soon as he can go to our post town he will have much pleasure in sending you a PO order

With my best regards

Believe me dear Sir

Very truly yrs

Mary C Llewelyn

Llan Vicarage

*   *   *   *

NLW, MS. 1808E, 1404
Thomas Stephens to Walter Davies (Gwallter Mechain)

Merthyr Tydfil
Sep 3 1849

My Dear Sir

I have been waiting to hear your opinion of my Llyfr,[55] as more ^than^ that of any man in Wales I respect your opinion. Ysgrifenwch Adolygiad yn yr Haul[56] a dywedwch *y gwir* am dano. Nid canmoliaeth, ond beirniadaeth. A Gadewch imi glywed oddiwrthych un waith etto.[57]

Very truly yours

Thos Stephens

---

[53] Book of Common Prayer, Psalm 45, line 5, 'Good luck have thou with thine honour: ride on, because of the word of truth, of meekness, and righteousness; and thy right hand shall teach thee terrible things.'

[54] Rev. R. Pendrill Llewelyn.

[55] 'Book'.

[56] *Yr Haul* (the Sun) was a the Welsh-language journal of the Established Church, published by William Rees, Llandovery who also published Stephens's *Literature of the Kymry*.

[57] 'Please write a review in *Yr Haul* [The Sun] and tell *the truth* about it. Not compliment, but criticism. And allow me once more to hear from you.'

NLW, MS. 965E, 266d
William Rees to Thomas Stephens

Llandovery Sept 5
1849

My dear Sir,

Your Book sells as fast as my Binder can turn them out of hand
Lingman has sold 50 & has had a fresh supply—Did you send a
copy to the Examiner as I find I have not marked it on my List as
sent, and I am told it has been favourably Reviewed therein. I am
expecting the Athenaeum & Lit Gazette to give a favourable notice
each of them.

I have not sent to any other reviews excepting those I wrote
to you viz the Quarterly, Blackwood Edinb. Review, Dublin
Magazine, & the two noticed above—So that you need not fear my
sending to the Standard of Freedom—I think one ought to be sent
to the Editor of the Archaeologia Cambrensis

I am *much pleased* with the Review of the Mabinogion in the
Guardian I hope that of the Lit of the Kymry may be equally
good—If you have a copy of the Examiner to spare let me have it
as I preserve all of the Reviews of my Works to extract recommendations therefrom—for the Prospectuses and I should like to
have a few of yours before the Prospectuses are issued

I have collected all the old proof sheets together for you—they
shall be sent by Wm Lewis who will call for the sheets next
Week—

Believe me to remain
　　My dear Sir
　Yours very faithfully
　　Willm Rees
The Dean's remarks shall go into the Prospectus-
　Did you sell them tolerably easy at Cardiff?

Inter nos[58]
　From what I can glean Mr Lockhart of the Quarterly is not not

---

[58] 'Between us'.

so favourable to the Work as I expected—If I had a downright good review fit for the Quarterly I would send it him and if he inserted it all would be right. Of course he would not accept it if not fully worthy. But if accepted it would most probably be paid for—Do you know any Literary Giant who would buckle to & write?

How would Mr Williams of Nerquis[59] do—provided he divested himself of Welsh prejudices?

How do you stand with the Vicar of Aberdare?[60] He has been reviewing Welsh Literature ere this and was a stout disbeliever of Iolo Morganwg's honesty

*   *   *   *

NLW, MS. 1808E, 1405
Thomas Stephens to Walter Davies (Gwallter Mechain)

My Dear Sir

I have been expecting to hear from you, that you would give me a *beirniadaeth*;[61] but whether you will or not, I have sent you by this days post a copy of my Llyfr, ~~and~~ which I trust you will do me the honour to accept. Dan obeithio cael *Verdict* yn yr Haul, ydwyf.

Yr Eiddoch yn barchus[62]
Thos Stephens

Merthyr Tydfil
Sep 29 1849

*   *   *   *

---

[59] John Williams (Ab Ithel) (1811–1862). His identification here as 'Mr Williams of Nerquis', refers to the fact that he was curate of Nerquis, Flintshire, 1843–1849.

[60] John Griffith (*c*.1818–1885).

[61] 'Criticism'.

[62] 'With the hope of receiving a *Verdict* in yr *Haul* [the *Sun*], I am, Yours respectfully'.

NLW, MS. 964E, 43
Walter Davies (Gwallter Mechain) to Thomas Stephens

Llanrhaiadr
Octr 1 49.

Dear Sir

I was compelled lately to forgo all literary correspondence owing to my shattered frame and that was the only reason your last favour remained unanswered. But by yesterday's post—your "Llyfr"[63] arrived, and of course I could not forbear, as it were by stealth, taking a peep into it *here and* ^*there*^ that ^and^ I must confess it *"surprised me"*. I will say no more at present, but that as soon as I pass the medical ordeal I am just now commencing I will undertake to what you require of ^me^ by writing to the Editor of the Haul—"approbatur" here, and "*dis*approbatur" there, but of the *latter*, I flatter myself that I shall have much less to do than of the *former*, by the glances I have already taken.

Have patience with me, as I hope to be able to accomplish what I undertake. In the mean time I remain

Dear Sir
    Your obliged Servant
       Walter Davies

Mr T. Stephens.
   Merthyr T^l

*   *   *   *

---

[63] 'Book'.

NLW, MS. 965E, 266g
William Rees to Thomas Stephens

Llandovery Oct 23
1849

Dear Sir

I hope you enjoyed your trip to Paris[64] as much as I did 13 years ago—Nothing of any moment has transpired since you left. The Arch. Camb. gave a short & very favourable notice of your Work which I shall copy into my next Lists of New Works—I wish I had a few more morceaux but must do the best with those we have as the Lists cannot be detained much longer.

I presume that I must pay for the advertisements in the Guardian & Principality

It is my intention to grapple with the Myv. Arch[65] as you may see by the enclosed—Can you give me any assistance in translating some of the Poetry

Mr Williams, late of Nerquis has translated the Gododin[66] and is going to publish the same immediately & not wait for the £40 prize at the Abergavenny Eisteddfod of 1851—should I place your name as a Subscriber to the Work?

When Mr Walter Davies' Review is sent to the Haul I will, if

---

[64] Stephens travelled to France in early October 1949. His passport is among his letters. NLW, MS. 965E, 388.

[65] Owen Jones (Myvyr), Edward Williams (Iolo Morganwg), and William Owen Pughe (Idrison) (eds.), *The Myvyrian Archaiology of Wales: Collected out of Ancient Manuscripts*, three vols (London, S. Rousseau, 1801–1807).

[66] John Williams Ab Ithel (ed. and trans.), *Y Gododin. A Poem on the Battle of Cattraeth, by Aneurin with an English Translation, and Numerous Historical and Critical Annotations* (Llandovery: William Rees, 1852). Stephen's own edition of Y Gododdin, in which he disagreed with Ab Ithel on several points, was published posthumously as Thomas Stephens, *The Gododin of Aneurin Gwawdrydd: An English Translation with Copius Explanitory Notes; A Life of Aneurin; and Several Lengthy Dissertations Illustrative of the 'Gododin', and the Battle of Cattraeth*, ed. by Thomas Powel (London: The Honourable Society of Cymmrodorion, 1888).

allowed, append his name to it. His name is worth having.

Have you sent any copies to London Reviewers? I ask this as no Review has yet appeared. One is sure to come out in the next Edinburgh Review, & the Quarterly promises an article.

Believe me to remain
Dear Sir,
    Yours faithfully,
      Willm Rees
Mr Stephens

*   *   *   *

NLW, MS. 964E, 43b[67]
Walter Davies (Gwallter Mechain) to Thomas Stephens

Llanrhaiadr
Oct 31. 49[68]

My dear Sir/

There is, said the wisest of all men, "A time for *all* things"—A *Time* for making promises—and a time for breaking or making void those promises. I am unhappily concerned in both these dilemmas.

On receiving your *Llyfr*, I was struck with its contents, and could not help wondering at the reading and assiduity of the Compiler: who, if he can be believed, is only 28 yrs old.

I happened to coincide with Casnodyn[69] in most of his assumptions &c &c and consequently made a hasty promise by

---

[67] This letter contained a lock of hair with the inscription: 'Gwallter Mechain's Hair cut off Nov. 1. 1849 by J. D.' who was identified by Stephens as 'Miss Davies'. Stephens further noted that 'The Hair is a nice brown with only a single grey hair.' Thomas Stephens to Daniel Silvan Evans, Merthyr Tydfil, 4 June 1868, NLW, Cwrtmawr MS. 919B, Letter 5.

[68] Davies died on 5 December 1849. Dictionary of Welsh Biography, s.v. 'Davies, Walter'.

[69] 'Casnodyn', which was Stephens's bardic name in the Merthyr Cymmrodorion Society, means 'bad note'. Taylor, 'Thomas Stephens of Merthyr', 138.

Letter, to send a kind critique to the Haul.

Youth and even Grey headed Manhood now surprisingly common among us, might have redeemed such a pledge given: but *Henaint*,[70] that formidable Hag would not give its consent; and has, as it were "perforce" thrust a quilsyn into my hand to re-call the promise hastily made

Casnodyn, some months ago, by post, lampooned *Henaint* rather freely, that may be right; As there is "a time for all things, Let him do so again: *Henaint* cannot kick, nor wince much: but he says—he is compelled by his superiors to relinquish *Criticism*; which he wishes to turn over to his Juniors

I am not a little vexed at this Conclusion by my compeer Henaint: but he is *inexorable* and will not stir "a *peg*". He states to me, rather too intelligibly his *reasons* for his non-compliance with my wishes, which are numerous, and *I feel them* grievously. This is no joke to me, tho' it may be to such as bask in the sunshine of pale youth

Now can even *Cas*nodyn wonder that I throw up the profession that one so kindly offered me by a friendly hand

The "Llyfr" sent to me, I must pay for, together with the half yearly payment for the Haul at Christmas next, the usual time.

I remain, in the mean time, while breathing –

Your humble servant—well and unwell—&c

Walter Davies

Thomas Stephens

(Casnodyn)

*   *   *   *

---

70 'Old age'.

NLW, MS. 965E, 201
Carl Meyer to Thomas Stephens

Windsor Castle
1/11/49

Dear Sir

In answer to your kind note (of the 16th l.m) I have the pleasure to inform you that Her Majesty the Queen has been graciously pleased to accept the presentation of the two copies of you Prize Essay for Herself & for H.R.R. the Prince of Wales. You had last sent the two volumes to Buckingham Palace from whence they will be speedily forwarded to Windsor Castle.

I have to apologize for the delay of this reply, which was owing to your note having been mislaid.

I am very anxious to read your volume and I hope I shall soon find leisure for giving myself that satisfaction.

I remain, dear sir,
Faithfully Yours
C Meyer

*   *   *   *

NLW, MS. 1808E, 1406
Thomas Stephens to Walter Davies (Gwallter Mechain)

Merthyr Tydfil
Nov 8 1849

My Dear Sir

I have delayed replying to your letter hoping to have time to write a long letter, in which I intend to take *Henaint* seriously to task on account of the following facts.–

1 The writer of the letter states that he is an old man—but the hair of Gwallter Mechain,[71] as silky in texture as the wearer is kind hearted, is not *white* but brown: *ergo* the letter is a forgery.

2. The letter complains of weakness; but on the seal are

---

[71] See note 67 above.

inscribed the letters "Fortiter et suaviter."[72] Now I should very much like to know how *Fortiter* can be reconciled to the weakness complained of. Besides what *suaviter* is there in refusing to review a fellow creature's Llyfr?[73]

Ergo. Is as clear as mud that the Rev Walter Davies is not the writer of the letter.

There is a piece of logic for you!

But seriously, I am not at all willing to let you off without writing the critique. I have set my mind upon it; therefore let me have it. But take your own time—if you cannot write it this month it will do the next. There is a pretty story told of an Italian artist who having completed a piece of sculpture invited his friend to see it. Many came, and were enthusiastic in their praise; one young ^man^ the ~~future~~ subsequent Michael Angelo, examined it minutely, and having finished his survey said, "It wants but one thing", and then abruptly left the room. Old Donizetti knew Michael's opinion to be worth having, and was very miserable for want of knowing what this was. In the meantime Michael had gone to Rome, and remained there for years. This deepened old Donizetti's grief until it last he got positively ill.

Now my case is something similar. I have received my flattering notices from many men eminent in Wales, and I have reason to hope for favourable notices in the great Reviews of England; but ~~there is no~~ English Critics cannot know whether I have or have not done well. And in Wales there is no man for whose opinion I have so much respect as I have for yours, and if you will do me the favour, you will greatly oblige me, and not improbably benefit Cambrian Literature. My ambition is to be the Historian of my Country's Literature; and if I meet with encouragement now, encouragement founded on desert mind— if I deserve it not—be it none of mine—I will probably not rest until I finish–

This History of the Literature of the Kymry.

Vol I.

---

[72] 'Strongly and sweetly'.

[73] 'Book'.

From the earliest period to the 12th Century
>   Vol II
The present work remodelled.
>   Vol III
From Daf Gwilym to Hugh Morris
>   Vol IV
From Hugh Morris to present time.
If I am fit to become the Sismondi[74] of Wales, let Gwallter Mechain say so; and if *he* says so, I shall engage in the task with renewed energy. Wanting his approbation, I shall want much, therefore if you will leave the arena of criticism, let your last act be the heralding of a younger successor, who is willing if he be deemed worthy to accept the office.

The Llyfr was a gift from *me*; to be kept whether you write or not. Pay for it eh? "No more of that Hal, an thou lovest me."[75]

Have you Pinkerton's Dissertation on the Goths?[76]

>   I am Dear Sir
>>   Very truly yours
>>>   Thos Stephens

*   *   *   *

NLW, MS. 965E, 343
John Williams (1792–1858) to Thomas Stephens

>>>>   Llandovery
>>>>   16. Nov 1849

Dear Mr. Stephens

It grieves me that I have not hitherto acknowledged the receipt of the handsome and richly bound copy of your work which you have been so good as to send me. But I really have been

---

[74] Jean Charles Léonard de Sismondi (1773–1842), a Swiss economist and historian.

[75] William Shakespeare, *Henry IV, Part I*, Act II, Scene 4.

[76] John Pinkerton, *A Dissertation on the Origin and Progress of the Scythians or Goths. Being an Introduction to the Ancient and Modern History of Europe* (London: John Nichols, 1787).

so much engaged with business of a various nature, the discharge of which I could not evade that this fact must plead my excuse for my previous negligence.

But if I have been negligent personally I have been very active in recommending your work to the first literary critics of our land and I expect that in at least two popular Reviews, a very impartial estimate will be taken of our cause and your work. Favour we cannot expect until we have proved more worthy, but I think even now I see the dawn of a better day when "The Literature of the Kymry" will ^rather^ confer honor *on* its patrons than receive honor *from* them. Watch the "Cromlech" question well and keep your mind free from prejudice and I will irrefragably prove that our "Megalithic" structures were the works of our civilized ancestors at least a thousand years before the christian Era. [77] Again I say, wait without prejudice for my illustration of the argument.

I never have boasted, and never will boast, but can honestly say that the solution of this much debated question is in my hand, and that I can solve it. Only wait.

Yours faithfully
John Williams.

To Thomas Stephens Esq

*   *   *   *

NLW, MS. 964E, 102
Charlotte Guest to Thomas Stephens

Lady Charlotte Guest, has on her return to Canford after a short absence, found the Copies of the Literature of the Kymry which

---

[77] A lively debate arose in the late 1840s amongst members of the Cambrian Archaeological Association, including several notable Irish figures, concerning the purpose and use of cromlechs. Williams led the more romantically inclined 'Welsh' camp who argued that cromlechs were druidic altars against an 'Irish' camp, led by James Henthorn Todd, who argued that they were sepulchral monuments. See pp. 69–70 below.

Mr. Stephens has been so good as to forward for Sir John and herself and which they have much pleasure in accepting.

Lady Charlotte is extremely pleased with the work in its complete form and admires the binding of the vellum copy very much.[78]

Canford Manor
1 Dec 1849

*   *   *   *

NLW, MS. 964E, 116[79]
Augusta Hall to Thomas Stephens

Abercarn Uchâf
Thursday Oct. 30th
1850

Lady Hall hastens to enclose the Checque for £15 & is very much obliged by the flattering reason given by Mr. Stephens for his originally undertaking the work in which he has been so successful.[80] Lady Hall *has* been very ill at different intervals this year & again last week was unable to leave the house—but she is not thank God! as yet incapacitated from working for the Cymry whenever she has an opportunity, tho' sometimes she works rather too hard for her health, having a good deal of extra writing from the still indifferent state of Sir Benj.'s Eyesight.

Lady Hall would be most happy to procure the Gododin for Mr. Stephens *if possible* but she foresees great difficulty from the Parties who unfortunately have possession of it. (Viz Mrs. Prichard & her daughter Mrs. Powell to whom Mr. Price left every thing)—However she will make the attempt on her return home

---

[78] This was also the style of binding which was sent to the royal family.

[79] This letter was written on black-bordered paper, likely indicating that the writer was in mourning.

[80] These remarks do not appear in *Literature of the Kymry* and therefore were likely made by Stephens to Lady Hall privately.

^to Llanover^ next week (She is now in her Mountain home)—&
Mrs. Powell & Mrs. Prichard reside at Abergavenny.

* * * *

NLW, MS. 964E, 99
Henry Griffiths to Thomas Stephens

Brecon College
Aug 30. 1851.

My Dear Sir

I attended the Archaeological Meetings at Tenby last week,—
and I cannot express to you, how delighted I was, to hear *your*
name so often quoted, and with such distinguished applause. Any
man might well be proud of honours, offered so spontaneously
and universally. The Secretary paid you a high compliment in the
Report[81]—on which the noble president enlarged, evidently con
amore—I suspect, it would make you blush to hear half of what
was said on the occasion.

Let me hope my, Dear Sir, all this will act more as a *stimulus*
than a *sedative*—a pen capable of doing so much—cannot be laid
aside, without *wrong*. There is a splendid field before you;—and
I heartily pray, that God may give you strength and perseverance
to reap it!

Now, with your leave, one or two words, by way of
enquiring.—very many of the Gentlemen at Tenby, seemed to
regret the absence of a Literary or Scientific Journal of some kind

---

[81] 'The Committee hail Mr. Stephens' labours as the first application of modern
criticism to works whose genuineness had been either received without
hesitation, or hastily rejected; and they cannot help noticing, as a new
illustration of the story of Columbus and the egg, the fact, that Mr. Stephens
has tried the poems of Taliesin by a simple and somewhat obvious test, which
had been previously overlooked—principle, namely, that a poem cannot well
have been written before the occurrence of the actions which it describes.'
'Cambrian Archaeological Association. Fifth Annual Meeting, Tenby, August
20th to 26th, 1851', *Archaeologica Cambrensis*, New Series, 8 (October 1851),
309–340 (312).

(besides the Archaeologica) in Wales. Of course, they meant, an *English one*,—either monthly, or quarterly, as circumstances may determine.—Would it not be possible, think you, to start one, with a fair prospect of success.? I know no one so well fitted as yourself for the Editorship:—and I feel persuaded you would find no difficulty in securing an effective staff of contributors. Surely there is a market opening just now for such a work; at any rate, such a work is most cryingly wanted in the present state of parties.

Pray, think over the matter—and see what ought to be done, and may be done—If in any way, my services can be of the slightest use, do not for a moment scruple to command them.— Let me know at your convenience, how you feel on the subject.— And with every sentiment of respect and esteem believe me in great haste

My dear Sir yours truly &c H Griffiths

*   *   *   *

NLW, MS. 965E, 267c
William Rees to Thomas Stephens

Llandovery Nov 9. 1853
My dear Sir,

I have put the enclosed Work in the Press—& enclose you a copy of the 1st Proof.[82]

It is my general practice when a Work is fairly committed to the Press, to look out for its successor, and for that purpose would not your continuation of the Literature of the Kymry be an appropriate Work?

I would propose to have it published by subscription as the only *safe* mode of publication—and in that mode I would take all risk of expense upon being allowed half profits—the usual mode of publishing.

---

[82] This is probably Jane Williams (ed.), *The Literary Remains of the Rev. Thomas Price, Carnhuanawc*, two vols (Llandovery, William Rees, 1854–55).

If such would meet your views, I would at once publish a Prospectus & collect names during the time that Carnhuanawc would be in Press so as to be ready to place its successor therein.

At the rate you have gained laurels at Abergavenny—there will soon be "no competition"—Proceed successfully, *but mind your health*. I was unable to attend the Eisteddfod in consequence of being under the hands of the Doctor. I am now all right once more—

Believe me to remain
My dear Sir,
Yours faithfully
Willm Rees.
T Stephens Esq

2

'BE KIND ENOUGH TO LEND ME A LITTLE OF YOUR LOCAL KNOWLEDGE': WELSH ENQUIRIES AND ANSWERS

IN HIS biographical sketch of Stephens, B. T. Williams remarked that '[a]fter the establishment of the fame of Stephens as a Welsh scholar and historian by the publication of "Literature of the Kymry," he became general referee upon all subjects relating to the Welsh language and antiquities.'[1] The letters in this section illustrate the truth and extent of that statement, focusing on knowledge exchange about various topics between Stephens and correspondents across Wales and wider Britain. As was pointed out in the 'Introduction', knowledge exchange and transfer, particularly asking and answering inquiries, was the primary theme and purpose of Stephens's collected correspondence. This took various forms. Books and journals were requested and sent, transcriptions and translations were made of sources which were inaccessible to the letter writer, and appeals for local or specialist knowledge were made. These letters therefore illustrate the diverse avenues and methods by which research was conducted and knowledge acquired in nineteenth-century Wales. Letters written by Stephens in 1856 requesting Thomas Wakeman copy a manuscript held by Lady Llanover for him, and by William W. E. Wynne in 1863 informing Stephens when he would be at home, both show the difficulties involved in accessing privately-held manuscript sources. Stephens's letter to Wakeman, which contains Stephens's translation of a poem by the fifteenth-century Welsh poet, Gwilym Tew, shows how requests for manuscript information could involve more than

---

[1] Williams, 'Life of Thomas Stephens', p. xxvii.

mere transmission. Although manuscripts and other sources could be difficult to access, the letters also appeal for information which could not be found in books. This included the letter recipients' opinions and specialist knowledge. An excellent example of the latter is provided by the correspondence between Stephens and Ebenezer Thomas (Eben Fardd) in which Stephens appeals to Eben Fardd's local knowledge of the toponyms and geography of Clynnog, Caernarfonshire, to inform his inter-pretation of medieval Welsh literature and history. Eben Fardd's letter to Stephens was found among notes in Stephens's own copy of *Literature of the Kymry* indicating that Stephens used these letters to prepare or revise his publications.

Many of the letters in this section preceded or followed publications or eisteddfod essays by Stephens and others, either seeking information whilst researching and writing or else asking for expansion on a subject which had appeared (or failed to appear) in print. Those sent to or by Stephens as part of the preparation of a book, essay, or article provide a view of the nineteenth-century research process and the evolution of scholars' deliberations on various subjects. Similarly, those which followed publications and the submission of eisteddfod essays show the continuing development of their ideas. Those correspondences which were prompted by essays, articles, or books, however, also show the interactivity of these texts, and can be read alongside the works to which they react and the public letters appearing in contemporary periodicals and news-papers to construct a wider view of nineteenth-century con-versations surrounding subjects of Welsh historical, literary, and cultural interest in both the public and private spheres. Indeed, as the letters discuss the relevance, importance, and use of works, they provide an idea of the 'impact' of a variety of nineteenth-century books, essays, and articles. This is true both for works by Stephens and those by others: letters mentioning prominent German scholars, for example, like Jakob Grimm or Johann Kaspar Zeuss, show awareness of their thought in Wales and wider Britain.

NLW, MS. 964E, 100
Charlotte Guest to Thomas Stephens

Lady Charlotte Guest would be much obliged to Mr. Stephens if he would spare her for a day or two the 1 Vol of the Myvyrian Archaiology[2] which Mr. Rees[3] mentions that he lent Mr. Stephens. Her own books are not in Wales. She would return it as soon as possible

Dowlais
14 Feb 1849

*   *   *   *

NLW MS 5175C, pp. 97–99
Thomas Stephens to George T. Clark

Merthyr Tydfil
Nov 13 1850

Sir/
I have read with much pleasure your article on Caerphilly Castle;[4] and have taken the liberty of sending to the Editor of the Archaeologia Cambrensis, some corrections of the historical part, for the next number. Iolo Morganwg and Malkin[5] have led subsequent writers astray, in having confounded the history of Senghenydd Castle in Gower with that of Senghenydd (Castell Coch?) near Cardiff.

One error I have not corrected. In connection with John

---

[2] [Owen Jones, Edward Williams, and William Owen, eds.], *The Myvyrian Archaiology of Wales, Collected out of Ancient Manuscripts,* Volume 1: Poetry (London: S. Rousseau, 1801).

[3] Probably the printer William Rees (1808–1873).

[4] G. T. Clark, 'Contribution towards an Account of Caerphilly Castle', *Archaeologia Cambrensis*, New Series, 4 (October 1850), 251–304.

[5] Benjamin Heath Malkin (1769–1842) was the author of *The Scenery Antiquities, and Biography of Wales* (London: T. N. Longman and O. Rees, 1804).

Giffard, the printer has made you write both bad grammar and non-sense. In the West of England Review you speak of "the castle of Glamorgan and Morganwg";[6] but in the Arch. the printer has put castle*s* while the context only treats of one.

The chief object however of this note is to call your attention to Ellis' Letters Vol I. ^first Series^ in the beginning of which he states ^that^ in the Cotton MSS,

"There is a French letter of Hugh le Despenser as early as 1319, giving orders for the defence of his castles; and several occur in the same language relating to the affairs of Edward the Third."[7]

This appears to have escaped your notice; but as it is likely to prove interesting, it will afford me and I doubt not others also, much pleasure to see it published as an appendix to your excellent article

I trust you will pardon the liberty of addressing you thus taken by an entire stranger,[8] and permit me to remain

Yours Respectfully

Thos Stephens

G. T. Clarke Esq

*   *   *   *

---

[6] Probably G. T. Clark, 'Essay on Caerphilly Castle', *West of England Journal of Science and Literature*, 1 (1835–6), 62–71, 101–4, 135–43, 185–99 (65).

[7] Henry Ellis, *Original Letters, Illustrative of English History; Including Numerous Royal Letters from Autographs in the British Museum and One or Two Other Collections*, three vols (London: Harding, Triphook, and Lepard, 1824), vol. 1, unpaginated.

[8] It is noteworthy that Stephens and Clarke did not know each other personally when their correspondence began: Clark would effectively become the controller of the Dowlais Ironworks, near Merthyr Tydfil, from 1852 and take an active role in social improvement throughout south Wales, both at Dowlais and as an inspector for the General Board of Health, in addition to his Welsh antiquarian activities. See *Dictionary of Welsh Biography*, s.v. 'Clarke, George Thomas'.

NLW, MS. 964E, 23
George T. Clark to Thomas Stephens

Athenæum Club
15 Nov 1850
Sir
I write to thank you for your note of the 13th past.

The letters to which you refer are part of a considerable mass of paper on the subject of Wales contained in the Cottonian Manuscripts in the British Museum.

They are in Norman French, full of contractions, & written in a hand which it requires much practice and time to decipher. There are two letters from Hugh Le Despenser the son to a certain John Jugg, sheriff of Glamorgan but I do not think they mention Caerphilly.

The printer Mr Mason, writes to me of a probable reprint of Caerphilly in which case I shall try and either copy or have copied the text of the above documents.

I am extremely obliged to you for your (flattering) criticism on the article on Caerphilly, the length of which I am much ashamed of as I must have excluded many matters of more general interest from the journal.

I remain
Sir
Your faithful servant
Geo. T. Clark
T. Stephens Esq

*   *   *   *

NLW, MS. 965E, 342
Jane Williams (Ysgafell) to Thomas Stephens

Llanover
January 27, 1851.
Miss Jane Williams, wishing to obtain the original Welsh of David ab Gwilym, for a translated passage of *a poem in w^h he reproaches*

a Clock for having disturbed him from a delightful dream; & finding that the Poems in Welsh are not in this Library, is referred by Lady Hall to Mr Stephens, as an eminent student of his country's literature, & requests that he will have the goodness, *to forward to her here* a transcript of the original passage. By sending it with the least possible delay the obligation will be enhanced.

*   *   *   *

NLW, MS. 964E, 168
W. Basil Jones to Thomas Stephens

Cambrian Archaeological Association
[printed letterhead]
St Davids Sept 6. 1851

Dear Sir

Mr Mason has sent me a proof of your paper;[9] which, I need not say is extremely interesting to me. Your additional evidence of the assassination of Iago ab Beli and of the Gaelic origin of Cadafael Wyllt,[10] is extremely important, and bears out what I have said about the condition of the Gael after their conquest of Caswallawn.[11] Allow me to suggest that the words I have marked in brackets should be omitted as Mr Aneurin Owen is just dead, and Mr Wynne Ffoulkes[12] is not a Welsh scholar. Mr Wynne[13] is more likely to give you information, as he is intimate with Sir R. Vaughan[14]—I will ask him about it.

---

[9] This was published as, Thomas Stephens, 'The Poems of Taliesin. No. III', *Archaeologia Cambrensis*, New Series, 8 (October 1851), 261–74.

[10] Ibid., 270.

[11] William Basil Jones, 'Vestiges of the Gael in Gwynedd', *Archaeologia Cambrensis*, Supplement, 1850 (London: W. Pickering, 1851), 1–85 (64 ff).

[12] Wynne Ffoulkes (1821–1903), was a Welsh judge and antiquarian.

[13] William Watkin Edward Wynne (1801–1880).

[14] Sir Robert Vaughan (1803–1859), 3rd Baronet, of Hengwrt, who would later leave W. W. E. Wynne the Hengwrt manuscripts.

I had not altogether overlooked Marwnad Aeddon,[15] although I cannot at this moment remember whether my attention was drawn to it before my paper went to press. However I could prove nothing from it, as I am a very poor Welsh scholar[16] and am so far from understanding the poems attributed to Taliesin that I always regarded it as a strong exercise of faith to believe that they mean anything. Your interpretation is on this account a great help, and I am looking anxiously for your comments on the Marwnad Cunedda, and the Cerdd Daronwy (if the latter is the exact title—I have no books at hand). Daronwy appears to have headed a revolt similar to that of Cadafael—but at ^an^ earlier period. I have mentioned this revolt in the "Vestiges", but I cannot remember whether I gave his name.[17] Now as far as I can make anything of the poem (and I can make very little of it) it appears to refer to this very fact.

One point in your valuable paper is not very clear, and, individually, I feel the necessity of its being made clearer. I mean your argument about a "pro-Gaelic theory",[18] and indeed, the exact meaning of those very words. Is it asking too great a favour to request you to re-model the sentence? Perhaps the obscurity is the result of conciseness.

I must wait until I return to Gwynfryn before I can give you any further information about Gors Fochno

I am, dear Sir,
Faithfully yours,
W Basil Jones

---

[15] In his article, Stephens remarked that 'Aeddon is certainly a Gaelic and not a Kymric name.' Stephens, 'The Poems of Taliesin. No. III', 268.

[16] This refers to his Welsh language abilities.

[17] He did not name Daronwy in connection with the rebellion. Williams, 'Vestiges of the Gael in Gwynedd', 67.

[18] In the article the 'pro-Gaelic argument' was that 'the land of Gwyddion' was 'interpreted to mean Ireland'. Stephens disagreed with this. Stephens, 'The Poems of Taliesin. No. III', 269.

P.S. I think your statement is far too sweeping about extermination[19] although, in this instance, I quite agree with it.

*   *   *   *

NLW Cwrtmawr 412B, 59
Thomas Stephens to Ebenezer Thomas (Eben Fardd)

Merthyr Tydfil
Jany 14 1852

Dear Sir/
I trust you ^will^ pardon the liberty taken by one who in person if not in name is to you an entire stranger, in troubling you with the following request.

About the 6th century, there was living in your neighbourhood a distinguished warrior; and Cynon ab Clydno Eiddin at that time made Clynog as celebrated, as it is made in the 19th by Eben Vardd. He was buried at *Rhyd Rheon*:

"Bet Kinon in Reon Rid"
Englynion Beddau

Rhyd Rheon in the middle ages was a place of much note; and it wais there that the great conference wais to take place when Cadwaladr comes again to drive the Saxons from this Island:—

"Yn y ddel Kadwaladr i gynnadl Rhyd Rheon
Kynan yn erbyn cychwyn ar Saeson
Kymry a orvydd kain vydd e dragon
Kaffant pawb ei deithi llawen fi Brython
Kaintor Cyrn elwch kathl heddwch a hinon."[20]
Merddin

---

[19] Stephens argued against the Irish having been driven from, or exterminated in, Anglesey. Ibid., 270–71.

[20] In *The Literature of the Kymry*, Stephens gives the translation of this passage, which he attributes to Iolo Morganwg, as 'But in vain until Cadwaladr comes to the conference of Rhyd Rheon / And Kynan advances to oppose the Saxons; / Then shall Britons be again victorious / Led by their graceful and majestic chief; / Then shall be restored to every one his own, and the sounder of the horn of gladness, proclaim / The song of peace, and days of happiness.' Stephens, *Literature of the Kymry*, pp. 225–26.

If Merddin tells no lies, there are good times coming and no mistake; and therefore we must find out where Rhyd Rheon is. Now Gwilym Ddu living about 1350, says in one of his poems: —
"Neud gewigion Arfonis Reon Ryd"[21]
From that line I should conclude that this ford was upon some river which divided upper and lower Arfon; and therefore, I conjecture that it must be in your neighbourhood.

Can you give me any aid to determine the position of this "Ford of Rheon"? Is there any river called Rheon? In the Gododin, Aneurin speaking of Cynon, calls him,
"Cynon lary vron *Clinion* Wledig"[22]
Is there any means of bringing Clynog and Clinion nearer to each other?

Be kind enough to lend me a little of your local knowledge, in order to clear up the works of our older Bards; and if you wish at any time to know anything respecting our Cinder tips, I shall at all times be glad to send you what information I may possess.

I am Dear Sir
Yours truly
Thos Stephens

[addressed to]
Mr Ebenezer Thomas
(Eben Fardd)
Clynnog Fawr
Caernarfonshire

*   *   *   *

---

[21] Stephens gives the translation of this line as 'Are not the people of Arvon become insignificant below the ford of Rheon?' Stephens, *Literature of the Kymry*, p. 270.

[22] Stephen gives the translation of this line as 'Cynon the gentle-hearted, Lord of Clinnion'. Stephens, *The Gododin of Aneurin Gwawdrydd*, p. 235.

NLW Minor Deposit 151 A[23]
Ebenezer Thomas (Eben Fardd) to Thomas Stephens

Clynnog fawr Jan 20/52

Dear Sir

I beg leave to assure you that the receipt of a letter from the great *Essayist* of South Wales has given me not a little gratification

I think I can give you some clues to the information you requested respecting

"_____ *"Rheon Rid"*

There is a Brook some mile and a quarter to the S. East of Clynnog Village called in colloquial Language—

"afon Rhyd Beirion"

The name has puzzled me very much some time ago to find out its etymology but I have been very long of opinion that it is the river you enquire about and I thus explain it—it might be very properly be termed <u>*Aber*</u>—*Rheon* then *Aber=rheon*, *'Ber=rh'on*, ^contracted^ like *rheol* into *rh'ol*, and by colloquial corruption *"Beirion"*. We have another river not far off, similarly contracted, vis. *Aber Erch—'Bererch—'Berach*, *'Berch*. *"Ieuan Brydydd Hir"*[24] you know, in a note to his translation of *Gwilym Ddu's* Ode, quoted by you, says—*"Rheon*, the name of a river in Carnarvonshire, often mentioned by the Bards, but it must have altered its name since, for I do not recollect any such river which has that name at present."[25] I might point out many other localities of ancient note in this parish which the above eminent antiquary confessed his ignorance of. However, your precision in regard to the situation of the above river does you immense credit, as you are at such a distance from the spot. I have not yet ascertained where is the exact position of the *"ford*," but I shall make further inquiries

---

[23] This letter was accompanied by a detailed map of the area entitled 'A rough sketch of The Parish of Clynnog', which appears to have been hand-drawn by Eben Fardd.

[24] Evan Evans (Ieuan Fardd or Ieuan Brydydd Hir) (1731–1788).

[25] Evans, *Some Specimens of the Poetry of the Ancient Welsh Bards*, p. 50, footnote.

when I find leisure: I almost hesitate to take *"Clinion"* in the line cited from the *Gododin* for *Clynnog*, is it not more probably *"Clydno"*?
[written across side of the page:]
The Boundary of arvon is some 2 or 3 miles to the South of Aber Rheon at present.

Aber Rheon flows from a mountain called *Bwlchmawr*, across the famous *"Pass"* of that name; and there are several localities close to this Brook recorded in ancient Poems as the scenes of terrible deeds of war. *"Graianog"* a very ancient Demesne; and in bygone ages, a considerable Lordship, is situated within about two miles of this Brook, King Cadwaladr, as you are perhaps aware, ~~gave~~ ^bestowed^ this lordship ~~to~~ ^on^ the Abbey of Clynnog fawr, which shows that he was not inaptly connected by *Merddin* with the "Ford of Rheon", the Brook Rheon must have been either a part and parcel of Cadwaladr's Lordship of Graianog, or a boundary of it.

My dear Sir
Yours most respectfully
Eben Fardd

T. Stephens. Esq
Merthyr
PS By the way, I find that *Merddin* could hardly be a contemporary of *Cadwaladr* the ^last^ British King, and that in his quoted prophecy he therefore must be understood to refer to some *Cad=waladr* (or General) who was to figure conspicuously at the Rhyd Rheon Conference. Excuse my desultory remarks and antiquarian blunders, if there be some, as I am snatching a moment in great hurry to acknowledge your kind letter just now in hopes of being a more correct and methodical narrator the next time.

E. F.

*   *   *   *

NLW, MS. 964E, 169a
W. Basil Jones to Thomas Stephens

Univ Coll.[26]

Feb. 13 1854

My dear Sir

The late editor of the Archaeologia Cambrensis[27] printed an abstract of your paper "on the Antiquities of Merthyr" &c in the report of the Brecon meeting.[28] I hope that this is not an indication of a wish on your part that the paper should not appear *in extenso*, a circumstance which I should regard as a real loss to the Journal. I should be very glad to receive, and forward it to the publisher.

Can you furnish me with a list of places bearing the name of the *Gwyddyl* in Wales, which do not appear in my "Vestiges",[29] and which you mentioned at Brecon.

Very truly yours
W. Basil Jones

*   *   *   *

NLW, MS. 964E, 169b
W. Basil Jones to Thomas Stephens

Cambrian Archaeological Association.
[printed letterhead]
Univ Coll. Feb 20 [1854]

My dear Sir,

I cannot regret that we are likely to lose your assistance for a time, as the archaeological world will receive compensation in

---

[26] University College, Oxford.

[27] This is a reference to John Williams (ab Ithel) who left in 1853 to form the Cambrian Institute and *Cambrian Journal*.

[28] 'Cambrian Archaeological Association, Seventh Annual Meeting, Brecon', *Archaeologia Cambrensis*, New Series, 16 (October 1853), 307–38 (317–320).

[29] Jones, 'Vestiges of the Gael in Gwynedd'.

another form.[30] When a writer is able and willing to give up his time to the composition of a systematic work, he evidently confers a far greater boon upon the subject on which he is engaged, than by communicating fragmentary contributions to a periodical.

I think it due both to the association and to myself to correct a misapprehension into which you appear to have fallen. The Cambrian Journal did not originate, as you seem to imply, in any "dissensions between the late editor and myself",[31] as it was announced in the last Number (Oct. 1853) of the Archaeologia Cambrensis,[32] and the only sort of disagreement which has ever occurred between Mr Williams and myself, had its origin in a notice published in the same number. Perhaps I ought to add that the "unfortunate dissensions" in question consisted simply of (what I thought) a rather hasty letter from Mr Williams to myself, and a certainly not uncourteous answer of my own, to which I have received no reply. Into the merits of the controversy I have no desire to enter at present; the concise history which I have given of it, will shew you that it is not, on my side at least, a very serious matter.

Meanwhile, I strongly depreciate rivalry between the two Journals. I confess I do not see that a new one was at all needed; but that is a matter of opinion.

Can you let me have any more "Gwyddyl".[33]

Faithfully yours,
W Basil Jones

---

[30] As *Literature of the Kymry* was the only volume published in Stephens's lifetime, this may refer to his 'Studies in British Biography' which was published in the *Cambrian Journal* between 1854 and 1857, although the following sentence seems to indicate otherwise. See Stephens, 'Dyvynwal Moelmud'; Idem., 'The Laws of Dyvynwal Moelmud'; Idem., 'Prydain ap Aedd Mawr'.

[31] See note 27 above.

[32] 'The Cambrian Institute', *Archaeologia Cambrensis*', New Series, 16 (October 1853), 338.

[33] See W. Basil Jones to Thomas Stephens, 13 Febuary 1854, above.

NLW, MS. 965E, 311[34]
Thomas Wakeman to Thomas Stephens

Graig 4th Decb 54

Dear Sir/

Many thanks for your prompt reply to my enquiries. I had forgotten that you have disposed of the question as to Arymes Prydain in your excellent work on the Lit of the Cymry.[35] I had some misgivings on the subject of its being a production of the 6th or 7th century had it been the expression Gwrtheyrn Gwynedd, would have been tolerable evidence that this celebrated character was a native of North Wales, as it is I suppose it amounts to nothing more that calling somebody in the 12th century _the_ Vortigern of N Wales, on account of his having entered into an alliance with the English. I have somewhere heard or read that Bedd Gwrtheyrn is a place in the parish of Llanhaelhaiarn, in Lleyn, Caernarvonshire, not far from Nevyn; the place I suppose alluded to by Price.[36] Unless the traditions of this description can be traced to some authentic source of early date I am not disposed to attach much credit to mere names, as I have known some very ingenious theories, based on _assumed_ traditions drawn from local appellations, imposed within my own recollection, through whim or wantoness. If Ystyvachau had been in Lleyn it would have been of some weight in support of the authenticity of the Bedd in Llanhaelhaiarn, but I think your etymology fixes the grave of Vortigern with greater probability in a district, with which we have at least some reason to believe, that he was connected. After all we really know so little about this

---

[34] This letter was written on black-bordered paper, likely indicating that the writer was in mourning.

[35] Stephens, _Literature of the Kymry_, pp. 285–94.

[36] Likely a reference to Thomas Price, _Hanes Cymru a Chenedl y Cymry, o'r Cynoesoedd hyd at Farwolaeth Llewelyn ap Gruffydd_ (Crughywel: Thomas Williams, 1842), p. 244: 'Rhai dybiant fod yr Englyn yma, yn cyfeirio at hen feddrod carneddawl, ar lan afon fechan, a elwir _Nant y Gwrtheryn_, gerllaw _Nefyn_, yn swydd Gaernarfon, yn hwn a agorwyd rhai blynyddau yn ol, ac y cafwyd ynddo gist-faen, yn cynnwys esgyrn gwr o gorffolaeth hir.'

personage that it may be doubted whether he was a Cymro[37] or not. Gale[38] thought he was of a Pictish family.

I have not seen Zeuss' Gramatica Celtica,[39] but I suppose like most German works it is very learned and very abstruse. The term Celtic as applied now a days to the Welsh, Breton, Irish &c is I think objectionable. No one knows what language the Celts of Gaul spoke, only Cæsar tells us, that it was different from that of the Belgæ, and Aquitani, and the Emperor Justinian likened it to the croaking of Ravens. I can't admit the justice of the similitude to either of the so called Celtic dialects as the term is used at the present day. I wish some other ~~term~~ name could be found for this family of language.

A very curious discovery has been lately made about half a mile from Caerwent. In cutting some drains the workmen came upon a cist formed as usual of flag stones within which was a stone coffin containing the skeleton of a tall man, but the extraordinary part of the affair was that the spaces between the coffin and the walls of the cist were filled with coal!

This must have been brought there from the forest of dean or our hills and must have been an expensive article when this internment took place. What could have been the intention of it I am totally at a loss to conjecture: The coffin is pronounced by some ~~to~~ ^who^ are considered judges in such matters "*decidedly Roman*"! It had been rifled by the workmen before the proprietor of the land was aware of the discovery, but from circumstances that have transpired there is strong grounds to believe some ornaments (rings or fibulæ) were found. If these could be recovered they might throw some light upon the probable age of this singular grave.

---

[37] Welshman.

[38] Thomas Gale (1635/6–1702) was an English antiquarian and cleric. Among his many works was *Scriptores quindecim* (1691) which contained the first published version of Nennius's *Historia Brittorum*. *Oxford Dictionary of National Biography*, s.v. 'Gale, Thomas'.

[39] J. C. Zeuss, *Grammatica Celtica* (Leipzig: Weidmannos, 1853). Thomas Stephens read and took extensive notes from this work. NLW. MS. 922C.

Yours Very truly
Thos Wakeman

T Stephens Esq

*   *   *   *

NLW, MS. 965E, 312
Thomas Wakeman to Thomas Stephens

Graig 26th Jany 1856
My Dear Sir)
Among the documents in the evidence room at Tredegar there is a MS poem addressed to Sir John ap Morgan by Gwilym Tew. Did you ever see this Cywydd. If not and you would like to have it I will send you a copy. The one at Tredegar is not the original, but a copy, by some one, from the hand writing I should think about a century ago to which the writer has appended some notes.
Your Very Truly
Thos Wakeman

Thos Stephens Esq

*   *   *   *

NLW Tredegar MS 1309[40]
Thomas Stephens to Thomas Wakeman

Merthyr Tydfil
Decbr. 8th 1856
Dear Sir
In turning over my papers to day, I have been reminded of my great remissness in not having sent you the desired translation of Gwilym Tew's ode to Sir John ap Morgan of Tredegar, which

---

[40] Stephens's annotations to the letters have been added after he wrote his translation. Some of the numbers denoting notes to the text which he inserted were therefore above the line of text while others were inserted in line with the text. All have been made uniform here for readability.

here I here subjoin.

An Eulogistic Cywydd to Sir John ap Morgan of
Tredegar.
The knight, armed all over,
Covered his blushes in gold, (A)
Sir John with the cross upon his seal, (1)
Whose knightly office is so high.
Much as is blamed, by Tafodwg! (2)
Morgan the widespread wine of Wentloog, (3)
The hay of Tredegar, (through fire)
Is (4) harvested by Jevan.
An arm and seal on Maesaleg
He went ᵂⁱᵗʰ꜀ from} his court eight hundred leagues (5)
Old age does not adjudge any one (anything?)
To be wanting to royalty at Aber-wysg.
In battle, I would not give anything I saw,
For an ~~spear~~ arrowhead without the spear of Einion
Sais.

[written across the side:]
A The plated band, passing under the chin, which fastened the
helmet.—probably
(1.) His arms, you say, bore a cross engrailed &c
2 Tafodwg—is Saint Tyfodwg (see Rees) Gwilym Tew was
connected with the monastery of Pen Rhys in Glyn Rhonddda,
which adjoins Ystrad-Tyfodwg.
3 Needs no explanation.
4 The poem was written in the father's lifetime. 5. To Jerusalem.

The great Dinas is under him,
Let him extend the power of Jestin yonder.
Higher than the ash of ^Early^ Brychan, (1) ~~in early
times~~
He is *square* in the bosom of Gwent.
Elen and her son, through the sea,
And Noah ʷᵉⁿᵗ꜀ were} like the nephew of Ivor.
On sea or land there was no tarrying,
But going like the image of Bonvil the grey. (2)

The Stars showed the blushes of Sir Bown
By measuring the world. (3)   }
By divination their successor   } Obscure 4
Waited to ^{give the stars to}₍shine on₎} Sir John.   }
A Noble Saint of Jerusalem, he is,
Who has the gold beneath his visage   (see note A)
Carrying the golden roll, as a gift,
Behind him, gave him strength.
Sir John loved the living Cross
Which purchased the pilgrims (salvation?)
His purpose was valourously
To serve two royalties
The divination of Israel went ~~with him~~
With him over those distant scenes.
The station of Christ, and his times,
At the end of a wood, there it was.

----

(1) I do not understand this allusion

2. Lord Bonville, created in 1449, and called "Old Bonvil" by Lewis Glyn Cothi. Works, p 102. What is the allusion?

3. Sir Bown or Bevis of Hampton—the hero of romance; but this reference is unintelligible,

(4) I do not understand the original here, and suspect some corruption.

He went not a foot without a prayer
He had make to the one and three,
~~Asking the tribute of Meredith~~
~~From the sea of Greece, I am with~~
I ask with serious face, the tribute
Of Meredith from the sea of Greece. (1)
A Wonderful sacrifice he offered
At the head of the grave—a live bird.
The gentle one became a pilgrim,
To turn gold and the blood to wine,
India the great showering
Gold instead of snow upon the host.
The silver of Sir Morgan and the steed,

And the *pedryw* (?) and the patriarch (of Jerusalem).
He showed gold upon a *benys*   }
On the side of his face, (after?) the Lord Rhys   }
Gold and a palm upon his *flower*,   }
Gold that encloses Saint Clears   }
If I divined the ages of men,   }   Heraldic
If there be gold on Sir John;   }
The hair of his head may be   }
Upon the Divination of the Jordan.   }

----

(1) I think this is an allusion to Meredith ab Rhys a contemporary poet, and ~~the~~ fisherman, he who wrote *in a poem*, asking for a present of a net, the allusion to Madoc ab Owen Gwynedd, which was afterwards pretended to be an epitaph found on his grave in America.[41]

The poem is one of the poorest I ever saw, and is quite inexplicable without a minuter knowledge of the heraldry of the family than I happen to possess. However, I have given a literal translation; line for line; from which with your more perfect knowledge, you will probably be able to make out the meaning; except indeed, where ~~the~~ words are used to suit the *cynghanedd*, not to convey any sense; From all that I have seen of Gwilym Tew's, he was but a poor poet. You say that there is a note in the Tredegar MS, that he lived at Cwm Taf: there is a similar note in the volumes of MSS poems purchased by Lady Hall, from the Iolo family,[42] stating that he was a "*Meddyg* ar lan Taf", a Doctor of Medicine on the Banks of the Taff

And while speake of these MSS volumes, I am reminded that you can do me a service. In one of these two MSS vols, there is a

---

[41] Madoc ab Owen Gwynedd was supposed to have discovered America in the twelfth century. This was disproved by Stephens in his controversial essay for the 1858 Llangollen eisteddfod. See section 6, 'Disproving the Madoc Myth', below.

[42] The Halls of Llanover purchased the Iolo manuscripts in 1853, after which time they could be viewed by Welsh antiquarians and historians by permission of the Halls.

poem by Gwilym Tew, to "Aberth yr Haul", the Sun Sacrifice, which I want to unfold the mystery of the /|\.[43] I wrote to ask Lady Hall for a copy, but as her ladyship has a pique against me, she gave me an evasive reply. If you could get me a copy, without mentioning my name, you would do me a service, as well as assist in exploding a semi-superstition.[44] The poem occurs not far from the commencement of the volume, and also among the Welsh Poems in the British Museum

Yours Truly
Thos Stephens

T. Wakeman Esq

*   *   *   *

NLW Tredegar 1310
Thomas Stephens to Thomas Wakeman

Merthyr Tydfil
Dec 16th 1856

Dear Sir/
    I find on examination of my papers, that my memory had deceived me, and that I had confounded the notes taken at Brecon of the Llyw. Sion MSS, which were there exhibited, with the notes made in the British Museum.

    Cywydd Aberth yr Haul is only to be found, I fear, in the Llywelyn Sion MSS now in the possession of Lady Hall. The ~~poem~~ volume commences either with "Thomas D Erllys, Cywydd i ddiolch am fwa" or "Llawdden i erchi Milgwn Gwynion" and the Cywydd i Aberth yr Haul is either the 11th or 12th in the volume.

---

[43] The 'nod cyfrin' or sacred symbol, symbolized God in bardic philosophy as well as forming the elements of the 'coelbren y beirdd' or bardic alphabet. See John Williams (Ab Ithel), *Barddas; or a Collection of Original Documents, Illustrative of the Theology, Wisdom, and Usages of the Bardo-Druidic System of the Isle of Britain* (Llandovery: Welsh MSS. Society, 1862), pp. 49-67.

[44] Stephens's critical attitude towards much Iolo-derived bardic material may have caused Lady Hall's reluctance to allow him access.

These are two volumes of the same size, being both small folios of about 600 pages each.

But, I find notes of two poems in the British Museum, which will I think interest you, be more worthy of translation than Gwilym Tew's poor cywydd to Sir John Morgan, and serve to illustrate the history of Wales in the ^14th &^ 15th ~~centures~~ centuries. They are both in MSS. Plut. CLXVII. No 14866—dated 1586. The first occurs at p. 70, and is a Cywydd by Iolo Goch to Edward y Trydydd, (the third), and the other at p. 440, by Dr John Kent, entitled a Cywydd ~~to~~ complaining of the oppression of the Cymry in the time of Henry IV. Should your leisure permit, I should be glad to get a copy of the latter, and should also feel great pleasure in supplying you with an English translation.

Yours faithfully
Thos. Stephens

Thos Wakeman Esq

*   *   *   *

NLW, MS. 965E, 279[45]
Charlotte Schreiber (née Guest) to Thomas Stephens

Lady Charlotte Schreiber has to apologize for having left Mr Stephen's note so long without an answer but she has hitherto been unable to lay her hands on the copy of the Greal which she had made for her. She hopes ere long to be able to do so and will then have much pleasure in lending it to Mr Stephens

  Exeter House
     Roehampton
        6 Oct 1857

*   *   *   *

---

[45] This letter was written on black-bordered paper, likely indicating that the writer was in mourning.

NLW, MS. 965E, 378
Thomas Stephens to John Williams (1792–1858)
Merthyr Tydfil. 20th Oct 1857
My dear Sir,

I am in receipt of your reply,[46] and am much obliged for the extracts quoted.

I propose to leave the Picts in peace, north of the Antonine wall; and to content myself with proving ~~that~~ or attempting to prove that the Lowlands were occupied by Cymry. My proposition is this: That in the 7th Century, the Lowland of Scotland were occupied by a people speaking a language identical with that of the Principality.

Now in reality this position does not render it necessary for me to discuss the question whether the Picts were Gael or Cymry; but it will follow as a matter of course that if the Lowland Picts spoke Cymraeg they must have been Cymry: and by the same rule, if the Highland Picts were identical with those of the Lowlands they were all Cymry.

That Cymraeg was the language of the Lowlands appears clear from the Gododin. The language of the Ottadini was that of the other tribes in all probability: and Aneurin's poem may be said to be living evidence of the fact that the Lowlands were occupied by Cymry. One passage will show the value of that poem:—

Gweleis y dull o bentir Adoen
Aberth am goelcerth a ddisgynnyn
Gweleis y ddeu oc eu tre Rygwyddyn
A gwyr Nwython ry gollesyn.

---

[46] This letter survives only in part. In it, Williams states that he has 'been lead to regard the Natives of Italy and of Gaul as the undoubted ancestors of our race', and directed Stephens to his 'On one Source of the Non-Hellenic Portion of the Latin Language', *Transactions of the Royal Society of Edinburgh*, 13:2 (January 1836), 494–563. He also provided Stephens with the address of William Forbes Skene (1809–1892), who he says enjoyed Stephens's *Literature of the Kymry* and would be happy to assist him. John Williams to Thomas Stephens, no place, no date, NLW, MS. 942C, Letter 145.

>Gweleis y wyr tylluawr gan wawr Adoen
>A phen Dyfnwal frych brein ae cnoyn[47]

These lines may be thus translated

>From the uplands of Doon, I saw men arrayed,
>While sacrifice descended on the beacon fire;
>I saw both (parties) by their town of Redegein
>And the men of Nwython lost the day.

Let us take these lines first: The uplands of Doon, are as you well know, the range of mountains in Ayrshire, ^to^ which Burns refer in "the banks and braes of bonny Doon". If so, here is Aneurin, in the West of Scotland; and occupied in such a manner as bespeaks him to have performing a very important duty: can we believe him to have been permitted to assume the priestly function among any other people than his own countrymen. Further, from the uplands of Doon, he commands a view of the town of Rhedegein, the capital of the Norantæ. In the MSS of the Gododin, this place is variously named Rhedegein, Fledegein (probably a misreading) and Rerygwyddyn and Rydwyddyn. Rhedegein corresponds exactly to the Retigonium of the Romans; and Rerygwyddyn very nearly to the Roman name for Loch Ryan— Retigonius Sinus. Retigonium stood on the present site of Stranraer in Wigtonshire, which is built on the banks of Loch Ryan. Aneurin then, saw two parties of armed men drawn up at Stranraer a fight ensued, and the men of Nwython lost the day. This was probably a local feud: history affords no notice of this fight, though singularly enough, a fact came to light some twenty 3 or 4 years ago strikingly confirmatory of Aneurin's statement; for in ploughing up the High St. of Stranraer with a view to its improvement, a large quantity of human bones were found strewed underneath. (If you would prevail with some of your learned Scottish friends to furnish fuller particulars respecting

---

[47] Stephens's transcription here differs markedly from that which was published in his translation of y Gododdin: 'Gweleis y dull o benn tir adoun / Aberth am goelkerth a disgynnyn / Gweleis oed kenevin ar dref redegein / A gwyr nwythyon ry gollesyn / Gweleis gwyr dullyawr gan awr adevyn / A phenn dyvynwal a breych brein ae cnoyn'. Stephens, *The Gododin*, pp. 310-14.

this fact you would greatly oblige me, and facilitate the illustration of the Gododin)—

To complete the case—Nwython was either the brother or
nephew of Aneurin! Ergo: Nwython's dominions were in
Wigtonshire & the Novantæ were Cymry.

Let me now take up the other lines: -

Gweleis y wyr dullyawr gan wawr adoen
A phen Dyfnwal frych brein ae cnoyn

English: -

I saw men arrayed by the dawn of Doon
And the head of Donald Bree gnawed by ravens.

Donald Bree was king of the Scots of Argyle. He was frequently at
war with the Strathclyde Kymry, and generally defeated. In 642
he invaded the dominion of the Norantæ, in the ~~dim---n~~ present
counties of Wigton and Aye, and the result is described by
Aneurin in this couplet, and is thus related in the *Annales
~~Ultronenses~~* of Ulster:—

DCXLII. Mors Domnail mac Aodha regis Hiberniæ, in fine
Jannarii. Postea Domnail Brec in bello Sraithe Cairuin, in fine
anni, m. Decembri, interfectus est ab Hoan rege Brittonum.

Fraithe Cairvin, is most probable Ystrad or Vale of the river
Girvan, which flows westward from the hills of Doon, and falls
into the sea at the town of Girvan midway between Ayr and
Stranraer; and therefore, the battle of which Aneurin was a
spectator, might easily have been seen from the hills of Doon. The
battle being fought in winter the bodies have been left unburied;
and the fact that ravens abound at Carnsmuir in that neighbourhood, shows the minute fidelity of the Bardic portraiture. The
Bard only mentions one of the Combatants—the other being his
own countrymen did not require to be named. Can ^Owen and^
the Britons of Ayr be ^of^ any other race than that of the Cymry?

At your leisure, I shall be glad to learn your opinion on this
point; for if I am not self deceived, the Cymric character of the
early Lowlander is as ~~clearly~~ as that of Wales. I shall also be glad
to learn your opinion respecting the terms Gael and Gwyddel. Are
they convertible terms?

All the Cymric documents show the contrary. The Gauls—Gal

of the Continent were Cymry; the triads classify all the British tribes as belonging to "Cyffredin Al y Cymry;" Llywarch Hen in two places calls Urien Rhegid—Eryr Gal; and Aneurin describes his countrymen to be Gal. But they carefully distinguish themselves from the Gwyddels. The Triads call the Scots—Gwyddelod, and describe the Picts as Gwyddel 'Ffichti and Gwyddel cochion,' and Aneurin thus classifies the people of North Britain: — speaking of ~~Gwen~~ Moryen Farfawc, he says.

> Goruchyd y Law Lovlen
> Ar Gynb a Gwyddyl a Phrydein:

The Britons were the Lowlanders I presume, the Gwyddyl—Scots & Southern Picts, and—Cynb—a remanent of the Cynebæ of Herodotus, ie the Cantæ of Ross, Sutherland &c

If these views are correct, Gal and Gwyddel are not convertible terms; but if Gal and Gael mean the same thing, Gallic and Cymbric ~~and~~ *are* kindred ~~terms~~ names—the distinction being between Gwyddel and Cymro, and not between Gael and Cymry. The resemblance between Gal and Gael, seems to furnish another proof of the identity of Picts & Cymry

What sound had the *u* in Gaul to Roman ears? Was it ~~like~~ *E* as in Welsh and German? Like *ee* in bee

Where can I find a copy of your Essay on "The Nonhellenic Elements of the Latin Language"?

> Waiting your reply I remain
> > Faithfully yours
> > > Thomas Stephens

P.S. The essay affair is in *statu quo*: the diversity of the judgments puzzles the Committee how to act. The Judges should agree upon an unanimous ~~reading~~ decision of some kind.[48]

---

[48] This most likely refers to Stephens's role as one of the adjudicators of a literary prize, proposed by Dr Rowland Williams, Vice-Principal of St Davids College in Lampeter, of £100 for the best essay, in Welsh, on Hebrew Prophecy. Stephens was to be one of five adjudicators — two churchmen, two dissenters and himself — as a judge purely of critical and literary merit. On 22 June 1857, David Williams, professor of Welsh at St Davids College, wrote to Stephens objecting to Stephens's Unitarianism. Stephens responded,

NLW, MS. 964E, 145a
Harry Longueville Jones to Thomas Stephens

Mr T. Stephens Merthyr Tydfil
Please to return in Dr. Williams's letter[49]
Cambrian Archaeological Association

Green Street
Neath
Ap. 29/58

My Dear Sir

I applied to the Rev. Dr. Williams[50] on your behalf as being a member of the Camb. Arch. Assoc. for leave to transcribe the *Ystoria Chyarlys*—and to publish it by means of the Association:—telling him that any condition the College might be pleased to name as to the place and manner of transcription would be gladly complied with, and the favour duly appreciated. I suggest that, through Mr Coxe[51] the sublibrarian of the Bodleian—a particular friend of Dr Williams and Myself,—a

---

countering Williams's comments in no uncertain terms. Although Rowland Williams interceded, apologizing to Stephens, David Williams withdrew as a judge as did all other judges except for Stephens and the Rev. David Lloyd. The prize was not awarded until 1860. David Williams to Thomas Stephens, Lampeter, 22 June 1857, NLW, MS. 965E, Letter 333; David Williams to Thomas Stephens, Pontarddulais, 30 July 1854, NLW, MS. 965E, Letter 334; Draft Letter, Thomas Stephens to David Williams, 12 August 1857, NLW, MS. 965E, Letter 335; Rowland Williams to Thomas Stephens, Lampeter, *c.* July 1857, NLW, MS. 965E, Letter 358 (2). Rowland Williams to Thomas Stephens, Mold, 18 August 1857, NLW, MS. 965E, Letter 359; Adjudications of Thomas Stephens and David Lloyd for the Essay on 'Hebrew Prophecy', NLW, MS. 965E, 396 (1–3). See also, Williams, 'The Life of Thomas Stephens'. pp. xxxv–xxxvi.

[49] This appears to be in a similar, but different, handwriting from the rest of the letter.

[50] This is most likely Charles Williams (*c.*1807–1877), who became principal of Jesus College, Oxford, in 1857. *Dictionary of Welsh Biography*, s.v. 'Williams, Charles'.

[51] Henry Octavius Coxe (1811–1881).

thoroughly competent transcriber might be found in Oxford.

I have the pleasure of enclosing you his reply by which you will learn that the College grant whatever we have asked—

In consequence of this I beg leave to propose to you as follows: (1) That we should ascertain carefully through Mr Coxe the probable *cost* and *time* of transcription:—that we should then make a formal proposal to the publishing committee of our Association to obtain the funds for paying the transcriber:—and for printing it in the Arch Camb

(2) That we should agree as to the number of copies to be printed off afterwards for yourself and as to the general form that the publication would assume.

If it is not too long it might come into *one* of our Numbers of the A. C.[52] together with your remarks, dissertations &c.:—or else it might form a separate volume by itself.

Be so obliging as to turn the matter over in your mind, and you can then write to me fully on the subject:—mentioning also the probable *time* of the whole being ready. I can then write to Dr Williams & the College.

I remain My dear Sir Yours very truly
H Longueville Jones

*   *   *   *

NLW, MS. 965E, 367
Bernard Bolingbroke Woodward to Thomas Stephens

Royal Library Windsor Castle,
22nd Augt 1860.

Sir,

I beg to acknowledge your very obliging & valuable communication, which I have forwarded to Mr Salisbury; from whom most probably you will hear soon. Any suggestions would be both welcomed & appreciated, from one so intimately acquainted with the Literature of the Kymry. Perhaps you would be able to assist

---
[52] *Archaeologia Cambrensis.*

in preparing a complete list of articles in high-class Periodicals on Wales, & the Border Counties, Welsh men, & Welsh affairs generally; or *by* Welshmen of mark. This would be a novel & very interesting feature in the Catalogue proposed.

 I am, Sir,
  Your most oblig'd servant
  B. B. Woodward

* * * *

NLW, MS. 964E, 112
Daniel Henry Haigh to Thomas Stephens

Erdington 6th October
1861

My dear sir

 Your kindness on former occasions induced me to trouble you on this. I have been asked to contribute a paper on the Fardell Monument to the Journal[53]—the Institute and I wish to notice the other ogham monuments in Wales. Can you introduce me to persons resident in the neighbourhood of Bridell Pembrokeshire, Clydai Cardiganshire, Kenfeggi, and Crickhowel from whom I could get information relating to the oghams there. If I have not given you a copy of a paper I contributed to the Kilkenny Transaction I will do so. I remain

 Yours very faithfully
  Daniel Hy Haigh

* * * *

---

[53] Haigh is likely referring to the *Archaeological Journal*, the organ of the Royal Archaeological Institute, to which journal he often contributed.

NLW, MS. 964E, 113
Daniel Henry Haigh to Thomas Stephens

Erdington 17ᵗʰ October
1861

Dear sir

I am aware that a paper on the Fardell stone has appeared in the Archaeologia Cambrensis but I have not read it,[54] nor shᵈ I, until I have done what Mr May has asked me to do. He has had an engraving made of the stone, and has asked me to write something for the Journal of the Institute about it.

I have had an opportunity of looking over the volumes of the Archaeologia Cambrensis of the first four years, and also several numbers of the last two years. The Llanfechan[55] and S. Dogmael's[56] stones are very well given, nothing more can be desired. About the Bridell[57] inscription I should write to ask some questions. The Clydai[58] inscription contains some of the same letters in Ogham & Latin, and I suspect has more Oghams than are represented. The Kenfegge[59] and Crickhowel[60] monuments are

───────────────

[54] E. Smirke, 'An Account of an Ancient Inscribed Stone Found at Fardel, near Ivybridge, in Devon, *Royal Institution of Cornwall*, Spring Meeting 1861', 1–16, printed as a supplement to *Archaeologia Cambrensis*, Third Series, 28 (October 1861).

[55] H[enry] L[ongueville] J[ones], 'Early Inscribed Stones of Wales. Llanfechan, Cardiganshire', *Archaeologia Cambrensis*, Third Series, 25 (January 1861), 42–45.

[56] Idem., 'Early Inscribed Stones of Wales. The Sagranus Stone at St. Dogmael's, Pembrokeshire', *Archaeologia Cambrensis*, Third Series, XXII (April 1860), 128–36.

[57] Idem., 'Early Inscribed Stones of Wales. Erect Stone with Oghams at Bridell', *Archaeologia Cambrensis*, Third Series, XXIV (October 1860), 314–17.

[58] J. O. Westwood, 'The Early Inscribed and Sculptured Stones of Wales', *Archaeologia Cambrensis*, Third Series, 23 (July 1860), 223–28.

[59] Idem., 'Ogham Characters in Glamorganshire', *Archaeologia Cambrensis*, 2 (April 1846), 182–3.

[60] Idem., 'The Turpillian Inscription, near Crickhowel, Brecknockshire, Welsh Oghams, Bardic Alphabet and Destruction of Ancient Monuments',

very imperfectly represented. In the numbers of the Archaeologia
Cambrensis which I have not seen, there may be others, but these
are all that I knew of.
I thank you for you obliging note and remain, dear Sir
    Yours very respectfully
    Daniel Hy Haigh

*   *   *   *

NLW, MS. 965E, 332
W. Walker Wilkins to Thomas Stephens

London. 16 June 1863
    Dear Sir, Pray accept my heartiest thanks for yr very prompt
& obliging replies to my last queries. I have never seen ab Iolo's[61]
"Colyn Dolphyn", or his "Cardiff Castle". Strange to say, the only
work of his in the Brit: Mus: is a Welsh ode on British Druids, with
a translation by Mr Bruce, 1835.[62]
    Concerning the ballad in praise of Glamorgan, attributed to Sir
Jo Stradling, author of Latin Epigrams, 1606, & Divine Poems,
1625,—in neither of wh. vols does it occur,—the hackneyed
quotation from it is as follows:—
        "And in Glamorgan's hillie parts
            Cole greatly doth abound;
        For goodness and for plenty, too,
            Its equal neuer was found.
        With wood & iren, ledde and salt,
            And lime aboundaint lie
        And every thing that mankind want,
            This land dothe it well supplie."
These stanzas certainly possess the ring of the early part of the

_____

Archaeologia Cambrensis, 5 (January 1847), 25–29.
[61] Taliesin Williams (Taliesin ab Iolo) (1787–1847).
[62] Henry A. Bruce, *Gwent and Dyfed Royal Eisteddfod, 1834: The Prize
Translation of the Welsh Ode on the British Druids by Taliesin Williams* (Cardiff:
William Bird, 1835).

16th century; but perhaps, after all, Sir John was *not* the author of 'em.

I have looked into Harl. MS. No 2273; wh, among several articles, more or less perfect (the Vol is in a tattered condition), contains a few brief extracts from the Book of Neath (so frequently quoted by Rice Merrick?) then (1595) in the possession of Sir Edw. Stradling of St Donat's, relating exclusively to the families of Mansel & Talbot. The full title of the article is:—
"6. Ex Libre abbathic de Nethe in cōm Glamorgan, jam en custodià Edwardi Stradlingo de St Donats, militis, anno 1595, cum aliis spectantibus ad familiam Talbotorum".

Your exposition of *gwynt a gwyden*[63] &c has set both my son & self a-thinking. Primarily, the reference, incorrect, is to the reserved fate of the criminal, who by his villanies has degraded himself to the level of a wolf, or beast of prey. By the old Roman law, a parricide was condemned to be sewn in a sack, together with a *wolf* & an adder, the sack with its strange contents was flung into the depths of the sea. Grimm, in his antiquities of German law,[64] stated that, in the very earliest times, "another aggravation of punishment was, that by the side of the hapless culprit (when hanged) they hung *wolves* or dogs". It wo^d seem that these beasts were usually (if not invariably) suspended *alive* by the side of the criminal, so that they might satisfy their hunger upon him. Grimm also quotes a German poet of the 13th century, who recommended his friends to put a rope about the neck of his worthless wife, "and hang thereby two wolves or three"!! Such may have been the fate of the adulteress.

Is there any affinity, think you, between "chwygy" and the Irish word cuilleasga, hazel rods or twigs? ^(The pronounciation is somewhat similar.)^ Before the advent of the Saxon in Ireland, who introduced hempen rope into that country, Irish criminals were hung in withs, or ozier bands—an additional ^(or the only)^ disgrace in their estimation! In ignorance of the history of

---

63 'Wind and withe'.

64 Jakob Grimm, *Deutsche Rechtsalterthümer*, zweite Ausgabe (Göttingen: Dieterichschen Buchhandlung, 1854) (originally published 1828).

Collyn Dolphyn, I cannot now conjecture the nature of the particular offence, which brought him to grief—i.e. the "twist". There wo^d seem, however, to be some allusion in, or resemblance to the ancient Briton's expression of horror against a very base criminal, to the commonly entertained detestation of an equal offence among the Romans.

Again thanking you for yr kindness, I beg to subscribe myself,

Dear Sir
Yr vry obliged & faithful Sert
W. Walker Wilkins

T. Stephens Esq

*   *   *   *

NLW, MS. 965E, 372a
William W. E. Wynne to Thomas Stephens

Peniarth
Machynlleth
[printed letter head]

Monday
[Postmarked August 25, 1863]

Sir,

I am not likely to be from home any morning excepting the 4 Sept:, & shall be glad to show you ~~any~~ such of the Hengwrt & Peniarth M.S.S. you may wish to see. I make the same rule that the late Sir Robert Vaughan did, of not lending ~~one~~ any of the M.S.S., excepting under very special circumstances.

In great haste,
Your's obedtly
Wm W E Wynne

*   *   *   *

NLW, MS. 965E, 373a
William W. E. Wynne to Thomas Stephens

Peniarth
Machynlleth
[printed letterhead]
Tuesday, Oct: 25 [1864].

Sir,

Upon looking for something else, in the Archaeologia Cambrensis, today I by accident ~~stumbled upon~~ observed a letter from you relative to the time at which the M.S. "B." ~~from~~ referred to in the Introduction to the Brut y Tywyssogion was written. I feel pretty certain that you are correct in ascribing it to a later date than the 13. Century. Mr Skene who is editing the Black book of Carmarthen, has been here for some time lately, & I have been ~~constantly~~ frequently in communication with him, relative to the work upon which he is engaged. He ~~have~~ has made out certain tests whereby to ascertain the ages of Welsh M.S.S. One of these is, that a letter representing w., very like the figure 6., did not come into use till about the year 1300. It occurs in M.S. "B.", ^of the Brut y Tywyssigion,^ Hengwrt M.S. 16., & in the "Llyfr Coch Hergest," M.S. "A." I differ from you however, in adjudicating M.S."A." to be of prior date to "B." There is a peculiar form of the letter g in the former which I believe shows it to have been of *later* date than M.S. "B."

I was sorry that you called here last summer when I was from home. Any time that you may be coming again into this neighbourhood & will give me notice, I shall be happy to show you any ~~here~~ either of the M.S.S. or printed books ^here^, if you take an interest in the latter. I have lately been so much engaged in attending & restoring this place, that I ~~cannot~~ have not paid the same attention to antiquarian pursuits that I did formerly. Can you tell me where *Hergest* is?—"Llyfr Coch Hergest". I am giving the decorators at Wynnstay some hints for restoring a curious set of heraldic panels from Llwydiarth, & Hergest occurs in them.

I am,
Your's obedtly
Wm W E Wynne

3

'WHAT HAS PREVAILED IN WALES, APPEARS ALSO TO HAVE PREVAILED IN IRELAND': THOMAS STEPHENS'S IRISH CORRESPONDENCE

THOMAS Stephens toured Ireland in August 1856. According to B. T. Williams, 'This tour was ever afterwards associated in his mind with many stories of Irish character, which he would recount at times'.[1] This was not, however, the beginning of Stephens's relationship with the 'emerald isle', as he corresponded with Irish antiquarians, exchanging information concerning Welsh and Irish history, language, culture, and antiquities, across his scholarly life. It is even probable that Stephens only met one of his Irish correspondents, the architect and antiquarian Richard R. Brash, before beginning to exchange letters and it should also be noted that his 1856 tour falls within a four-year gap in his Irish correspondence (although he did subscribe to the *Ossianic Journal* in 1859).[2] The value of his travel notwithstanding, it seems to have had little impact on his Irish correspondence which began, as was stated in the 'Introduction',[3] on the intro-duction of a fellow Welshman, and resumed after a hiatus through a mutual acquaintance with another Welshman, Robert John Prys (Gweirydd ap Rhys), and involvement with the Welsh Cambrian Archaeological Association.

Stephens's Irish correspondence began in 1849 as a result of the 'cromlech question'. A heated debate about cromlechs arose at the Third Annual Meeting of the Cambrian Archaeological

---

[1] Williams, 'Life of Thomas Stephens', pp. xxxiii.

[2] John O'Daly to Thomas Stephens, Dublin, 17 February 1859, NLW, MS. 964E, Letter 30.

[3] See p. xxiii, above.

Association, a society well-connected with Irish and Breton scholars and societies. At the meeting, a paper by James James (Iago Emlyn) on the relationship between the different Celtic languages prompted James Henthorn Todd, who was in attendance as part of an 'Irish delegation' of eminent anti-quarians, to comment that the word 'cromlech' was not, in fact, derived from their supposed use as altars to the Irish god 'Crom'.[4] This led to a debate over whether cromlechs were sepulchral monuments or druidic altars which soon spilled out into the local newspapers, particularly the *Cardiff and Merthyr Guardian*. In a series of letters, an 'Irish' camp, led by Todd, argued for sepulchre against a native, romantic 'Welsh' camp led by John Williams, Archdeacon of Cardigan, arguing for druidic use.[5] Although he did not comment publicly on the issue until 1856,[6] Stephens was appealed to for information on Todd's behalf and on that basis established a correspondence with him.

Although the correspondence began with megalithic monu-ments, it soon moved on to other topics, exploring the diverse offerings of Welsh-Irish knowledge exchange. Stephens's Irish correspondence illustrates a wide range of topics and opinions, with correspondents ranging from some of Ireland's most scien-tifically and critically inclined antiquarians, such as Eugene O'Curry and John O'Donovan, to those with more romantic views, such as Brash. It is also a rich source for accessing the networks and connections between Welsh and Irish scholars in the period, demonstrating how systems of introduction and reputation facilitated knowledge exchange even if the letter writers never met in person.

---

[4] 'Cambrian Archaeological Association, Third Annual Meeting, Cardiff, August 27th to September 1st, 1849', *Archaeologia Cambrensis*, 16 (October 1849), 294–320 (311-13).

[5] See various articles in *Cardiff and Merthyr Guardian, Glamorgan, Monmouth, and Brecon Gazette*, September 1849–January 1850, available via *Welsh Newspapers Online*.

[6] T. Stephens, 'On the Names of Cromlechau', *Archaeologia Cambrensis*, Third Series, 6 (April 1856), 99–109.

NLW, MS. 965E, 241a
J. Bruce Pryce to Thomas Stephens

Dyffryn Golych—Cardiff Sept. 24. 49

Dear Sir

Can you help the Irish Antiquarians to the *first* appearance of the word Cromlech?

I enclose you a letter[7] from Dr. Todd[8] of Dublin University to me on that subject.

If Ffili *was* the son of Cennydd after whom our "Lordship of Senghennydd" is called, it is a strong *primâ facie* proof of the soundness of your derivation.

But I believe the Breos family, for 3 or 4 generations (though not recorded by the scanty writers of the day) *were* at Caerphilly—one of them *had* a son called Philip—one of them (William) was selected Bishop of Llandaff in 1265, and died 1287—his tombstone, perfectly legible, may now be seen within the altar Rails of "our Ladye's Chapel" at Llandaff Cathedral—

Now the family of Breos, or Bruce were well known to be at Gower & at Brecon—both these places were then, as they now are, in the Diocese of *St David's*—would not his being elected for Llandaff be a (collateral) proof of local influence arising from local power?—Think of this and give me information, if you please, of the oldest manuscript in which you can find the word Cromlech—Yrs Sinc

J Bruce Pryce

*　　*　　*　　*

---

[7] This letter does not appear among Stephens's collected correspondence. It was probably returned to Pryce.

[8] James Henthorn Todd (1805–1869).

NLI, MS. 2252, 23
Thomas Stephens to James Henthorn Todd

Merthyr Tydfil
Nov 10 1849
Rev Sir,

Having some time since hastily promised Mr Bruce Pryse to take part in the melee raised by the Comlech question, I am, now that the disputants are falling off, beginning to think of what I shall write. And at the outset I am met by a difficulty, which you only can remove.

In the Dictionaries of O'Reilly,[9] Vallancey,[10] and Armstrong,[11] the Dict.—Scoto-Celticism,[12] and Shaws Analysis of the Gaelic,[13] occur the words *Crom*, God, *Cromchmach*, a famous Irish idol, *Cromthear, Cromleac*. Now. I wish to know how these authorities are estimated in Ireland, and by such scholars as yourself, Dr. Petrie,[14] and Mr ODonovan.[15] In Welsh literature, and particularly in lexicography we have had an immense amount of quackery, but there are reasons to believe that a better spirit is about to prevail, and that our language and literature will henceforth be subjected to the test of a more scientific criticism. What has prevailed in Wales, appears also to have prevailed in

---

[9] Edward O'Reilly, *An Irish-English Dictionary* (Dublin: J. Barlow, 1817).

[10] Possibly Charles Vallancey, *Prospectus of a Dictionary of the Language of the Aire Coti, or Ancient Irish* (Dublin: Graisberry and Cambell, 1802); or Idem, *A Grammar of the Iberno-Celtic or Irish Language to which is Prefixed an Essay on Celtic Language* (Dublin: R. Marchbank, 1782).

[11] R. A. Armstrong, *A Gaelic Dictionary, in two Parts: I. Gaelic and English.–II. English and Gaelic* (London: James Duncan, 1825).

[12] *Dictionarium Scoto-Celticum: A Dictionary of the Gaelic Language*, two vols (Edinburgh: William Blackwood under the direction of The Highland Society of Scotland, 1828).

[13] William Shaw, *An Analysis of the Gaelic Language* (Edinburgh: W. and T. Ruddiman, 1788).

[14] George Petrie (1790–1866).

[15] John O'Donovan (Seán Ó Donnabháin) (1806–1881).

Ireland; and now that more severe principles of study are being applied to antiquities, the fanciful etymologies of your old writers are getting into disrepute. With respect to General Vallancy you have said that such is the case; but are O'Reilly, and the Scotch Shaw, Armstrong, and the writers of the Dict. Scot. Celticism— also men of straw? Does not the word *Crom* occur in any of your old bards in the sense—God? *It does not in ours.* Will you be kind enough to favour me with a reply at your leisure, ~~and~~ in return I shall be happy to place at your service, the small stock of Cymric knowledge which has fallen to my share.

You are quite right in your conjecture that we know but little upon the question, and I have been not a little amused at the perplexity into which you have thrown our antiquarians: The Archdeacon[16] has disappointed everybody, and made a very Bobadil of himself; while you have not made as good a case for the sepulchral theory, as ^was^ expected. On this subject however more anon. I am not sure, that I shall say anything now, but my epistle shall at least be good tempered, and if possible brief.

I am Sir
    Very respectfully Yours
        Thos Stephens
The Rev Dr. Todd.

P.S. In Llwyd's Arch Brit.[17] Lit. Irish-English Dictionary are the following entries –

Crom, Crooked: crom chonail, a plague in Ireland 540 A.D. (what meaning has <u>Crom</u> here?)

Ag Cromadh, Bowing or bending, Do Chromadh Sios dhi, to bow down unto it; to <u>worship it</u>.

---

[16] John Williams (1792–1858).

[17] Edward Lhuyd, *Archæologia Britannica Giving some Account Additional to What has been Hitherto Publish'd of the Languages, Histories and Customs of the Original Inhabitants of Great Britain, Vol I: Glossography* (Oxford: Printed at the Theatre for the Author, 1707), unpaginated. Thomas Stephens's copy of this book is now at Dowlais Library.

What ~~significance~~ ^importance^ would you attach to these interpretations?

*   *   *   *

NLW, MS. 965E, 300a-b
James Henthorn Todd to Thomas Stephens

Trin: Coll: Dublin
Nov. 14. 1849

Dear Sir

I am very glad to find that you intend entering the lists, & taking a share in the Cromlech controversy

O Reilly's Dictionary is compiled from various sources, & amongst the rest from Vallancey's MSS. O Reilly was not himself an original or vernacular Irish scholar. He was a man of great industry & learned all he knew of the language from books. Hence it came to pass that he transcribed into his Dictionary many words for which there is no authority—& they have been copied from his work into the Dictionaries compiled by Armstrong, Shaw, & other Scotch lexicographers of the Celtic.

You will see a curious instance of O Reilly's ignorance in the word *Croimlin*, which he interprets thus (from a MS. note of Vallancey's,) —

"Croimlin, the temple of Crom; the name of several places in Ireland".

Now there is no such name as Cromlin, except in the Anglicized spelling of the names of some places in Ireland. In Irish these places are called Cromglinn,[18]—Crom=glinn, bent or crooked *valley*. Moreover if there were such a word as Crom signifying a God, or idol, & if we wished to say temple of Crom, (using the old word *lann* for church or temple) we would have said lann an Chroim, not Crom=lin.

And now with respect to the famous Irish idol Crom=chruac. The authority for the word is the tripartite Life of St Patrick, lib.

---

[18] Written with Irish letters.

ii. c. 3, where this idol is said to have been destroyed by the saint—But in Joceline's life, where the same story occurs, the idol is called not Crom=cruach, but Cean=cruithi, which name is there interpreted to signify *caput omnium deorum*. In the annals of Ulster &c the four Masters the same idol is mentioned, but the lives of St Patrick are the original source of the name: & if Jocelin be correct then Crom=cruach is an error for Cean=cruithi, which signifies literally bloody head, (for cruach & cruithi are the same word in Different spellings) & the idol is described as surrounded by twelve other idols that are sunk in the earth, so that this was the chief, & is so called caput omnium deorum.

Crom cruach signifies bloody stooped (thing); it was probably Cean crom cruach, bloody stooped head, or chief, which would reconcile the two accounts.

In the Duin Seanchus, or History of Forts, castles, &c. in Ireland, a work of great antiquity the following account of the Crom cruach is given—"Magh sleacht (Plain of slaughter) is so called because it is there was the chief idol of Ireland, viz the Crom-cruach, & twelve stone idols round it, & its face was of gold, & this was the god of all the people that possessed Ireland until the coming of St Patrick."

If the face of the idol was covered with gold, this may account for its being called bloody head - & if the head was inclined or stooped this would be a reason for calling it crom.

This word crom is ~~off~~ often used as a sort of surname or appellation for ~~those~~ men who are remarkable for a stoop or inclination of the head. Thus O Donovan Crom, or the stooped was a famous chief of the O Donovan's who was often called "the Crom" or the stooped one. There is a Glen in the County Cork, in the O Donovan country called Glenn an Chruim, or the valley of the Crom, i.e. of the stooped O Donovan. If Vallancey had got hold of this he would of course have made it the valley of his God Crom: & it w^d have been much more plausible than some other of his instances, inasmuch as it would have been correct Irish.

There was also a Castle in the Co Limerick called Crom Castle from the same Crom O Donovan: & this is the Crom mentioned in the Duke of Leinsters motto—That Castle was taken by the

Fitzgeralds from the O Donovan's & hence they assumed for their motto Crom a boo, or in correct spelling Crom a buaidh, i.e Crom conquered, alluding to O Donovan Crom & his Castle. See Gough's Camden. iii. 518.[19]

The supposition that the word Cromlech signifies the stone of the God Crom, has been suggested by O Halloran[20] & others who have been infected with Vallanceyism. But no Irish scholar could imagine such a thing—for if we wanted to say stone of Crom, we could only express it by Leach an Chroim—whereas the position of crom in the word cromlech clearly shews it to be an adjective, whatever be its meaning.

The name which Llwyd quotes for the great plague of 540—is a mistake—it ought to be cronchonaill. Cron or Cruan signifies yellow, & the words are translated flava ictericia the yellow jaundice, by Colgan, Acta Sanctorum Hibernia, p. 831. col. 2–

Cromadh is a living Irish word signifying to bend, to stoop, to bow down. It may be used for worship, not primarily but just as we use the word bow down, for worship—It occurs frequently in our Irish version of the Bible, & is still in vernacular use.

By the way the Annals of Ulster & of Tighernach, describing the great pestilence of 543, say "anno post quam Papa Vigilius——obiis, mortalitas magna que. Blefed dicitur"

The word Blefed is unintelligible to us—has it any meaning in Cymric ears?

I am very sorry archdeacon Williams could not write with a better tone. I did not enter into the question of the sepulchral theory of the cromlechs, because I was anxious only to know what Welsh tradition said respecting them. My friend Dr Petrie

---

[19] William Camden, *Britannia: or, a Chronographical Description of the Flourishing Kingdoms of England, Scotland, and Ireland, and the Islands Adjacent; from the Earliest Antiquity*, ed. by Richard Gough, three vols (London: John Nichols, 1789).

[20] Sylvester O'Halloran (1728–1807), was an Irish surgeon, antiquarian, and historian, whose historical works include *An Introduction to the Study of Antiquities of Ireland* (1770), *Ierne Defended* (1774) and *A General History of Ireland* (1775).

has fully investigated that subject, I would rather it was discussed by him. I hope he will be persuaded to mingle in the fight. The discussion I hope will do good

    I remain, dear Sir
        Very truly yours
           J. H. Todd

*   *   *   *

NLI MS, 2252, 21
Thomas Stephens to James Henthorn Todd

                         Merthyr Tydfil
                        Nov. 17th 1849

My dear Sir,

    I am not sure that I shall be able to answer your question satisfactorily, but as the following facts may be suggestive of something better, I hasten to reply to your note.

    Blefed, in that form certainly carries no sense to Cymric ears; yet it is possible to evoke meaning out of it. In Wales, the yellow plague of 543, was as early as the 12th century, the subject of a myth, and I suspect from this word that such was also the case in Ireland. In the poem called "Mabinogi Taliesin", a production formerly supposed to belong to the 6th century, but now known to belong to the 12th or 13th (see my Lit of the Kymry p 425) occur the following lines,—

      E ddaw prŷv[21] rhyvedd
      O vorva Rhianedd
      I ddial enwiredd
      Ar Vaelgwn Gwynedd
      Ei vlew, ei ddannedd
      A'i lygaid yn eurwedd
      A hwn gwna ddiwedd
      Ar Vaelgwn Gwynedd.

This romance may be seen at length in either the last number of

---

[21] The accent over the 'y' is a straight horizontal line.

Lady Charlotte Guest's Mabinogion,[22] or in Vol v of the Cambrian
& Caledonian Magazine (1833). In the latter, these lines are by Dr.
W. O. Pughe, ~~are~~ thus Englished,—

> "A most strange creature will come
> From the sea marsh of Rhainedd
> As a punishment of iniquity
> on Maelgwn Gwynedd;
> his ^hair^, his teeth,
> And his eyes being as gold;
> and this will bring destruction
> upon Maelgwn Gwynedd."[23]

This plague is called "y Vad Velen", *the yellow pest.* you will
perceive that with you, as with us, the yellowness forms an
essential part of the description. But we do not know what "y vad
velen" signifies. Mâd with us generally ^means^—kind, gracious.
Dr Pughe says it is also a general name for reptiles; but gives no
authority. Dr Davies a much older, in fact our oldest
lexicographer, states the *Vad Velen* to be the fabulous animal
called the basilisk.

This plague was usually called the yellow Plague of Rhos,
~~which~~ and was said to have been caused by the number of
unburied bodies of the slain that remained ~~buried~~ on that spot,
and that whoever went within the reach of the effluvia fell dead
immediately. Thus Davydh ab Gwilym a bard living between 1350
and 1400, describes it (p 279 Works) as the cold yellow plague of
Rhos—

> "I'r oer Fad Felen o Ros."

There is a story that Maelgwn Gwynedd King of Wales to avoid
the effects of this pestilence retired from his castle of Dyganwy to
the Church of Llanrhos, (NB all these places are in North Wales)

---

[22] Lady Charlotte Guest (trans), *The Mabinogion, from the Llyfr Coch o Hergest, and Other Ancient Welsh Manuscripts*, three vols (London: Longman, Brown, Green, and Longmans, 1849).

[23] [Idrison], 'The Mabinogi of Taliesin. (Continued from the Cambrian Quarterly for April)', *The Cambrian and Caledonian Quarterly Magazine*, 5: 19 (July 1833), 366–382 (368).

where he hoped to be safe, "but says Lady Charlotte (Vol 3 p 399) being impelled by curiosity, he looked out through the keyhole of the door and thereby caught the infection," from which he died. Her Ladyship's version is a little confused. There could have been ^no^ gratification of curiosity in peeping through a keyhole at a pestilence! There is however a more perfect form of the story; but where I read it, I cannot now recollect. It is:—The Vad Velen ~~wa~~ (ie the supposed basilisk) being about to pass the church of Llanrhos, Maelgwn was told not to look at it, as the sight of it was fatal. He looked nevertheless, and reaped the consequences. He died of the Vad Velen, whatever it was.

In all these cases we perceive that the pestilence is personified. The fact that the pestilence was ^by^ *malaria* from the marsh of Rhianedd, aggravated if not caused, and that the pestilence was characterized by yellowness are sustained throughout; but it is evident that much difficulty was felt in personifying it. The author of the lines attributed to Taliesin can only speak of eyes, hair, and teeth, ~~and~~ nor has there been any account given of what the story states Malgwn to have seen. He saw the Vad Velen passing; but what sort of thing the Vad Velen was—the deponent saith not.

So much for tradition; now for criticism. You say the position of crom in the compound Crom-lech indicates it to be an adjective. What is the rule by which you determine that? Be kind enough to inform me at your leisure, as I propose to introduce something on the grammatical structure of Crom-lech into my proposed letters. To return to "y Vad Velen". and the bearing upon it of this rule. In Wales, in *single words* the adjective invariably *follows* the noun, as Ceffyl *du*, a black horse; but though I have not seen it mentioned in any Welsh grammar, this rule is reversed in compound words, as crogbren, a gallows, Crog-lên, a suspended curtain, Cronglwyd, and would be in Crom-lech. Is your rule in this respect general, or only specifically applicable to compound words?

Now for the application supposing the rule to require the adjective first, the Welsh *Vad Velen* would in Irish be Velen-Vad. Drop the *n* and you have Velevad, by contraction Vlevad, & Blefed.

This is the best answer I can give. How far it is correct you are the best judge.

The *Vad velen* is with us also called *y Vall Velen*, and this is considered to be the correct form—Y fâll or vall means Evil, a plague, or ~~an~~ Evil spirit—demon: In an early part of this note I gave a story from recollection; since that I have found my authority to be Geoffrey of Monmouth, two Welsh copies of which refer to the Vad Velen as follows,—

"Ac yn Eglwys y brodyr y by varw (ie ≠ Maelgwn Gwynedd) pan welas er y *vall velen* drwy dwll ar drwys yr eglwys"

And he (M.G.) died in the church of the brothers when he saw the Vall Velen through a hole in the door of the church.

"Ac ymewn Eglwys en emyl Dygannwy eu bu farw pan weles e *vat velen* drw dwl dor er eglwys"

And in a church in the neighbourhood of Dyganwy, he (M.G.) died when he saw the Vat Velen through a hole

[The remainder of this letter is missing]

*   *   *   *

NLW, MS. 965E, 301b[24]
Thomas Stephens to James Henthorn Todd

Dear Sir/

Some time ago I sent you a long note on the meaning of the word "blefed", which occurs in the following entry:—

"Mortalitas magna quæ 'blefed' dicitur". *Tigernach.*

It has just occurred to me that after all, this is only our common name for sickness or disease—clevyd—which in Welsh orthography—the f being soft could be written Clefyd, Clefid, or Klefid. Sounded Klevid.

I do not know whether the letter *k* occurs in some of your MSS. It does occur in ours. If so the b in *blefed* may be a mistaken k. Which according to Llwyd was introduced into our MSS about the

---

[24] This letter was probably returned to Stephens with Todd's reply.

year 1200, and was discontinued about 1500. We have no *k* in the Kymric alphabet, and the letter in our old MSS was probably derived from the Normans. The initial consonant changes as follows: —

		sounded
Nom. Case.	Clefid—	Clevid
Gen.	glefid—	glefvid
a Chlefid—		with sickness
yn nghlefid		in sickness

Please to accept this attempt to explain the word and believe me Dr Sir
   Yours faithfully
      Thos Stephens
Dr Todd

*   *   *   *

NLW, MS. 965E, 301a
James Henthorn Todd to Thomas Stephens

Athenaeum
London
Sept. 6. 1851

My dear Sir
   Your letter followed me here. I believe the word 'blefed' is correct. We have no k in Irish. The pestilence referred to by Tighernach is elsewhere generally called the yellow pestilence (flava- or in Irish buidhe)—this leads me to conjecture that blefed is connected with the root of an English word *blue*, which in Anglo Saxon had a more enlarged meaning & was applied to colour in general. Bleofah, & Bleofag in Anglo Saxon signifies versicolor, & might very well be applied to a disease whose characteristic was coloured blotches or spots over the body. Wachter gives the root *blaw*, cosius, glaucus, coruleus, & gives the Islandic synon. *blafain*, in which the w, as in Anglo Saxon has become f.[25]

---

[25] Johannis Georgii Wachteri, *Glossarivm Germanicvm Contens Origines et Antiqvitates Totius Lingvæ Germanicæ, et Omnium Pene Vocabulorum,*

If the final d were aspirated the word ~~bfe~~ blefed would be identical in sound with the A. Saxon *bleofah*.

Your conjecture however is very ingenious & plausable; & I will not undertake to say that it is not correct, but the parallel passages in the Annals lead me to the conclusion that blefed must be synon[s]. with the Irish buidhe, & therefore that it signifies colour of some kind.

    I remain, dear Sir
      J H Todd

*   *   *   *

NLW, MS. 965E, 322a
William Wilde[26] to Thomas Stephens

Dublin Westland Row [printed]
23rd June 1854

Sir/

My friend Dr. Todd of Trinity College has frequently promised to give me a letter of yours upon the word *Blefed*, applied to the plague styled in our Annals the *Buidhe Connail*, the great yellow plague of 548, which appeared in Ireland and also in England as Bede states.

I am at present engaged in compiling a history of Irish epidemic pestilences and would gladly enter into communication with you or any friend in Wales respecting contemporaneous plagues in that country.

An answer at your earliest convience will confer a compliment upon,

Yours faithfully
W Wilde

Vigentium et Desitorum (Leipzig: Joh. Frid. Gleditschii B. Filium, 1737), p. 175 (s.v. 'Blaw').

[26] The majority of Wilde's letters to Stephens were written in a much finer and more legible handwriting than Wilde's own.

NLW, MS. 965E, 322b
William Wilde to Thomas Stephens

Dublin Westland Row [printed]
24 July 1854

Dear Sir

Accept my best thanks for your prompt and learned reply to my former communication respecting the *Blefed*. You have I think fallen into some trivial errors respecting the dates at which it appeared in Ireland, but as they are comparatively of little consequence I will not trouble you about them. I will with your permission have some further communication with you on your Welsh *Clefyd*, but for the present permit me to ask you for the extracts from the Welsh Annals respecting it and the *Crom Connail*, which with us means the same disease.

I am profoundly ignorant of your Welsh Annals and would therefore ask you to put me in the way of procuring any Works which refer to them, that is, provided they are English or Latin as I do not know any Welsh Scholar here.

Our Irish Annals viz those of Tigernach—the Annals of Ulster, Annals of Clonmacnoise—An. of Innisfallen; An. of Kilronan. Annals of the Four Masters, And the Chronicon Scotorum &c &c abound with notes of plague, pestilence, and famine, and these I am having extracted and arranged chronologically: And the whole history of Irish Epidemics printed as a fitting Preface to the Analysis of our late fearful Epidemic of 1826–8. I intend to give the words of the respective Authors as far as possible and then write a dissertation upon the whole. I will print in chronological order this history of pestilences and Cosmical phenomena in four columns containing the date—the event and circumstance—(chiefly quotations)—the authority from which the foregoing was taken—and lastly some brief references to contemporaneous Epidemics. In this latter Column your Welsh Annals would be of great use.

I likewise have included Epizootics and Vegetable diseases.

Allow me to refer you to the following names which possibly the Welsh Annals may throw some light upon

AD 550 The Chronicon Scotorum gives an Account of a "Pestis qua Vocatur *Samtrug.*" Other Authorities style it *Samthrose,* and others again *Santrusk.* It raged about the middle of the Sixth Century. Do the Welsh Annals allude to this?

Under the year 949 the Annals of the Four Masters give an Account of the *Clamhtrusgadh* a sort of Scaly leprosy or Mange, which O'Donovan has translated "Great Lues",[27] and in the annals of *Clonmacnoise* it is called *Dolor Gentilum* having been introduced by the Danes who then swarmed upon the coast of Ireland ^I think it was syphilis^. Have you any Welsh term for disease similar to the foregoing?

About the beginning of the 16th Century we had an Epidemic of a disease called the *Kings Gain* ^*chuche au* riogh^ which carried off many persons of distinction and among the rest the celebrated Dr O'Cassidy in 1504.[28] I am inclined to think that this was some nervous affection like the Dancing Mania. Can you enlighten me thereon?

The week before last I directed a copy of our Census Report upon the Status of Disease to be forwarded to you. It has I hope reached you. Toward the end of it you will find a Nosological table in which the Irish terms for disease are given. If you have anything of the kind in Welsh I would feel obliged by being referred to it.

By this Post I send you a Copy of a little Work of mine upon Irish Popular Superstitions.[29]

I remain

Yours faithfully

W Wilde

*   *   *   *

---

[27] John O'Donovan, *Annala Rioghachta Eirann: Annals of the Kingdom of Ireland, by the Four Masters,* second edn, six vols (Dublin: Hodges, Smith, and Co. 1856), vol. 2, p. 667.

[28] See O'Donovan, *Annála Rioghachta Éireann,* vol. 5, p. 1275.

[29] W. R. Wilde, *Irish Popular Superstitions* (Dublin: William S. Orr and Co., [1852]).

NLW, MS. 965E, 323
William Wilde to Thomas Stephens

Dublin 21, Westland Row [printed]
4. January 1855

My Dear Sir:/
Allow me to revive our correspondence by asking you to refer me to such Cambrian Annals as relate to "Plague pestilence and famine" in the early times. In a work published lately by Dr Bascome he frequently alludes to plagues in Wales of which the following is one example A.D. 327 "The inhabitants of Wales suffered from Pestilence;" but as he has not given any authorities I find some difficulty in acknowledging that part of his book which I am myself unable to verify.[30]

When I had had the pleasure of hearing from you, you said you would make some further enquiries for me respecting *Blefed* or as you call it in Welsh *Vel Vellen*.

    I have the pleasure to
        remain,
           Yours faithfully
             W Wilde

      *   *   *   *

NLW, MS. 965E, 324
William Wilde to Thomas Stephens

21 Westland Row,
Dublin 23rd June 1855

My Dear Sir/
Allow me to renew our correspondence by asking your opinion with respect to the date of Sampson one of your Welsh Bishops mentioned in the Itenarary of Baldwin. So far as I can

---

[30] Edward Bascome, *A History of Epidemic Pestilences from the Earliest Ages, 1495 Years before the Birth of our Savour to 1848 with Researches into their Nature, Causes, and Prophylaxis* (London: John Churchill, 1851), pp. 22–3.

make out Sampson flourished early in the tenth century say about AD 913; but the "yellow Plague" which raged in Wales in his time had been referred by some chroniclers to the period of the *Buidhe Chonnail* in the 6th and 7th centuries. If you can assist me in fixing the date of Sampson I shall feel much obliged.

Yours Faithfully
W Wilde

[Thomas Stephens, in pencil:]
The date of Sampson may be fixed without any difficulty. He was born abbot of Lantwit Major in this county in the middle of the 6th century. He left Glamorganshire about 550, for Armorica (Brittany), where he was made bishop of Dole, and in that capacity he attended an Ecclesiastical council at Paris in 557. Died Etat 68 in 566 or 592

*   *   *   *

RIA, MS 12 N 23/1/52/
Thomas Stephens to William Wilde

Merthyr Tydfil
June 26 1855

Dear Sir,
Your question as to St Samson is easily answered.
He was the son of one Ammon the Black, who was descended from a royal family, of the district of Meath (according to the *Lib. Landavensis*.[31] p 287), or of the district of Graweg in Brittany. (^according to the^ Iolo MSS.[32] 501); but whether his ^birth^

---

[31] W. J. Rees, *Liber Landavensis, Llyfr Teilo, or the Ancient Register of the Cathedral Church of Llandaff; From MSS. in the Libraries of Hengwrt, and of Jesus College, Oxford* (Llandovery: William Rees, 1840).

[32] Taliesin Williams (ab Iolo), *The Iolo Manuscripts: A Selection of Ancient Welsh Manuscripts, in Proze and Verse, from the Collection Made by the late Edward Williams, Iolo Morganwg, for the Purpose of Forming a Continuation of the Myfyrian Archaiology; and Subsequently Proposed as Materials for a new*

~~death~~ took place in 496 or 524, or at either, is uncertain. He was abbot of Lantwit Major in this county ^in^ ~~about~~ the middle of the 6th century. He left Glamorganshire about 550 for Brittany, where he assisted Ithael a native prince in throwing off the yoke of the Frankish kings. He was made Bishop of Dole in that coun‐ try; and (*this much is certain*) in that capacity, he attended and subscribed the Act of the second council of Parish in 557 (*Concilia Galliæ* cited by Usher). He died at Dole at an advanced age, according to the *Lib. Landav*; According to another account he re‐ turned to Glamorganshire, and died at Lantwit. He was 68 years when he died; but whether he died in 564 or 592 is undecided.

The central and fixed date of 557 will suffice to prove that the flava pestis that took place in his day was your *Crom Chonaille* of 550 (*Tigernach*), and our *Vall Velen*. However, to remove any doubt, I may mention, that the story given by Giraldus is told of *Bishop Teilo* in the Liber Landarvensis,—that he fled from Wales, ~~and~~ was received at Dole by Samson, and that he remained in Brittany for 7 years until the "Pestis autem illa *flava* vocabatur"— had abated.

The insertion of Artmael and Samson as bishops of St Davids, is a holy fraud on the part of Giraldus, to serve the great contro‐ versy or rather contest in which he was engaged; and having only the colouring of fact:—Samson either before going to Brittany, or after returning (if he did)—erected a cross at Lantwit for the sake of his own soul, that of Irthael the king (of Brittany), and Artmael (decani)—the deacon? There never were any such bishops of St Davids.

There is a much fuller account of this *flava pestis*, in our accounts than in any where else. The whole history of St Samson, and the *flava pestis*, is ~~state~~ recorded in circumstantial detail in the *Liber Landavensis*.—Latin pp 101. ^&^ 123 English Translation pp. 343. ^& 371^ I presume it is in the Library of Trinity College.

Yours truly
Thos. Stephens

History of Wales (Llandovery: William Rees, 1848).

NLW, MS. 965E, 327[33]
William Wilde to Thomas Stephens

21 Westland Row
[Postmarked 29 July 1855]
Dear Sir
I received your note of the 26th Together with the proof—for which I send you my best thanks.

I procured a copy of the Iolo MSS. from Dr Todd but am stupid enough not to be able to find the quotations you have given me under AD 220 307. 334. 5. & 410

The *"Yellow pestilence"* recorded under this latter I don't understand as *the first* Welsh pestilence (of the 3 recorded) was in 466, when the bodies of the Gwyddalans (were they not _Irish_) caused the plague.

Your Welsh Antiquarian Works want indeces very much

I will send your introduction to Dr O Donnovan (now at Oxford) & E. Curry[34] now in London. & also answer your other queries forthwith, but I write this in haste as I have the first sheet going to press. & I also want if possible the authorities for dates in Iolo MS
Yours
W Wilde

*   *   *   *

NLW, MS. 965E, 385a
William Wilde to Thomas Stephens

21 Westland Row
Dublin, 30th July 1855
My Dear Sir/
I yesterday wrote you an authograph letter I fear has afforded

---

[33] This letter was written in Wilde's own handwriting, which is less legible than that handwriting in which most letters from him were written.
[34] Eugene O'Curry (Eoghan Ó Comhraí) (1794–1862).

you some difficulty to decipher.[35]

I had a letter from Dr. O'Donovan today from Oxford where he has been for some time past transcribing our Irish Brehon Laws. He will return here tomorrow or next day. He is not only the most learned Irish Scholar by far—but one of the most liberal men of his knowledge I ever came across. Next to the accumulation of knowledge his chief delight seems to be the distribution of it. I will see him as soon as he comes home and mention your wish for an introduction so you may at once address any questions you please to Professor O'Donovan, 35 Upper Buckingham street Dublin.

Mr Curry as present resides at 11 Judd st. Brunswick square London being still engaged transcribing some of our Brehon Laws from MSS. in the British Museum. He is a very critical Irish scholar and especially well versed in old readings of the Irish language and in the desciphering of MSS. I will write to him tomorrow stating your wish for his acquaintance and requesting him to attend to your behest.

Enclosed I send you such answers ~~contained~~ ^concerning^ to the queries in your last letter as I can at this moment make out but when I see O'Donovan I will speak to him on the subject.

I have to thank this wearisome history of our Irish Plague Pestilence and Famine (the Construction of which I may say I imposed upon myself) for some acquaintance with Welsh history at least with the books relating thereto. Can these works published by your Antiquarian Societies be procured from a bookseller? I mention in yesterday's letter that it was to be regretted that the transactions of your societies were not supplied with copious Indexes at least of persons and places; and in the case of the Iolo MSS. the want of an introduction is greatly felt by persons as unlearned as myself. In yesterday's letter I asked for page references for extracts from the Iolo MS. work inserted by you from one of the proofs sent from the Census Office and I also wish to know how you arrived at the dates that you placed opposite each quotation.

---

[35] See NLW, MS. 965E, 327, p. 88 above.

I hope some day to make your personal acquaintance, but I am sadly deficient in topographical knowledge of Wales except that scene from the London and Holyhead Railway. How are you to be got at from here. Are there any antiquities in your neighbourhood worth a visit. Is there any trout fishing in your vicinity. Are you far from Stonehenge. Is there any Railroad from your neighbourhood thereto?

*   *   *   *

RIA, MS 24 O 39/JOD/354
Thomas Stephens to John O'Donovan

Merthyr Tydfil
Nov. 2. 1855

Sir,

Having some time ago, given Dr Wilde of your city, some assistance, from the Welsh Annals; in the compilation of the Census Report, I expressed a wish to have an introduction to yourself and Mr Currie, knowing you to be the chief Irish scholars of the day, and he was kind enough to inform me that I might take the liberty of addressing you directly.

The point on which I wished to obtain your opinions and assistance were the following. There are several legends of foreign origin blended with our traditions; and I suspect them to have come from Ireland, either directly, or mediately through the romances of the 12th century. One of these has reference to the family of one _Llyr_ Llediaith or Broadspeech. This Llyr is said to have been taken prisoner in war; and his detention is called one of "the three grievous captivities of the Isle of Britain." Again our poets allude to a story respecting "the three sons of Llyr." But the story as we now have it, appears to be a more recent form of this, and treats of two sons—namely Bran and Manawydan, and a daughter named Branwen. Now, from my slight acquaintance with Irish literature, I am led to identify _Llyr_ with your Leary or Leogaire ^?^ _circa_ 458. And I also find that you have a story respecting "the three sons of Lir"; but that is the whole of my information. Could you enlighten me on the subject. Is Leogaire and Lir the same person? Is the story extant of the sons of Lir, or are there any details known respecting them?

Another question I wish to ask has reference to one Alon, Allon, or Albon, a musician. He is named as one of our three primitive bards, namely Plennydd, Alon, and Gwron; and our writers are not content ~~wi~~to identify ~~aigluin~~ ^Alon^ with any body less ancient than the Olen of the Greeks. I suspect him to have been an ^Irish^ musician, *temp.* Murketach Prince of Aileach (or Glyn Achlach as we have it). Does Irish History know a person of this name? On *Plennydd* I think you could throw some light. You are aware that "a Saracen hero from Ireland", figures in Morte de Arthur, and the Romance of Tryst~~os~~an, under the name of Palamedes, or Palemides. The person thus named is of course the Greek hero of the same name ^revived^; but I should be glad to see the Irish form of the name, and thus be enabled to determine whether he is to be identified with our Plennydd.

Your answers to these questions, at your convenience will be gratefully received; and I need scarcely add that I shall be glad to reciprocate the kindness, should you at any time wish to obtain any on Welsh antiquities.

Have you determined the age of Cuchullin? We have a poem in Welsh, addressed as to a living person, to Correy ab Dairw (your Garraidh Mac Dairw) in which he is named as the opponent of Cuchullin. Our traditions locate these two heroes in the 6th century; and this poem is attributed to Taliesin. Should it be of any interest, I shall be happy to send you a copy with translation.

I remain Sir
Yours very Respectfully
Thos. Stephens
author of
"The Literature of the
Kymry."

Prof. O'Donovan
Dublin   }

*   *   *   *

NLW, MS. 964E, 47
John O'Donovan to Thomas Stephens

Dublin, 36 Buckingham St
upper, Novr 5th 1855

Sir,   I have received your letter of the 2nd instant, and write to say that we have an Irish story called the Death of the Clann- Lir,: but I never saw a copy of it on vellum, and I am of opinion that its present form is not very ancient. The children of Lir are said to have been contemporary with our St. Brendan of Inis Gluairé in Erris, who flourished in the sixth century. The story is *rather modern* and looks rather Scandinavian than Irish!

Our Mythic musicians were all of the Tuatha De Danann colony, but our Bards have pushed their era so far back into the night of time that it is difficult to form any idea of their *real* period. All the monuments however ascribed to this magical colony, such as the tumuli situated along the river Boyne and elsewhere, would indicate that they belonged to the Homeric age. They certainly had not the use of letters. We think that we have fixed the age of our *fortissimus heros* Cuchullin to the first century. His mortal enemy *Curoi Mac Dari* was king of the Degads of Desmont, and lived in a strong Cyclopean fort in Kerry. They are said to have plundered the Isle of Mann, and to have carried off from thence the celebrated beauty *Blathnaid* (Florina). We have very old stories about this Curoi Mac Dari. They call a mountain in Kerry—*Cathair Conroi* (^Caer^36 munitio Curaii) after his name. It would be necessary to translate all these stories (and the various modifications of them) before any comparison could be made with the Welsh legends about characters bearing the same or similar names.

I have the honor to be, Sir,
your obedt servt
John O'Donován
Thos Stephens Esq,
&c &c &c

---

36 This may have been inserted by Stephens as a gloss on 'munitio'.

NLW, MS. 964E, 28
Eugene O'Curry to Thomas Stephens

'Brehon Law' office
T. C. Dublin
March 11th 1856

Dear Sir

The discharge of pressing duties prevented my answering your note of the 19th ult long before this.

Curaoi Mac Daire and Cuchulann were contemporaries, flourishing in the reign of Connor Mac Nessa King of Ulster, in whose reign Christ was crucified.

I have no recollection of the poem in Keting that makes Curaoi the contemporary of St. Patrick and Laeghaire, there must be some mistake in the matter.

Curaoi, Cuchulann, and Conall Cearmach were the chiefs of the Ulster 'Heroes of the Red Branch.' They were all of the Rudrician Race of Ulster, but Curaois tribe passed into Munster where they made a large settlement before the Incarnation. Curaoi himself became king of West Munster about this time, and a mountain in Kerry, near Tralee, near which he had his residence, bears his name to this day, as *Cathair Conravi—Con* being the genitive form of *Cu*.

Curaoi was treacherously slain by Cuchulann in his own Court in Kerry. for his possession of the[37] fair lady Bathmal and Keting gives the tale accurately. On Curaois death his poet, the celebrated Ferceirtne, wrote an elegy on him of which there is a very ancient and obscure copy preserved in an old vellum MS in this College. I have some reason to think that you have got a version of this poem among your old writings, and should be glad to know if such be the opinion of Welsh scholars

I remain Dr Sir, Yours very
Faithfully
Eugene Curry

Thos Stephens Esq

---

[37] O'Curry has written 'possession of the' twice, at the bottom of one page and the top of the next. The duplication has been omitted for readability.

NLW, MS. 965E, 275a
William Rushton to Thomas Stephens

Glanrafon
Ruthin
2 July 1861

Dear Sir

Having frequently heard of you from my friend Gweirydd ap Rhys,[38] I venture to address you without further introduction.

Dr. William Smith,[39] the editor of Classical Dictionaries and other works, is making arrangements for a Biographia Britannica. He requested me to furnish a list of those gentlemen in Wales, who might feel disposed to contribute; and among other names I mentioned your own.

In a letter of the 29th June he writes to ask whether you would undertake an article on "Aneurin"; and in desiring me to send some other articles as specimens, he adds, "I am unwilling to insert any articles till I see them."

He is a cautious man and does not like to commit himself; but he is fair in his dealings, and as the work is extensive, the proposition is worth considering, with a view to the future.

I am very anxious that the Cymric portion of the Biography should be treated in a philosophical spirit, and shall be very happy to learn that you think well of the design.

I am, Sir
Yours faithfully
Wm Rushton

Thomas Stephens Esq
    Merthyr Tydfil.

*   *   *   *

---

[38] Robert John Prys (Gweirydd ap Rhys) (1807–1889).
[39] William Smith (1813–1893).

NLW, MS. 965E, 274
William Rushton to Thomas Stephens

Glanrafon
Ruthin
8th July 1861

Dear Sir

I am glad to learn from your letter of the 5th instant, that you think well of Dr. Smith's proposition; I will send your letter to him, recommending him to adopt your suggestions, and requesting him to correspond with yourself.

This week I expect to be able to send a few articles as specimens, including one of on Ambrosius Aurelius, of whom Price says much in his Hanes Cymru.[40] But the traditions of the early time are so very vague, that it is like walking amid quicksands. I think that with the assistance of Gweirydd ap Rhys, I shall venture upon *Arthur*, and I am very much pleased with the view given of the *romantic* Arthur in Price's Remains.[41] The only fault of Price is, that he is too discursive, and seems to have lacked the faculty of working up his thoughts into one connected discourse. He must have been rather desultory in studies.

Gweirydd has an article on Arthur in the Gwiddoniadur,[42] but it is an enlargement of the view given by Williams in his Biog. Dict.[43] If I feel the want of additional refrences, I shall make bold to consult you.

I am not of Dublin, as you suppose, but of Queen's College, Cork where I hold the chair of History and English Literature; and it is in order to study the early history of Britain, that I have

---

[40] Thomas Price (Carnhuanawc), *Hanes Cymru a Chenedl y Cymry, o'r Cynoesoedd hyd at Farwolaeth Llewelyn ap Gruffydd* (Crughywel: Thomas Williams, 1842).

[41] This is probably Jane Williams (ed.), *The Literary Remains of the Rev. Thomas Price, Carnhuanawc*, two vols (Llandovery: William Rees, 1854–55).

[42] John Parry (gol.), *Y Gwyddoniadur Cymreig: gan Ysgrifenwyr Enwocaf y Genedl* (Dinbych: Thomas Gee, 1856–1879).

[43] Robert Williams (ed.), *Enwogion Cymru, A Biographical Dictionary of Eminent Welshmen* (Llandovery: William Rees, 1852).

endeavoured to acquire the Welsh language. I can now read with some degree of comfort, but the colloquial part of the language gives me great trouble. I never had so much difficulty with any spoken language, arising principally from the fact that I have not been thrown among persons who could speak nothing but Welsh. But for literary purposes, this is not of much moment; and of this I am certain, that unless the English scholars lay aside their prejudices, they will be left far behind by the Germans. I have sent a long extract from "Das Alte Wales" by Ferdinand Walter of Bonn,[44] to Ab Ithel for the Cambrian Journal; and that will afford a slight proof of what the Germans are doing.

With kind regards,
I am, Sir,
Yours very faithfully
Wm Rushton
Thos Stephens Esq
Merthyr Tydfil.

*   *   *   *

NLW, MS. 964E, 9
Richard R. Brash to Thomas Stephens

College View Cork
Nov 2 1861

Dear Sir
I sent you some papers containing sketches of the last Archl. Con at Swansea,[45] did you get them.

I am informed that there is a work entitled "The Gael in

---

[44] Ferdinand Walter, *Das alte Wales. Ein Beitrag zur Völker-, Rechts- und Kirchen-Geschichte* (Bonn: Adoph Marcus, 1859).

[45] The Fifteenth Annual Meeting of the Cambrian Archaeological Association took place in Swansea in August 1861. See 'Cambrian Archaeological Association. Swansea Meeting, 1861', *Archaeologia Cambrensis*, Third Series, 28 (October 1861), 333–372.

Cymru"[46] do you know anything about it, or where I could purchase it, as I don't know either Author or Publisher. It is a book might help me on a subject I am at present writing about. I had a litterary party with me last night, and should not wonder if your ears were tingling far as you were from us. Proffessor Rushton and Mr Windele[47] were with us and your name was honourably mentioned in connection with Welsh Antiquities and Literature. We had a very pleasant evening the major part being devoted to the above subjects as we are very cosmopolitan, and don't confine ourselves exclusively to our native antiquities, a habit, I fear too prevalent among your Savans as I sometimes see traces of narrow prejudice and a confined spirit in the way some of your controversies are handled. Mrs Brash[48] having a pleasing recollection of our social Swansea trips desires to be remembered.

Yours very faithfully,

Richard R Brash

Thos Stephens Esq

P.S. I should like to know your opinion on the probability of a preoccupation of a portion of Wales by the "Erse" or else a temporary Colonization My last visit has filled my mind with the idea the appearance manner and accent of your peasantry is intensely Irish and many topographical denominations very suggestive of the fact

RB

---

[46] Brash is referring to William Basil Jones, 'Vestiges of the Gael in Gwynedd', *Archaeologia Cambrensis*, Supplement, 1850 (London: W. Pickering, 1851), 1–85. See NLW, MS.964E, Letter 10, p. 98 below.

[47] John Windele (1801–1865).

[48] Brash's wife seems to have also had antiquarian interests and accompanied him in his research trips. The dedication of his work on *The Ecclesiastical Architecture of Ireland to the Close of the Twelfth Century with Historical and Antiquarian Notices of Numerous Ancient Remains of that Period* (Dublin: W. B. Kelly, 1875), describes her as 'the congenial companion of many a pleasant pilgrimage in search of the materials from which [this volume] was compiled'.

NLW, MS. 964E, 10
Richard R. Brash to Thomas Stephens

[printed letterhead, Oval with figure, 'Faithful and hopeful']

College View Cork
Feb 6 1862

Dear Sir

I was agreeably surprised to find that though silent you had not forgotten me. I am much obliged in your kind present of the "Gael in Cymru" or rather in "Gwyned" to me it is a most interesting and suggestive book and proving already some startling points in connection with that subject the occupation of the whole or a portion of England by a Gaedhelic population it was most welcome as corroborating views I had long held on the subject. The discovery of Ogham monuments in Wales and Devon has added greatly to the probability of such an occupation for beyond all manner of doubt our Oghams are Pagan. I find that the ancient literature of Wales is full of allusion to the Ogham though not so designated My opportunities in consulting such authorities are meagre The quotations in Davies's "British Druids"[49] and "Celtic Researches"[50] are the only ones I could avail myself of I have written a paper upon the "Ogham writing of the Gaedhil" at the request of Mr Barnewell.[51] But I find that the Revd H L Jones[52] thinks that it is not local enough for the Archol- Cam I shall therefore hand it to one of our local Antiquarian Societies and shall send you a copy when it is published

Should you have met any thing in your readings in your ancient literature referring to the subject I would feel obliged for the information hoping to hear from you soon

---

[49] Edward Davies, *The Mythology and Rites of the British Druids* (London: J. Booth, 1809).

[50] Edward Davies, *Celtic Researches on the Origin, Traditions & Language, of the Ancient Britons* (London: Printed for the Author, 1804).

[51] Edward Lowry Barnwell (1813–1887).

[52] Harry Longueville Jones (1806–1870).

I am Dear Sir
Very Truly Yours
Richard R Brash

Thomas Stephens Esq
Merthyr Tydfil

*   *   *   *

NLW, MS. 964E, 15
Richard R. Brash to Thomas Stephens

Sundays Well Cork
    Jany 13th 1870
Dear Sir   See Book of Judges[53]
In Davies's Celtic Researches at p 258 to 268 there are a number
of quotations from a poem of Taliesin's named the "Battle of the
Trees"; would you kindly inform me if I may depend upon the
translations there given; if the original is of any authority; If the
poem is of authority and that Davies's translations are not safe
quoting; would you kindly direct me to a better translation. And
also are you aware of any other allusions to the same subject—
The tree alphabet—the Alphabet of the Bards &cc.[54]

    It would appear to me as if the Bards of Western Britain had
some knowledge of the Ogham at a remote period and that the
mention of Trees, Sprigs &[c] are obscure allusions to it. I send
you by next post a paper of mine

                                Yours very truly
                                Richard R Brash
Thomas Stephens Esq

---

[53] 'See book of Judges' is written in pencil in a different hand from the rest of
the letter.

[54] 'Coelbren y Beirdd'. Two years later, Stephens published 'An Essay on the
Bardic Alphabet Called "Coelbren y Beirdd"', *Archaeologia Cambrensis*, Fourth
Series, 11 (July 1872), 181–210. See section 5, 'Revolutionising Welsh
Scholarship' below.

NLW, MS. 964E, 13
Richard R. Brash to Thomas Stephens

Sunday Well Cork
  Feb 19 1870
Dear Sir
Respecting your enquiry about the Kenfegge stone. The Ogham is incomplete in both angles but there is sufficient evidence in what remains to shew, that the Ogham was not a rendering of the Roman British inscription, nor the latter a rendering of the former; this you may rest certain of, if the published copies can be relied on. I am going to propound what will be deemed an awful piece of Blasphemy from studying the inscribed stones of Wales both Ogham and otherwise, and comparing them with the names found on the Ogham mon[ts] of Ireland, as also from an examination of the topography of Wales, I am led to the con-clusion that the Gaedhal at the remote pre-historic period crossed from between Hook Point and Carnsore in Wexford, to St Davids head or there abouts, and occupied Cardiganshire, Pembrokeshire, Carmarthenshire, Glamorgan, & that the occu-pation lasted in a considerable period down to Roman times, and that they were subjugated by the Romans and adopted their letters and partially their language; that on the decline of the Roman power, the Cymry, who I believe to have been originally Picts, forced their way Southwards from the eastern counties of Scotland, occupying first the borderlands of Scotland & England, and subsequently Wales; either ~~day~~ driving out the Gaedhal, or reducing them to subjection. The Picts a powerful people could not have disappeared at the late period of their occupation of the borders, they must have turned up somewhere a race and a language could not have been extinguished suddenly, leaving no trace. We have here two mysteries Where did the Picts go to, and where did the Welsh come from. The mystery would be solved if we could prove that both are the same race, under different names. Zeuss[55] propounds that the Welsh & Gaedhelic languages

---

[55] Johann Kaspar Zeuss (1806–1856).

~~are of~~ ^were^ originally one, but separated at a remote period, this suits the Gaedhelic traditions respecting the Cruithine or Picts, namely that they spring from the same ancestry as themselves. On the strength of their relationship the Picts came to Erein in settlements, their Gaedhelic cousins informed them they had little enough room for themselves, but recommended them to cross over to Albyn, where there was room enough and to spare; the Picts say they have no women to multiply their race, and beg wives of the Gaedhal, which is granted; they occupy Scotland, multiply, and become a nation, they are invaded by the Gaedhal, pushed from Argyle and the West Coast over to the east, from the east coasts they are ultimately forced by their perceiving enemies southward to the borders where in their turn they harass and annoy the Romanized Britons-

Such is an outline of my views of this interesting subject one requiring learned leisure time and assiduity to develop

I am Dear Sir
Very Truly Yours
Richard R Brash

Thos Stephens Esq

*   *   *   *

NLW, MS. 942C, 127
Richard R. Brash to Thomas Stephens

Sunday Well Cork
April 19—1870

Dear Sir
A short time since I procured some of the earlier vols of the Arch Camb in which are a series of papers by yourself on early Welsh poems—one of these papers struck my attention very forcibly as having a very Gaedhelic aspect—That one attributed to Taliesin namely the "Elegy on Corroy the son of Dairy"[56]—These names

---

[56] Thomas Stephens, 'The Poems of Taliesin. No. 1', *Archaeologia Cambrensis*, New Series, 6 (April 1851), 149–55.

were exceedingly familiar to me and on investigation I find that
the poem refers to Curoi Mac Dairé the chief of the Clanna
Deghaid or Ernaans of Munster a warlike tribe who inhabited
west Munster namely the County of Kerry and part of the County
of Cork and who bore great sway in the south his name being the
theme of the story-tellers through the Country districts to this
day—the chief seat of his power was at Cathair Couree in the
neighbourhood of Tralee in Kerry—Where his fort is still pointed
out on a spur of one of the Iliable Mis Mountains—There can be
no mistake about the identification as Curoi Mac Dairé is a
historical personage and his pedigree given in the Book of
Clanmacuoise—Curoi the son of Daire the son of Deagha the son
of Sen the son of Celill &cc The Cocholyn you were at such a loss
to identify is the celebrated Cuchullin the chief of the Craobh
Ruadh ie the warriors of the Red Branch between whom and
Curoi there was a deadly feud which ended in the death of the
latter. I have forwarded to the editors of the Arch Camb a paper
on this subject giving an account of Curoi and Cuchullin and the
legends connected with them which are very interesting when
you see the paper I am sure you will be much interested in it.[57]
The question is how it found (the elegy) its way into your
collection of Welsh Poems. I have a strong suspicion that your
Cymric Literature is largely indebted to Gaedhelic Bardism. I am
most anxious to procure an authentic translation of the works of
Taliesin. Aneurin, Lywarch Hen and Myrddin, would you kindly
direct me to the purest source—

I am Dear Sir
Yours very Truly
Richard R Brash

[On the reverse, in Thomas Stephens's hand:]
Copy
Am
    I will make you a proposition. If you can send me post paid, a

---

[57] Richard Rolt Brash, 'On an "Elegy of Corroy, the son of Dairy," An Ancient
Gaedhelic Poem Attributed to Taliesin', *Archaeologia Cambrensis*, Fourth
Series, 3 (July 1870), 234–51.

clear second hand copy Curry's Evidence of the Ancient Literature of Ireland[58] (I doubt if this is the exact title) I will send you Nash's Taliesin[59] and Owen's Llywarch Hen.[60] The books are of about equal value (I think) You will a translation of Aneurin in several forms, one in Davies' Mythology of the Druids.

*   *   *   *

NLW MS 964E, 14
Richard Rolt Brash to Thomas Stephens

21 South Mall.
Cork.
[printed letterhead]
April 26 *1870*
Dear Sir
I presume the work you are anxious to procure is Dr O Currys "Lectures on the MS Materials for Irish History" if so it is a most valuable and useful work without which you can have no idea of the untranslated and unpublished matter on Gaedhelic history and literature lying on library shelves it is a thick closely printed large octavo containing 720 closely printed pages and with the second vol now I believe in the press on a kindred subject helped to kill time. I shall write to my Dublin Bookseller and try if I can procure you a copy I have missed it from the *Cat* for some time past and know that it has got scarce

As to "Curoi Mac Daire" I have let you down very easy;[61] in

---

[58] Eugene O'Curry, *Lectures on the Manuscript Materials of Ancient Irish History Delivered at the Catholic University of Ireland during the Sessions of 1855 and 1856* (Dublin: James Duffy, 1861).

[59] D. W. Nash, *Taliesin; or, the Bards and Druids of Britain* (London: John Russell Smith, 1858).

[60] William Owen, *The Heroic Elegies and Other Pieces of Llywarç Hen, Prince of the Cumbrian Britons* (London: Printed for J. Owen and E. Williams, 1792).

[61] In the beginning of this article, Brash focuses on Stephens's inability to identify Corroy, son of Dairy as the Irish Curoi Mac Dairé, naming Stephens

truth, in your paper,[62] you expressed strong doubts as to the poem being attributable to Taliesin; before I wrote mine, I looked through the succeeding numbers of the Arch Camb, to ascertain, if you had discovered this Cymric robbery, and acknowledged it, but not finding any such I then went in for it. I think you will be pleased with the paper, in which I give a sketch from Gaedhelic sources, of the sayings and doings of the real Curoi and the real Cuchullin. Only yesterday, I discovered a name on a Ratti an Ogham pillar, in a Ratti Cave, in the Co of Kerry, identical to the letter with one on an Ogham pillar in Wales one of many such I have identified

I am Dear Sir
Very truly Yours
Richard R Brash

Thos Stephens

*   *   *   *

NLW, MS. 964E, 17
Richard Rolt Brash to Thomas Stephens

Sunday Well Cork
July 28th 1871

Dear Sir

When I did not receive an answer to my letter in course I surmised that you must be unwell and am indeed much concerned to find that it really was the case and under so severe a form Alas it is the penalty that men of zeal and enthusiasm in literary pursuits too often pay. I sincerely hope that your health will

---

and quoting from his article on the subject at legnth. As O'Donovan and O'Curry had provided Stephens information about Curoi in 1855–6, Stephens presumably knew of this connection prior to the publication of Brash's article. Moreover, this discussion and the article illustrate Stephens's continued interest in the subject. Brash, 'On an "Elegy of Corroy, the Son of Dairy,"'.

[62] T. Stephens, 'The Poems of Taliesin. No. 1', *Archaeologia Cambrensis*, 6 (April 1851), 149–55.

improve if you never wrote another line you have done enough for fame and have left your mark in the history of Welsh literature

As you are so anxious to have O Curry I shall do my best to procure you a copy but not on the score mentioned in your former letter. I shall be too happy to be the means of adding to your gratification under present circumstances I hope to be in Swansea in about a week as I want to complete my survey of the Welsh Oghams

My own book is nearly ready for the press, had I been aware of the labour involved in it I should never have begun. There will be a long chapter devoted to early Welsh history as deduced from the inscribed stones I think it will mark a new era in the mode of treating these matters

I am Dear Sir
Very truly Yours
Richard R Brash

Thomas Stephens Esq

4

'CHER MONSIEUR STEPHENS': THOMAS STEPHENS'S CONTINENTAL CORRESPONDENCE

THOMAS Stephens's letters travelled across the English Channel as well as the Irish Sea, and, like his Irish correspondence, many of those with whom he exchanged letters on the European mainland participated in wider networks of knowledge exchange. Stephens travelled on the mainland at least twice and passports exist for two trips—to France in October 1849, and 'the Continent' in September 1851—although, as his extant Continental correspondence does not commence for some time after, it is not apparent whether he met any of his future correspondents on his travels.[1] Indeed, his first trip seems to have been undertaken for pleasure and as an opportunity to rest on his laurels after his success at the 1848 Abergavenny Cymreigyddion Society Eisteddfod and the subsequent publication of *Literature of the Kymry*.[2]

As was shown in the 'Introduction', nineteenth-century Welsh scholarly society was well connected with Continental European scholarship. The Abergavenny Cymreigyddion Society was particularly well connected, and two of the letter writers in this section, Théodore Hersart de la Villemarqué and Albert Schulz (San Marte) were directly involved with that society.[3] Moreover,

---

[1] Passport for France, issued to Thomas Stephens 3 October 1849, NLW, MS. 965E, Letter 388. Letter recommending Stephens for travel on the Continent., London, 29 October 1851, NLW, MS. 965E, Letter 388 (2).

[2] Williams, 'Life of Thomas Stephens', p. xxvi.

[3] See Gregory, 'Cymdeithas Cymreigyddion y Fenni'; Thomas, *Welsh Spirit of Gwent*, pp. 8–9; Thorn, 'Cymreigyddion y Fenni'.

Stephens met the eminent French Historian Henri Martin at the 1861 Aberdare Eisteddfod and at a meeting of the Cambrian Archaeological Association at Neath. Martin was travelling with the French writer Alfred Erny, who published an account of his and Martin's Welsh tour, and with whom Stephens also corresponded.[4]

Stephens's international correspondence depended heavily on his reputation, and B. T. Williams noted that 'Nowhere was the learning of Stephens more appreciated than it was among the scholars of France.'[5] Stephens's impact on Continental scholarship is apparent from the letters in this section, and in acknowledgements and citations in the publications of his correspondents. Martin, for instance, acknowledged Stephens's kindness and guidance in his investigation of Welsh traditions in his *Études D'Archéologie Celtique* (1872),[6] while Schulz discussed the revolutionary importance of Stephens and *Literature of the Kymry* at some length in *Die Sagen von Merlin* (1853).[7] This

---

[4] Alfred Erny, 'Voyage dans le pays de Galles', *Le Tour de Monde*, 15: 1 (1867), 257–88.

[5] Williams, 'Life of Thomas Stephens', p. xxxiii.

[6] 'Mes recherches sur ces traditions avaient été fructueuses, grâce à l'extrême obligeance et aux lumières d'un savant à qui j'aime à payer ici une dette de reconnaissance, l'auteur de la *Litterature des Cymrys*, M. Thomas Stephens, un de ces hommes qui, entourés au début des conditions les moins favorables, se créent entièrement eux-mêmes et sont les fils de leur courage et de leur persévérante volonté.' Henri Martin, *Études D'Archéologie Celtique Notes de Voyages dans les Pays Celtiques et Scandinaves* (Paris: Librairie Académique, 1872), p. 41.

[7] 'Stephens hat durch seine verdienstliche Schrift, die ebenso von warmer Liebe für jenes Volk und dessen früheres reges Geistesleben, als von klarer unbefangener Anschauung der Erzeugnisse desselben zeugt, einen Riß in den celtischen Götterhimmel schonungslos gebrochen, ... und den celtischen Mythologen bleibt nichts übrig, als das Werk ihrer Forschung von neuem, und mit der Besonnenheit, Gründlichkeit, Umsicht und Vorsicht zu beginnen, wie dazu ihnen Jacob Grimm in seiner Deutschen Mythologie die Wege gewiesen und Anleitung gegeben hat.' San Marte [Albert Schulz], *Die Sagen von Merlin. Mit wälschen, bretagnischen, schottischen, italienischen, und lateinischen*

influence was celebrated at home and abroad, augmenting the reputation of both Stephens and wider Welsh scholarship. In 1854, Schulz sent copies of his *Die Sagen von Merlin* and *Gottfried von Monmouth Historia Regum Britanniae* (1854) to show Stephens his impact on German scholarship. Soon after, Stephens wrote excitedly to an unknown recipient, likely his publisher William Rees, about Schulz's praise, including a translation of the passage from *Die Sagen von Merlin* in which his work was discussed.[8] A few months later, an English translation of the same passage appeared in the *Cambrian Journal* under the heading 'Welsh Literature in Germany'.[9] A few years later, Schulz further ensured the impact of Stephens's work on the continent, translating *Literature of the Kymry* and publishing it as *Geschichte der wälschen Literature von XII. bis zum XIV. Jahrhundert* (1864), which he prefaced with an account expounding on the importance of Stephens's work, his translation, and Welsh literature generally.[10]

The majority of letters which were written to Stephens in languages other than English and Welsh were translated contemporarily in whole or part, either by Stephens or someone else.[11] It is likely however, that Stephens could read much of what was sent to him. His education at John Davies's academy would have given him a good Classical educational grounding, including

---

Gedichten und Prophezeihungen Merlins, de Prophetia Merlini des Gottfried von Monmouth, und der Vita Merlini, lateinischem Gedichte aus dem dreizehnten Jahrhundert (Halle: Verlag der Buchhandlung des Waisenhauses, 1853), p. 5.

[8] Thomas Stephens to Unknown, Merthyr Tydfil, 22 May 1854, NLW, MS. 942C, Letter 111.

[9] 'Miscellaneous Notices', *Cambrian Journal*, 1: 2 (Alban Hevin 1854), 192.

[10] San Marte [Albert Schulz] (Trans.), *Geschichte der wälschen Literatur vom XII. bis zum XIV. Jahrhundert Gekrönte Preisschrift von Thomas Stephens* (Halle: Verlag der Buchhandlung des Waisenhauses, 1864), pp. v–vii.

[11] While the handwriting of a few of these letters resembles Stephens's, most do not.

Latin.[12] He also studied German from the 1840s,[13] and his detailed notes on Johann Kaspar Zeuss's *Grammatica Celtica* survive.[14] He also seems to have studied French, as the *North Wales Chronicle and Advertiser for the Principality* noted in their reporting of the 1861 Aberdare Eisteddfod that Martin 'addressed the meeting in the French language, which was translated into English by Mr. Stephens, of Merthyr'.[15] In this section, therefore, Stephens's correspondence evidences knowledge transfer across both national and linguistic borders.

*　　*　　*　　*

---

[12] Taylor, 'Thomas Stephens', 135–36'.

[13] Löffler, 'Failed Founding Fathers', p. 73.

[14] Notes on *Grammatica Celtica* by Thomas Stephens, NLW, MS. 922C.

[15] 'Grand National Eisteddfod at Aberdare'. *North Wales Chronicle and Advertiser for the Principality*, 24 August 1861, 5, accessed via *Welsh Newspapers Online*. See also Martin, *Études D'Archéologie Celtique*, p. 60.

NLW, MS. 965E, 227a
William Owen[16] to Thomas Stephens

Rhyllon, St. Asaph
Oct 29. 1853

My dear Sir/
I have just read in the "Star of Gwent" of Oct 21st. the proceedings of the Fenni Eisteddfod. The "judgement" of Chevalier
Bunsen[17] ^in the great prize^ is a masterly composition.[18] It
would be no mean praise to any author, that his work had been
even favourably noticed, by this learned and distinguished man.
I cannot therefore refrain from offering my heartiest congratulations that your essay has elicited so noble a eulogy from his
Excellency.[19] Your other success at this great meeting must have
been very gratifying; still the awards were made by local judges
& your own countrymen. Not so with regard to the Essay in
question. The adjudicator was a foreigner, a man of exalted
station, a profound theologian, an accomplished scholar, a deeply
read jurist — one in short, whose brilliant attainments & world-
famed writings have won for him the very foremost place in the
literary ranks of Europe. We sincerely hope this Essay with the

---

[16] This is probably William Owen (d. 1859), a Welsh antiquarian, magistrate
and advocate of Welsh issues, who was the son of Aneurin Owen and the
grandson of William Owen Pughe. Note his use of his grandfather's orthography in the signature. See 'William Owen Esq. of Tan y Gyrt', *Cambrian
Journal* (Alban Eilir 1859), 62.

[17] Christian Carl Josias von Bunsen (1791–1860).

[18] Stephens won three prizes at the 1853 Abergavenny Cymreigyddion Society
Eisteddfod, including a prize for his essays on 'Names of Places Designated
from Remarkable Events' and a 'History of Welsh Bards'. Owen is here
referring to his essay on the 'History of Trial by Jury in Wales', for which he
was awarded a prize of £70. 7s. by Bunsen. The adjudication, which was highly
complementary of Stephens's ability as a critical historian, was printed in
several accounts of the eisteddfod in newspapers, as well as in Williams, 'The
Life of Thomas Stephens', pp. xxx–xxxi.

[19] Probably a reference to Bunsen.

judgement prefixed, may be published as soon as may be.

We purpose forwarding the "*Star*" of the 21st inst to our valued friend *Profr* Ranke at Berlin.[20] The Profr takes a warm interest in all that relates to Wales.

Lady Hall[21] was good enough to invite us to Llanover, but circumstances, beyond my control, put it out of our power to avail ourselves of her Ladyship's kindness. It was a ~~great~~ grievous disappointment. Our great pleasure we had proposed to ourselves was to renew the acquaintance which we had so happily made with the Author of the "Literature of the Cymru" at Rhuddlan.

Repeating my own & Mrs Owen's hearty congratulations,

Credwx fi Anwyl Syr
Yr Eiddox
Yn ddifuant[22]
W. H. Owen

*   *   *   *

NLW, MS. 965E, 280b
Albert Schulz (San Marte) to Thomas Stephens

Magdeburg. 14 Avril.
1854

Monsieur:

Le soussigné se sent obligé à dire beaucoup de rémerciments à l'auteur savant de la "*Literature of the Cymry*" à cause de l'information multiple, que cet oeuvre, plein de mérite, lui a fournit. Celui-ci désire, outre cela prouver la récon[n]aissance par le fait, en se permettant de vous présenter les oeuvres ci-joints: "Les Traditions de Merlin, "[23] et l'"histoire de Gottfried v.

---

[20] Leopold von Ranke (1795–1886).

[21] Lady Augusta Hall of Llanover (Gwenynen Gwent) (1802–1896).

[22] 'Believe me Dear Sir Yours Sincerely.'

[23] Schulz, *Die Sagen von Merlin*.

Monmouth."[24] A mon savoir, c'est que vôtre oeuvre soit le premier et l'unique, qui soumet la litérature des Gáules ouvertement et sans préjugé à une critique, qui lui manquait tout à fait jusqu'ici. Vôtre excellent ouvrage a allumé et répandu la lumière dans les régions, regnés par une obscurité impénétrable, ou moins seulement d'un clair obscure et lueur pale. C'est pourquoi que les fruits ne manqueront pas à paraitre ni pour la litérature nationale des Gaulles, ni pour les sciences entières.—Un de mes plus agréables devoirs ait été, de répandre sur les champs de la litérature allemande vos doctrines et vos résultats.—Que de temps viendra encore de passer jusqu'à ce que la Myvyrian Archaiology[25] paraitra dans une traduction et complète, et parfaite, qui pourra supporter une critique sévère!

Je vous prie infiniment de m'avertir de l'existence d'une telle traduction. Le Continent ne se réjonit pas de sa connaissance.

Puisse continuer les études scientifiques se tendre la main pour un effort aussi grand, non séparé ni par la nationalité, ni par les mers!

Agréez donc l'assurance de mon estime pour Vous, Monsieur, avec laquelle j'ai l'hon[n]eur de rester
Monsieur
Vôtre très humble
Schulz, conseiller de régence.

[**NLW, MS. 965E, 280a,** a contemporary translation of the above. This translation contains many crossings out and amendments, likely by Stephens, and is presented here with these revisions incorporated:

---

[24] San-Marte [Albert Schulz], *Gottfried's von Monmouth Historia Regum Britanniae, mit literar-historischer Einleitung und ausführlichen Anmerkungen, und Prut Tysylio, altwälsche Chronik in deutscher Uebersetzung* (Halle: Eduard Anton, 1854).

[25] Jones, Williams, and Pughe (eds.), *The Myvyrian Archaiology of Wales.*

Magdeburg
14 April 1854

Sir/

The undersigned feels himself obliged to express many thanks to the learned author of the "Literature of the Cymru" for the abundant information which this work, full of merit, has furnished him

He desires, besides, to prove his gratitude, in fact & deed, by permitting himself to present to you the accompanying works, the "Traditions of Merlin" and the "History of Geoffrey of Monmouth"

To my knowledge (as far as I know) your work is the first and only one, that submits the literature of the Gauls (Welsh) openly and without prejudice, to a criticism, which was hitherto entirely wanting to it.

Your excellent work has kindled and spread a light over regions, where reigned an impenetrable obscurity or at least only pale dim and glimmering light and therefore it as that fruit cannot to appear for the national literature of the Gauls as Welsh nor for the entire sciences {the original translator wrote, 'therefore it cannot fail to be fruitful to the national literature of the Gauls as well as to all sciences'}.

One of my most agreeable duties has been to spread your doctrine and results over the fields of german literature.

How much time shall pass ere the Myvyrian Archaeology shall appear in a complete and perfect translation, that shall stand a severe criticism.

I pray you infinitely to give me notice of such a translation. The continent does not rejoice in its acquaintance.

May scientific studies continue to join hands for so great an effort, unseperable by nationality or the seas!

Accept the assurance of my esteem for you, Sir, with whom I have the honour to remain

Sir

Your very humble
      Schultz
            Councillor royal]

NLW, MS. 965E, 305
Théodore Hersart de la Villemarqué to Thomas Stephens[26]

Au Cháteau de Keransker
près Kemperlé, (Bretagne)
le 17 mai 1856

Monsieur,
Quand même il n'existerait pas une *république des lettres*, dont tous les membres sont frères, il y aurait pour nous, Bretons-armoricains, et pour vous, Kymrys-*britons*, une mères-patrie commune dont nous sommes les fils; nous devons donc nous aimer et vous entre-aider. Vous m'avez prouvé que ces sentiments sont les votres, en voulant bien parler de moi d'une manière aimable dans votre excellent livre, *The Literature of the Kymry*, et moi-même j['']ai été tres heureux de pouvoir louer ce livre dans ma traduction française des *Poèmes des bardes bretons du VIe siècle*, publiée à Paris par Renouard, rue de Tournon, en 1850. Dernièrement encore, j['']ai en occasion de citer vos travaux, comme des modèles du critique, dans une lecture que jai faite à l'Institut de France, sur les monuments de la langue des Anciens Brêtons.

C'est donc avec un véritable chagrin que jai lu dans le *Cambrian Journal*, revue distinguée, éditée par un homme si intelligent et si impartial, ce me semble, une lettre à l'editeur où vous êtes traité d'une manière inqualifiable. [27] Non! quelques dissentiments qui puissent exister sur certains points de détail vos *Studies upon ^in the^ british biography*[28] ne sont point indignes de vos études précédentes; vous continuez à marcher dans la bonne et large voie, et vous y marchez même d'un pied

---

[26] This letter was written on black-bordered paper, likely indicating that the writer was in mourning. A copy of this letter was printed in Williams, 'Life of Thomas Stephens', xxxiii–xxxiv.

[27] La Villemarqué is probably referring to [Caradoc ab Bran], 'Dyvynwal Moelmud'. *Cambrian Journal*, 1 (1854), 269–71.

[28] For discussion of this series of articles by Stephens, published in the *Cambrian Journal*, see Chapter 5, 'Revolutionising Welsh Scholarship', below.

plus assuré et plus indépendant vous perpétuez la saine école de Edward Lhuyd à laquelle appartenait aussi mon excellent et à jamais regrettable ami Thomas Price, et vous partagez avec d'autres l'honneur de cette Renaissance Cambrienne qui attire sur votre beau et intéressant pays les regards de l'europe savante. Mais j'espère que ce nuage élevé entre compatriotes c'est dissipé depuis longtemps, et que vos contradicteurs auront fini par juger, comme les etrangers, qu'une sévérité même pousser à l'excès, vaut mieux qu'une complaisance fâcheuse ou qu'une déplorable flatterie. Je serais bien aise de l'apprendre de vous, car je n'aime point les querelles de famille :

Cas bethau *Breton*:
Gwrth ac ymryson
Rhwng cydvrodorion[29]

Vous savez qu'on attribue ces vers à un de vos sages et de vos saints qui vint vous prêcher au vie siècle, et qui est mort chez nous! je les cite souvent.

Pour vous, Monsieur, si, comme je n'en doute pas, vous avez fait la paix avec vos critiques revenus à des sentiments plus équitables, à ceux du temps où ils vous regardaient "with pride as the future historian of Wales", vous pouvez dire, en le leur prouvant, avec le sage des Kymry:

Nerth cryv, ei drugaredd.[30]

Veuillez agréer l'assurance de mon estime et de la sympathie avec la quelle jai l'honneur d'être, votre serviteur

Le Directeur de l'Association bretonne
Vte Hersart De la Villemarqué

---

[29] Hateful Breton things /opposition and strife / between compatriots
[30] The power of the strong is his mercy

[**NLW, MS. 942C, 37**, a contemporary translation:
{Different Hand: Chateau de Keransker}

Chepisker Castle
Near Kemperlé
(Brittany)
May 17. 1856

Sir/
Even if there did not exist a republic of letters whereof all members are brothers, there would yet be for us Amoricain-Bretons and for you Cymry-Britons a common mother country, whose children we are; we ought then to love and mutually aid one another –

You have proved to me that these are your sentiments, by speaking of me in so amiable a manner in your excellent book, The Literature of the Cymry, and I myself have felt happy in praising this book in my french translation of the Poems of the Briton Bards of the 6th century, published at Paris by Renouard, Rue de Tournon, in 1850. Recently too I have had occasion to cite your works, as models of criticism, in a lecture which I delivered at the Institute of France upon the monuments of the language of the Ancient Britons.

It is therefore with unfeigned sorrow, that I have read in the Cambrian Journal, a distinguished review edited, as appears to me, by an intelligent and impartial man, a letter to the editor, where you are treated in an unjustifiable manner: No, whatever differences of opinion may exist upon certain points of detail, your Studies in the British Biography are not unworthy of your previous studies; you continue to walk on the good broad path and your tread even with a firmer and more independent step, you are perpetrating the sound school of Edward Lloyd, to which also belonged my excellent and ever to be regretted friend Thomas Price, and you are partaking with others of the honour of this Cambrian Revival which attracts the eyes of learned Europe to your beautiful and interesting country.

But I hope that this cloud, raised between fellow countrymen, has long since been dispersed and that your opponents will ultimately praise, as foreigners do, that severity, even pushed to excess, is of more value than mean complaisance or deplorable flattery. I should be glad to hear it from yourself for I like not family quarrels.

{In Welsh:
Hateful Breton things
opposition and strife
between compatriots}

You know these words are attributed to one of your sages and saints, who come to preach to us in the 6th century and died here; I often quote them.

For yourself Sir, if, as I doubt not, you have made peace with your critics, who shall leave returned to more just sentiments, to those sentiments they had when they looked upon you "with pride as the future historian of Wales", you even say in proving it to them, with Cymry's sage

{In Welsh: The power of the strong, his mercy}

Pray accept the observance of my esteem and of the sympathy with which I have the honour to be your servant

The Director of the Bretonian association
Vcte Hersart De la Villemarqué]

*   *   *   *

NLW Facs 854
Thomas Stephens to Théodore Hersart de la Villemarqué

Merthyr Tydfil
July 4. 1856

Dear Sir

I have to apologize for not having taken an early opportunity to acknowledge the receipt of your of very acceptable letter, and to thank you for the manner in which you have spoken of me therein; but I had hoped to have something to write more than a merely courteous reply. You rightly conjecture that I entertain a sincere respect for yourself and your writings; and I was glad to find from the *Poemes de Bardes Bretons* in 1850, as well as subsequently from your letter that the feeling was reciprocated.

I procured the "Poemes" as soon as the work became known in England, and have perused it with interest. It is probable that in my next public appearance as an author, I may have to travel over the same ground, where it is probable that I may find many valuable suggestions in your work. At present, speaking merely of the general impression from a cursory perusal, it seems to me to a decided advance on your previous works; and the mastery displayed over the difficult language of the old bards, appeared to me very remarkable. But I may have more to say on this head hereafter. There was a notice of the "Poemes" in the *Quarterly Review* Sept. 1852, in an article entitled "British Bards and Stonehenge",[31] and supposed to have been written by the Rev. Rowland Williams, Vice Principal of Lampeter College. The translations given in the article, were English versions of your French translations.

I thank you for your sympathy with respect to the letter in the *Cambrian Journal*, and more especially, ~~felt~~ I am pleased to find that the *Studies in British Biography*, have elicited your commendation. The remarks of the writer seemed to me impertinent, but had made no further impression on my mind, and had been quite forgotten when your letter recalled them. Whether or not there was a falling off ~~under~~ in my writing was not a question for me to determine, ~~but~~ I was content to refer the matter to the

---

[31] Anon. 'Bards of the Sixth Century–Stonehenge', *The Quarterly Review*, 92 (September 1852), 273–315. This article discussed three works: La Villemarqué's *Poèms des Bardes Bretons du VI Siècle* (1850), Algernon Herbert's *Cyclops Christianus* (1849) and the Supplement for 1850 to the *Archaeologia Cambrensis*. Interestingly, Stephen's *Literature of the Kymry* was frequently mentioned in the article, occasionally when discussing La Villemarquè's work, the author even noting that 'A study of the three [works] preceded by Sharon Turner's "Vindication of the Bards" as an introduction, and followed if the sacred hunger is not yet appeased, by Mr. Stephens's "Literature of the Cymry," ... would furnish our readers in general with a far greater idea of the most venerable antiquities of their country than they probably now possess.' Ibid., 273.

judgment of the public; and am glad to find that your opinion is still favourable.

In a recent conversation, ~~from~~ a member of the Cambrian Institute expressed a desire to have your name, as one of the Vice Presidents. If you would be good enough to consent, it will do good here, and keep alive the remembrance of your services to Cambrian literature.

You are probably aware that a translation of the Gododin issued from the Llandovery Press in 1852. This ~~wais~~ by the Rev John Williams, (Ab Ithel), the Editor of the Cambrian Journal, but in my opinion fails to do justice to the original, and displays a total misconception of ~~spirit,~~ the subject, and spirit of the poem. However, on this head you have doubtless formed your opinion.

 I remain, Dear Sir
  Yours Faithfully
   Thos Stephens
M. le Count Villemarque

* * * *

NLW, MS. 965E, 306a
Théodore Hersart de la Villemarqué to Thomas Stephens

Au Chateau de Keransker près Kemperlé
(Bretagne) le 14 juillet 1856

Cher Monsieur,
Jai reçu votre lettre du 4 juillet, et je ne saurais assez vous remercier de ce que vous me dites d'aimable, je suis particulièrement flatté de l'honneur que le *Cambrian Institut* veut bien me faire en m'offrant de placer mon nom parmi ceux de les Vice-président; je l'accepte avec beaucoup de plaisir, et je vous prie de remercier pour moi cette Société Savante, en attendant que je la remercie moi-même, à la réception officiele de ma nomination. Etre loué par vous, dont les travaux sont si justement estimés en France et en Allemagne, était déjà un grand succès. Jai souvent

parlé de vous à mon illustre ami Augustin Thierry[32] dont les
souffrances & les infirmités, jointes à la perte de ses yeux,
n'altéraient en rien le génie: il avait été lui même très sensible à
l'éloge que vous faites de lui dans votre excellent ouvrage *The
Literature of the Kymry*, et peu de temps avant sa mort, qui est,
pour la France & pour ses amis, une perte irréparable il me
demandait quelle était votre opinion sur une assertion très
importante du Cambrian register for 1791, p. 241, concernant le
ressentiment conservé en Galles des appropriations de la
conquête. Il me demandait également le que vous pensiez du
Kyvrinach y beirdd que M. Pictet de Genève[33] a récemment
exhumé et mis en credit, d'après un texte de 1792 d'iolo
Morganwg, [34] et qui me parait à moi non un *mystère* mais une
mystification. J'aurais été bien aise de pouvoir lui répondre pour
vous, et de l'éclairer de lumières meilleures que les miennes mais
vous n'en parler point dans la ~~Literature of the Kymry~~; et vous
qualifiez seulement, avec beaucoup de bon sens & d'esprit, dans
le cambrian journal, les MSS d'iolo, de *Slipshod documents.* [35]
Comme on continue en France à s'occuper de l'authenticité du
Kyvrinach, vous m'obligeriez beaucoup de me dire s'il en existe
une copie ^datée^ antérieur au manuscrit qu'on attribue à
Edward Davydd, mort en 1690, et si ce manuscrit de Davydd
existe réellement dans la bibliothèque de Llanharan, dans le
Glamorganshire, maintenant la propriété de la famille
Turberville. Je ne sais si je me trompe, mais jai bien de
soupçonner Edward Davydd et ses confrères d'avoir fabriqué
tout le Kyvrinach ^on de moins la partie^ *théologique* du livre, à

---

[32] Augustin Thierry (1795–1856) was a prominent French historian and
liberal.

[33] Adolphe Pictet, *Le Mystère des Bardes de l'Ile de Bretagne ou la Doctrine des
Bardes Gallois du Moyen Age* (Genève: Joël Cherbuliez, 1856).

[34] Probably the Introduction to William Owen, *The Heroic Elegies and Other
Pieces of Llywarç Hen*, which contained detailed descriptions of druidic and
bardic orders and ceremonies.

[35] See Stephens, 'Laws of Dyvynwal Moelmud', 47, where he refers to 'the
slipshod documents in the *Iolo Mss.*'

l'exception des vieilles triades des Cercles. Qu'en pensez-vous? Je me suis exprimé dans ce sens en adressant mon opinion écrite à mon savant collègue de l'Académie du Berlin, M. Jacob Grimm; je serais heureux de la voir confirmée par un juge aussi compétent que vous: Les recherches que jai faites, au mois de décembre dernier, dans la bibliothèque de Sir Robert Vaughan, à Rhug, [36] n'ont pas changé ma manière de voir à cet égard. J'aurais été aussi très aise d'y trouver quelque document ancien et portant une date certaine de nature à confirmer l'important passage cité par Iolo Morganwg, p. 630, [37] sur l'origine armoricaine de la table-ronde; Taliesin Williams[38] me l'avait montré en 1839, dans les papiers de son père, mais je doutais de l'ancienneté de la tradition avant de l'avoir vue adoptée par vous, (p. 336) [39] et il me

---

[36] Sir Robert Vaughan (1803–1859), 3rd Baronet, of Hengwrt, then custodian of the Hengwrt manuscripts.

[37] 'After that Rhys son of Tewdwr, prince of Dinevor, and Dyved, and Keredigion, having from necessity been some time in Brittany, returned to Wales, and brought with him the system of the Round Table, where it had become forgotten, and he restored it as it is with regard to minstrels and bards, as it had been at Caerlleon upon Usk, under the Emperor Arthur, in the time of the sovereignty of the race of the Cymry over the Island of Britain, and its adjacent Islands; and it was placed under the protection of the church of Cattwg, in the vale of Neath, in Glamorgan, which was from the time of St. Teilo possessed of the privilege ecclesiastically confirmed, that neither war nor weapons of slaughter could be brought into the parish of Cattwg, neither by the people of the adjacent country, or any other whatever, under bond and pledged hand throughout all the districts of the Isle of Britain.' Taliesin Williams (ab Iolo), *Iolo Manuscripts*, p. 630.

[38] Taliesin Williams (Taliesin ab Iolo) (1787–1847).

[39] 'We have already noticed the Eisteddvodau said to have been held by Cadwaladr, Asserius Menevensis, and Bleddyn ab Kynvyn. These occurred prior to the time treated of here; but subsequently a considerable impetus had been given to such meetings by Rhys ab Tewdwr, who assumed the sovereignty of South Wales in 1077. On his return to Wales from Brittany, "he brought with him the system of the Round Table, which, at home, had become quite forgotten, ..."'. Stephens, *Literature of the Kymry*, p. 336. Stephens cites the *Iolo Manuscripts*, p. 630, although the quote differs slightly from what appears

parait que M. Albert Schulz en doute encore, car il vous cite avec un point d'interrogation à ce sujet, lui qui d'ordinaire vous emprunte vos opinions. Le fameux Llyfr o grefft yr holl vordd gron où j'espérais trouver tant de lumières et que Lady Vaughan m'a ~~permis~~ de lire, (celui-la même dont vous parlez p. 438 avec une si juste défiance de la date), [40] est la traduction pur & simple d'un roman du st Graal en prose française. Le traducteur cambrien le dit expressément, et nous apprend que l'auteur français a drosses yr ystoria honn o ladin yn ffranghec (fol. 36 verso).

Voilà une lettre bien longue, cher Monsieur, et bien des questions; je veus pourtant vous en adresser une dernière. Je vois dans un de vos articles si intéressants du Cambrian Jl que vous placez la bataille de Cattraeth en 608, [41] voserai je vous demander la source de cette date très précieuse pour moi? Mille pardons de mes importunités vous y trouverez j'aime a le croire, une preuve de plus de ses sincères considérations de votre bien devoué
Vcte Hersart De la Villemarqué
P.S. Seriez-vous assez bon pour offrir des homages à M H. A. Bruce M.P. dont jai garde le plus agréable Souvenir, et qui m'a parlé de vous.

[Written across the side of third page:]
Je n'ai pas l'article dont vous avec l'obligeance de me parler sur les ~~British Bards~~ mais on m'en a cité des passages: quand je la connaitre j'en remercierai l'auteur.

---

there.
[40] 'The latter [Y Greal] is evidently the MS. noticed by Lhwyd; and possibly may be the identical MS. of Trahaearn ab Ievan ap Meuric. It is a most interesting document; and if the date A.D. 1106 be correct, it must be the first of the Arthurian cycles; and it is hoped, that Lady Charlotte Guest will not allow her work to remain incomplete, while this important work remains unpublished.' Stephens, *Literature of the Kymry*, p. 438.
[41] See Stephens, 'Dyvynwal Moelmud', 163.

[Written across the side of the last (fourth) page:]
Comme vous le pensez avec raison, j'ai lu la traduction du Gododin par le Rev John Williams Ab Ithel, j'en dois une copie à un ami du Jesus college je partage tout à fait votre sentiment sur la traduction & sa critique: c'est avec la plus vive impatience que j'attends votre nouvel ouvrage à vous-même.

[A contemporary translation of the above, probably by Stephens:

Chateau de Keraskier près Kemperlé
Bretagne
The 14th July 1856

Dear (Monsieur) Sir
I received your letter the 4th of July, and I am unable to compensate you sufficiently for the friendly terms in which you speak of me. I am particularly flattered by the honour which the *Cambrian* Institute thought proper to allow me, in offering to place my name among the number{?} of its Vice Presidents; I accept it with much pleasure, and I pray you to thank that learned society for me, until I can myself thank them, on the official reception of my nomination. To be praised by you, whose labours are so justly esteemed in France and Germany, is already a great success.

I often talked of you to my illustrious friend in suffering and infirmities, the hardship of losing his eyes did not alter his genius in life: he was himself very sensible of the eloge {praise} which you made of him in your excellent work the *Literature of the Kymry*, and a little before his death, which is for France and for his friends an irreparable loss; he demanded of me what was your opinion, respecting a very important assertion, in the Cambrian Register for 1791. p. 241, concerning the slight remains conserved in Wales of the expropriation of the conquest. He equally demanded what you think, of the *Kyvrinach y Beirdd*, which Mr Pictet of Geneva has recently exhumed & with credit, after the text of 1792 of Iolo Morganwg, and which appear to me, not a mystery but a mystification. I should have been well able to reply to him for you, and to explain the more clearly that you do not speak on the point in the *Literature of the Kymry*: your qualifying solely, with much sense and spirit, in the *Cambrian Journal*, the Iolo MSS as *slipshod* documents. However we continue in France to occupy ourselves with the authenticity of the Kyvrinach, you would oblige me much by informing me if there exists a copy of a date anterior to the MS attributed to Edward Davydd who dies in 1690, and if the manuscript of Davydd exists really in the library of Llanharan, Glamorganshire the property of the Turberville family:—

I am not, unless I am deceived, without ground for suspecting Edward Davydd and his confreres, to have fabricated the whole of the Kyvrinach, or at least the theological part of the book, with the expression of the old Triads of the Circles. What think you? I have expressed myself in this sense in addressing my written opinion to my learned colleague of the Academy of Berlin, Mr Jacob Grimm: I shall be happy to see it confirmed by so competent a judge as yourself: The researches I made, in the month of December last, in the Library of Sir Robert Vaughan at Rhûg, do not change my desire to see it this regard. I should have been very easy {glad} to find an ancient document bearing a certain date, of a nature to confirm the important passage cited by Iolo Morganwg p 630, respecting the Armorican origin of the Round table. Taliesin Williams showed me this already in 1839, in the papers of his father; but I doubted the antiquity of the tradition, before seeing the view adopted by you (p 336). And it was I who caused Mr Albert Schulz to doubt also, inasmuch as he cites you with a point of interrogation on the subject, whereas he ordinarily borrows {adopts} your opinions. The famous *Llyfr o grefft yr holl ford gron*, in which I hoped to find every light, and which Lady Vaughan permitted me to read (it is the same that you speak of p 438, with such defiance distrust of the date), is a pure and simple translation of the Romance of St Graal in French Prose—The Cambrian translator says this expressly, and we learn that the French author, adresses yr ystoria honn o Ladun yn Ffranghec (fol 264, verso)

Here is a very long letter, Dear Sir, and full of questions: your will bear me to address you one more. I see in one of your interesting articles in the Cambrian Journal, that you place the battle of Cattraeth in 608 may I ask you the source of this date, very precious to me? A thousand pardons for my importunities, you will find, that I love you

P.S. I press you to be good enough to offer my homages to Mr H. A. Bruce MP of whom I have the most agreeable souvenir, that he spoke to me of you.

Comme vous le perchez, avis restons.

I saw the translation of the Gododin by the Rev John Williams, Ab Ithel, I was given a copy by a friend of Jesus College; I partake your sentiment respecting the translation and the criticism. It is with many turns of impatience that I await your new work from yourself.

I did have not seen the article, of which you obligingly spoke to me, on the Br respecting the British Bards in which the passages from me were cited, though I knew and thanked the author.]

*   *   *   *

NLW, MS. 965E, 308
Théodore Hersart de la Villemarqué to Thomas Stephens

Chateau de Keransker, le 29 juillet 1861.
Cher Monsieur Stephens,

Permettez-moi de vous présenter mon ami, notre éminent historien français, M. Henri Martin, qui a lu et admiré votre bel ouvrage Sur la littérature des Kymri, et qui désire faire votre connaissance et recourir à vos lumières. Je regrette de n'avoir pu l'accompagner dans votre cher et beau pays et lui envie le plaisir qu'il aura de vous voir & de ? vous entendre

Votre bien dévoué
    Vte Hersart De la Villemarqué
    Membre de l'institut
M. Thom. Stephens, Merthyr Tydwyl

[A translation of the above by Nely van Seventer:
Keransker Castle, July 29, 1861.
Dear Mister Stephens,
Allow me to introduce my friend to you: our eminent French historian Mr Henri Martin, who has read and admired your beautiful work On the Literature of the Kymri, and who would like to make your acquaintance and resort to the light of your knowledge. I regret that I have not been able to accompany him into your dear and beautiful country, and I envy him the pleasure he will have to see & hear you.
    Yours faithfully,
    Vte Hersart de la Villemarqué
    Member of the institure
Mr Thom. Stephens, Merthyr Tydwyl.]

*   *   *   *

NLW, MS. 964E, 188
Henri Martin to Thomas Stephens
Royal
Victoria Hotel
Llanberis
[printed letterhead]
18 August[42]
My dear Sir
    I write at you from ^the foot of^ Eryri,[43] where we are pute out by great tempest of wind and rain: i was to go on Conway the third day of Eisteddfod of north-Wales, but too late, I seen a little moment the reverend J Williams ab Ithel, ~~and~~ but between a much people and much occupations, and ^it^ was means between us that i should to write at him upon any interesting questions.
    I am to come back from holy-head ~~and~~ or Bangor at the 20 at morning, and i ~~may~~ shall to be at Merthyr at evening of the same

---

[42] 1861.
[43] Snowdon.

day. I ~~should~~ shall to leave the luggage at Merthyr and ~~go~~ to go to Aberdare, the 21 at morning, with hat and umbrella, *expeditus in armis*, and to arrive toward you at Eisteddfod.[44]

Since you are so generous so at me to offer to translate in Welsh any words of a French ^and Gaul^ traveller at his brothers of Cymru, i shall to prepare some words ~~that at you~~ i shall to communicate at you before the last seat of Eisteddfod.[45] I therefore shall to have again the pleasure of seeing you at the 21 at evening.

Yours very truly
H Martin

The doctor Th. Stephens
Aberdare

*   *   *   *

NLW, MS. 964E, 189
Henri Martin to Thomas Stephens

Yères (Seine et Oise), 11 7 61[46]
Near Paris,

Dear Sir,

I have laboured during any days amongst the MSS. of Llanover. You not are mistaken upon the being of various documents of the

---

[44] Martin attended the 1861 Aberdare Eisteddfod. See 'Aberdare Eisteddfod. (Continued from Sixth Page)', *The Cardiff Times*, 23 August 1861, 8; 'Grand National Eisteddfod, Held at Aberdare, continued from Page 8', *The Cardiff and Merthyr Guardian Glamorgan Monmouth and Brecon Gazette*, 24 August 1861, 6, accessed via *Welsh Newspapers Online*.

[45] While Stephens did provide an English translation of Martin's address, Martin spoke to the eisteddfod in French about the ethnic unity of the Welsh and French peoples: '...we all, French, Italians, Spaniards, are all called by the Germans—by the one name—Welsh, like yourselves. Welsh we are then and Welsh we will remain, —if not in tongue, yet in heart.' Ibid.

[46] Postmarked at London, 14 September 1861.

same kind as the theological triads. One Ms. include several of such writings; in many others as allusions and fragments in the same spirit; and many remains that i not have ~~seeing~~ seen; it was at me necessary to return at Paris, and the Rev. ab Ithel have wrote at me that he would to publish near Christmas a volume including this documents with much things concerning the bardic mysteries. This was at me the essential thing.

As for "MS. of the triads" Iolo had up it many times wrote in his notes; what is summed up this words: "I have a transcript the origin of it is in the possession of M. R. Bradford, of Bettws, near Bridgend, in Glamorgan, son of the late M. J. Bradford, who, for skill in ancient british bardism left not his equal behind." Therefore, the MS. of Llywelyn Sion remains even into the hands of any John and Richard Bradford's heir, if this heirs have preserved their family's library.

The questions concerning the MS. have losed great ~~portion~~ party of their importance, since the discovery of other documents of the same kind have proved the being of a tradition and collective doctrine, with various interpretations. Which documents not may to be writing by one same writer, since they offer ^some^ valuable differences of ^theological^ belief. Whatever I have seen of Iolo's notes ~~and~~ of his ^of^ work and study means, had most confirmed and augmented my ~~ast~~ esteem for its personality and its undoubted sincereness. Whole attest his probity until the scruple.

Alas, he learn us of what the theological triads, ~~what which~~ whose he had accepted passionately the doctrine, ~~have~~ are presented to the bardic gorsedd of year 1680, but no sanctioned; nothing was to compelling him at this fair and faithful notification. Iolo not explain why the gorsedd not had admitted the triads[1]; we may to day to it comprehend, i think; the bards are divided between the doctrine of the triads and the doctrine of Llyma Rol Cof &c[47] which differs up the creation's system. They no may to agree concerning the decision. The triads and Llyma

---

[47] 'Llyma Rol Cof a Chyfrif' or 'The Roll of Tradition and Chronology'. See Williams. *Iolo Manuscripts*, pp. 45–9, 424–29.

Rol &c, both are between the MSS. of Llywelyn Sion, who had transcribing this from the MSS. of another more ancient bard, Edeyrn Dafod Aur. It at me seems most probable that this surer documents are wroteing between the XIVth and XVth centuries, from the ~~tradition~~ before oral tradition. This remove entirely whole suspicion that Dafydd Edward of Margam had tooke hand up the theological triads; it is up the poetical triads only that the gorsedd had authorized him to add any examples and explanations.

Nothing rather explain the Iolo's sincereness, that the questions, that the doubts of himself before himself; for instance, your opinion up the bardic alphabet[48] he had inclined at him; only retained by the ~~a~~ consideration that any bards more ancient of the XIVth century have wroting allusions at the alphabet. But, at length, he had entirely abandoned that opinion, by this consideration, what at me seems much notable, that many words touching at the ground of the cymric language, indicate the symbolic affinity of the letters, and of the whole knowledge with the trees as means; for instance, *gwydd*, plant, tree, and knowledge;— afterwards, the numerous derivations.

Our friend La Villemarque has published his *Myrddhin*[49] ~~there~~ what I have ^begined^ the reading; excellent method; clearest light in most complicate matters; as pleasing as utile book, and deserving to be approved by the learned author of *Literature of the Cymru*.

Will you me recall ~~at~~ to ~~of~~ mind of our common friends, especially of the excellent Mr James's family; never i would to forget their amiable and cordial hospitality. I was to regret that i no may to taking my way at return by Merthyr; but i was retained at Park-Gwern, ~~for~~ by a meeting of the Cambrian archaeologic

---

[48] These were later published as Thomas Stephens, 'An Essay on the Bardic Alphabet Called "Coelbren y Beirdd"', *Archaeologia Cambrensis*, Fourth Series, 11 (July 1872), 181–210.

[49] Hersart De La Villemarqué, *Myrdhin ou l'Enchanteur Merlin son Histoire, ses Œuvres, son Influence* (Paris: Librairie Académique, 1862).

society,[50] that had me admited between his correspondence members. I have carried away from your country a remembrance that ~~you~~ leave on me great desire of to see again ~~him~~ she.
 Yours very truly
  H Martin
P.S. I add the following note from Iolo's MSS, that I recover between my papers.

 "The language of Llwelyn Sion himself is full of anglicisms and modern idioms, but that of the Triads _Llafar_ gorsedd &ca, is of the most antique cast" Iolo believe the triads wroting in XIIth century, at length, "The language of the triads seems to be that of the XIVth century, and the Silurian dialect."

2 P.S. Iolo says to be some triad's copies interpolated in the XVI century, and there to be repeating the tales up the false Trojan origins. It is remarkable that in secret documents such as the Llyma Rol Cof &ca, this tales are entirely put out.

(1) It not seems that the triads are rejecting, but that the gorsedd ~~had~~ was silent up.

*   *   *   *

---

[50] The fifteenth annual meeting of the Cambrian Archaeological Association was held in Swansea in August 1861. At this meeting, Stephens read a paper on the inscribed stone at Cefn Brithdir, Gelligaer, near Merthyr Tydfil and was active in the meeting's discussions. Martin, conversely, was only mentioned in the report in relation to the vote to admit him as an honorary member. 'Cambrian Archaeological Association. Swansea Meeting, 1861'.

NLW, MS. 965E, 309
Théodore Hersart de la Villemarqué to Thomas Stephens

Château de Keransker près Kemperlé
(Bretagne)
8 7bre 1861

Mon cher Monsieur

Il y avait bien longtemps que je n'avais eu de vos nouvelles et je suis heureux d'en recevoir par le *Cambrian daily*; j'ai lu avec plaisir votre excellent *Speech* à l'Eisteddfod d'Aberdare, et votre non moins excellente traduction du discours de mon ami Henri Martin. Il m'écrit que vous l'avez accueilli à bras ouverts et qu'il a eu autant à se louer de votre bienveillance que de votre science; je n'en doutais pas, et je vous remercie. Plus heureux que moi, il vous connaît maintenant personnellement, et je compte recevoir prochainement de lui d'intéressants détails sur ce qu'il a vu & appris grâce à votre recommandation; Je m'applaudis extrê-mement, dans l'intérêt de vos études celtiques, qu'il ait fait votre connaissance; il emportera du Pays de Galles des notions justes sur toute chose, et votre esprit droit l'aura mis en garde contre des documents qu'il était trop disposé à admirer sur la foi d'enthousiastes peu éclairés & sans critique, qui croient faire preuve de patriotisme et ne font que nuire à leur cause.

J'aurais été heureux de revoir avec Henri Martin votre cher pays pour la troisième fois, et si j'avais été prévenu à l'avance de la réunion d'Aberdare je m'y serais peut-être rendu. Les récits du mon ami me donnent des regrets: Il est vrai que j'en aurais éprouvés aussi de ne plus retrouver tant de personnes que j'aimais et qui m'aimaient:

> Pa le mae Price, vy anwyll Price?
> Vy mrawd, pa le yr wyt ti?
> Pa le mae *Tegid*? Pa le ych chwi,
> Owen, Williams, parchedig Rice?[51]

---

[51] Where is Price (Thomas Price, Carnhuanawc), my dear Price? / my brother, where are you? / Where is Tegid (John Jones)? Where are you, / Owen, Williams, Rev. Rice.

Parmi les vivants, j'aurais été étonné de ne pas trouver à Aberdare mon excellente amie Lady Augusta Llanover (*Gwenynen Gwent*); je vois qu'elle s'y est fait représenter par un Telynwr[52] de son village que vous avez couronné, et Henri Martin m'apprend qu'elle a acquis et qu'elle fait mettre en ordre par M. Williams Ab Ithel les papiers d'Iolo pour les publier: sont-elles les pièces que vous avez qualifiées de *"Slipshod documents"* dans le *cambrian journal* de mars 1855 (part. V. p 46)? [53] Les deux volumes ^de Price^ qu'elle a intitulés *The literary remains* et mis au jour en 54 sont audessous de la réputation de Carnhuanawc, [54] et de son vivant, il ne les eut pas publiés tels qu'ils sont; son *hanes Kymru* est bien supérieure. [55] J'espérais y trouver quelques nouveaux renseignements pour un livre que je viens d'achever *"Myrdhin, Son histoire, ses oeuvres, Son influence,* (Paris, Didier ed.) mais je n'en ai point trouvés. Veuillez me dire, chez monsieur, par quelle voie vous adresser cet ouvrage où je vous cite souvent avec reconnaissance et que je serais très flatté de vous juger dans quelque Revue l'Angleterre

    Votre bien dévoué

      Vte H. De La Villemarque

P.S. Si vous n'aviez pas de correspondant à Paris, je prierais Didier de vous adresser directement ce livre.

---

[52] Harpist.

[53] Thomas Stephens, 'The Laws of Dyvynwal Moelmud', 47. See Thomas Stephens to Théodore Hersart de la Villemarqué, Merthyr Tydfil, 20 Nov 1856, NLW Facs 854, in section 5, 'Revolutionising Welsh Scholarship', below.

[54] Williams, *The Literary Remains of the Rev. Thomas Price, Carnhuanawc.*

[55] Thomas Price (Carnhuanawc), *Hanes Cymru, a Chenedl y Cymry o'r Cynoesoedd hyd at Farwolaeth Llewelyn ap Gruffydd; ynhyd a rhai Cofiaint Perthynol i'r Amseroedd o'r Pryd Hynny a Waered* (Crughywel: Thomas Williams, 1842).

[A translation of the above by Nely van Seventer:

> Château de Keransker near Kemperlé
> (Brittany)
> September 8,1861

My dear Sir,

It has been a long time since I had any news from you, and I am happy to receive such via the *Cambrian Daily*; I have read with pleasure your excellent *Speech* at the Eisteddfod of Aberdare, as well as your no less excellent translation of the speech of my friend Henri Martin. He has written to me that you have welcomed him with open arms, and he had as much praise for your kindness as for your knowledge; I expected no less, and I thank you for it. He is luckier than me now that he knows you personally, and I expect to soon hear interesting details from him about what he has seen & learned thanks to your recommendation; I am extremely gratified, for the sake of your Celtic Studies, that he has made your acquaintance; he will take from Wales the correct ideas about everything, and your upright spirit will caution him against the documents of the kind he was all too ready to admire based on the faith of little-enlightened enthusiast without critical judgment, who believes they show their patriotism but does nothing but harm their cause.

I would have been happy to see your country with Henri Martin for the third time, and if I would have been informed about the gathering in Aberdare beforehand I would maybe have made my way there. The stories of my friend make me feel sorry: it is true that I would have felt the same for not being able to see again so many people I loved and who loved me:

> {In Welsh:
> Where is Price, my dear Price?
> my brother, where are you?
> Where is Tegid? Where are you,
> Owen, Williams, Rev. Rice?}

Among the living, I would have been surprised not to find my excellent friend Lady Augusta Llanover (*Gwenynen Gwent*) in Aberdare; I understand that she had herself represented by a {In Welsh: harpist} from her village, whom you have crowned, and

Henri Martin tells me that she has acquired the letters of Iolo and has them put into order by Mr Williams Ab Ithel to publish them: are these the documents you qualified as *"Slipshod Documents"* in the *Cambrian Journal* of March 1855 (part. V. p 46)? The two volumes ^of Price^ that she titled *The Literary Remains* and updated in 54 are beneath the reputation of Carnhuanawc, and while he was alive he did not publish them as such. His *Hanes Kymru* is far superior.I hoped to find some new information in it for a book that I just finished, "*Myrdhin*, *Son histoire*, *ses oeuvres*, son *influence*" (Paris, Didier ed.), but have not found it. Would you please tell me, dear Sir, by which way I might send you this work, in which I cite you often, and with gratitude, and I would be very flattered to appreciate your work in some Journal from England.

    Yours Sincerely,

       Vte H. De la Villemarqué.

P.S. If you do not have any correspondent in Paris, I will ask Didier to send the book to you directly.]

*   *   *   *

NLW Facs 854
Thomas Stephens to Théodore Hersart de la Villemarqué

Merthyr Tydfil

Sept 23 1861

My Dear Sir

    I am glad to find from you that Mons Martin has been pleased by his visit to Wales. He was fortunate enough to come at the right time—just at the autumnal season when learned societies, in Wales as well as in England, hold their annual meetings, and when, therefore, there is most probability of coming into contact with the principal *Savans*. The Eisteddvod at Aberdare was a grand affair, it lasted over four days, and was attended by 3000 to 4000 people. Mons Martin's speech was addressed to a very numerous audience; it ~~was~~ elicited much applause; and was greatly admired. It was a complete success.

    At the Eisteddvod, Mons. Martin was introduced to the Welsh

people—the popular element being there predominant. The succeeding week, he met quite a different body of men, at the meeting of the Cambrian Archaeological Society; and in a Series of excursions visited Margam Abbey, Neath Abbey, Swansea Castle, Arthur's Stone, The Flemish Settlement in Gower &c. We had a splendid luncheon given to us, *in the ancient refectory of Neath Abbey*, where about 200 ladies and gentlemen sat down together; the Bishop of St David, as the representative of the old Abbots of Neath said grace; and there we enjoyed ourselves very much. What would the old monks have thought of us, and especially of 70 or 80 ladies, dressed in the height of fashion, dining in their refectory? C'est la dernier refecteon dans la Abbaye de Neath. But it was a very *jolly* affair; ~~and~~ worthy of the Abbey, whose abbot loved to read the Romance of the Greal; and it is a pity you did not come over with Mons Martin.

What you say about "The Remains of Carnhuanawc"[56] is quite correct; these volumes are much inferior to "Hanes Cymru"; and they were not calculated to throw any new light on the subject of Merddin. Since his return to France M. Martin has written to me. He is greatly delighted with your Myrddin; and I do not doubt I shall be equally so. I shall have much pleasure in reviewing it in one of our periodicals. I have no correspondent in Paris; and therefore it had better be sent direct. ~~The~~ you should also send a copy to The Editor of the Atheneum, London, where you will be sure of a fair and favourable review. I presume you have seen the "Sagen Von Merlin" of San Marte[57]

What you are told respecting the Iolo MSS, is probably correct. Lady Hall bought all the MSS of Taliesin ab Iolo from his widow; and they are now at Llanover. Ab Ithel has been engaged for a long time in arranging them, and a volume of them on the subject of *Barddas* or the theosophy of the Bards, is promised about Christmas.[58] ~~A~~ It will probably be acceptable, *as additional*

---

[56] Williams (ed.), *The Literary Remains of the Rev. Thomas Price, Carnhuanawc.*
[57] [Schulz], *Die Sagen von Merlin.*
[58] John Williams (ab Ithel), *Barddas; or a Collection of Original Documents, Illustrative of the Theology, Wisdom, and Usages of the Bardo-Druidic System of*

material; but like all the Iolo MSS, it must be received *cum grano salis*;[59] and, but little attention must be paid to the opinions of Ab Ithel, who ~~is dis~~ believes them to be the veritable traditions of the British Druids, descended from the remotest ages to our time. On this point we must all form our own conclusions, when the volume appears.

   Yours very truly
      Thos Stephens
M le Comte de le
   Villemarque

*   *   *   *

NLW, MS. 964E, 62
Alfred Erny to Thomas Stephens

Paris 22 Jan 1863

   Dear Sir
When I have had the pleasure of seeing you with Mr Henri Martin some months ago[60] you had the amiability to promise me a few

---

the Isle of Britain (Llandovery: Welsh MSS. Society, 1862).

[59] 'With a grain of salt'.

[60] An account of Erny's tour of Wales, undertaken largely in the company of Martin, who split from Erny in Barmouth, in 1862, was published as Erny, 'Voyage dans le pays de Galles'. Erny's visit was highly cultural, and he mentions traditions and literature in connection with Llanover as well as commenting on Guest's Mabinogion when visiting Merthyr. He also comments at length on eisteddfodau and gorseddau in connecting with his attendance of an eisteddfod at Caernarfon and includes several folktales and legends, including the fairy bride of Llyn y Fan Fach, the Pwca at Llanover, the death of Llewelyn's dog Gelert, and the discovery of America by Madoc. Martin is mentioned often in the text and also provided notes and commentary. This account is available via the *European Travellers to Wales* website. See also, Heather Williams, 'La construction du Moyen Âge dans les récits de voyage français portant sur le pays de Galles, ou: Alfred Erny, celtomane en Galles en 1862', in Hélène Bouget and Magali Coumert (eds), *Enjeux épistémologiques des recherches sur les Bretagnes médiévales en histoire, langue et littérature*

legends that you told me you'll be able to send me. I come now to ask you if you are kind enough to send them me, for I am collecting them in order to publish them, which I'll do only when they are complete, ~~and~~ I suppose that in the small book you showed me, intitled if my memory is exact tales and superstitions of Wales,[61] you'll be able to find some interesting things, nevertheless in order to prevent your taking any unuseful pain, I'll tell you all the legends I have, in order to prevent you sending me a double. For the superstitions I have the curious history of the Tolaeth, ~~Cyrarth~~ Cyhiraeth, Corpse-candles, Spectre funeral, Goblin fire, Vale of glooms, Torrent Spectre,[62] & for the legends I have one of Dunraven, one of the Donatts Castle, the Lady of the Lake, Carn Cafall, Legend of Gwen & Lancarvan, Gitto Bach, Lewellyn's Dance & Fairy money.

I am most anxious to have other ones & I'll be most obliged if you can find some curious ones, perhaps in the reviews & papers already published you'll be able to find something. I thank you before hand for the little pain I give you & hope it'll be only a little one, for I'll be very sorry to prevent any serious occupation of yours. I have seen somewhere that once at an Eisteddfod ~~one~~ a prize ~~should~~ had been proposed for an Essay on Prince Madoc's settlement in America, & that on account of your Essay which proved, it appears, that he never settled in America, the prize was not given you. What is true about this; As the history of Prince Madoc interests me very much and that I have found many things

---

(Brest : CRBC-UBO, 2018), pp. 1–17. I am thankful to Heather Williams for providing me with a copy of this paper.

[61] Possibly *Celtic Fables, Fairy Tales and Legends Versified* by Jane Williams (Ysgafell) which was published in 1862, or W. Howells, *Cambrian Superstitions, comprising Ghosts, Omens, Witchcraft, &c. To which are added a Concise View of the Manners and Customs of the Principality, and some Fugitive Pieces* (Tipton: Thomas Danks, 1831), which Stephens is known to have owned.

[62] This list of folktales and their phrasing suggests that Erny was familiar with [Charles Redwood], *The Vale of Glamorgan: Scenes and Tales among the Welsh* (London: Saunders and Otley, 1839).

which show very likely that he settled or if not Welshmen did, I'll
be very much obliged to you to give me your idea about this.[63]
Believe me dear Sir

Yours very truly

Alfred Erny

40 Rue St Georges.

I have not seen yet Mr Martin, but I hope he'll be soon in Paris.

*   *   *   *

NLW, MS. 942C, f. 101
Albert Schulz (San Marte) to Thomas Stephens[64]

Geehrtester Herr Collega in lauro,
So darf ich Sie nennen, dem die Ehre des Preises, welcher im
Jahre 1848, für Ihre so sehr wertvolle Literature of the cymry zu
Theil ward, auch mir im Jahre 1840, von der selben geleehrten
Gesellschaft, wenn auch weit weniger verdient, zu erkannt ward.
Gestatten Sie mir die Ehre und Freude, Ihnen durch die Anlagen
den Beweis zu liefern, daß Ihr herrliches gelehrtes Werk auf dem
Kontinent seine Ehre gefunden, und daß Ihre rühmliche Arbeit
auch hier weitere nützliche Prühfg. tragen wird. Denn hier ist die
Literatur von Wales noch eine fast völlige terra incognita und
doch hängt sie mit einem Theile so eng mit der Literatur des
deutschen Mittalalters zusammen. Reichen sich die Königlichen
Hoheiten von Großbrittanien und Preußen zum heiligen
Ehebund die Hände, wie sollten nicht die Gelehrten beider
Länder in gleichem Studienkreise sich freundlich begegnen, und
ihre Arbeiten fördern und nach Kräften unterstützen.

Dies war mir eine theure liebe Pflicht, und ich wünsche auf-
richtig, daß meine Bemühung Ihre Zufriedenheit erlange.

Genehmigen Sie die Versicherung der ausgezeichnetsten
Hochachtung, mit welcher ich die Ehre habe zu verharren,

Geehrtester Herr,

---

[63] See section 6, 'Disproving the Madoc Myth', below.

[64] 27 March 1864. I am grateful to Dr Marion Löffler for transcribing this letter.

TS
Ganz ergebenster
Dr Schulz Regierungsrat

[**NLW, MS. 965E, 306a**, a contemporary translation of the above:

Honoured Sir Collega in lauro—
So may I call you since the honor of the prize which was awarded
to you in 1848 for your so very valuable work on the Lit^r of the
Cymry was also in the year 1840 awarded to me tho' far less
deserved, from the same learned society. Allow me the honor &
joy thro' the enclosed to give you the proof that your excellent
learned work has met with honor on the continent & that your
famous work also here will bear further useful fruits. For here the
Welsh literature is still almost a terra incognita, yet it is so nearly
connected in part with the Literature of the German Middle Ages.
As the Royal Families of Gr^t Bt. and Prussia give the hand in holy
Mat^y so should also the scholars of both lands in the same circle
of study meet friendly & further their labors & assist them
according to their powers. This was a precious duty to me & I
sincerely hope that my labor meets with your approval. Receive
the assurance of the highest esteem with which I have the honor
to remain
    Most esteemed Sir yours very humbly]

*　　*　　*　　*

NLW, MS. 964E, 192
Henri Martin to Thomas Stephens

Paris Passy 15 Juillet 67

Dear Sir

Excusez-moi de vous écrire très brièvement et en français. J'ai en ce moment une fatigue de tête qui m'émpêche de faire aucun effort et de lire et d'écrire. Je puis vous recommander une bonne maison d'éducation pour le but que cherche votre ami; l'adresse est Mr Keller, rue de Chevreuse, no 4; près le boulevard du Montparnasse.

Je regrette bien que vous ne puissiez accompagner à Paris notre excellent Mr James, que j'aurais très grand plaisir á revoir. Je regrette doublement que vous ne puissiez venir en France cette saison, parce que nous aurons un Congrès breton à St Brieuc vers le 10 7bre. Je voulais précisément vous en donner avis ces jours-ci. Nos Bretons ont adressé aux Gallois un appel qu'ils m'ont fait signer avec La-Villemarqué. On veut tâcher de resserres les liens entre les *celtisants* des deux côtés de la mer. [65]

Je vous envoie, pour vous et Mr James, ma nouvelle adresse, qui est, de: *Rue du Ranelagh, no 54; Passy, Paris.* Je voudrais bien qu'elle pût vous servir à tous deux, pour faire le voyage de Passy, qui est maintenant un quartier de Paris.

Tout à vous bien cordialement et veuillez présenter tous mes affectueux souvenirs à la bonne famille James.

H. Martin

---

[65] This meeting was attended by several Welshmen and reported on the in *The Cardiff and Merthyr Guardian, Glamorgan, Monmouth, and Brecon Gazette*. The meeting was opened by 'a Breton cantata—"The Bretons to the Welsh." [...] The words sung were extremely thrilling and pathetic, being a most cordial welcome of the Welsh to Brittany. We are spoken of as "brothers," as "sons of the same mother"'. 'The Breton Congress', *The Cardiff Guardian, Glamorgan, Monmouth, and Brecon Gazette*, 8 November 1867, 6, accessed via *Welsh Newspapers Online*.

[A translation of the above by Nely van Seventer:

                                        Paris Passy, July 15 67
Dear Sir,

Excuse me for writing you very briefly in French. At this moment, I have a head fatigue that stops me from making any effort, and from reading and writing. I can recommend you a good education house for the purpose your friend is looking for: the address is Mr Keller, rue de Chevreuse, nr. 4; near de boulevard de Mont-parnasse.

I am very sorry you will not be able to accompany our excellent Mr James, whom I will have the great pleasure of seeing again, to Paris. I am doubly sorry you will not be able to come to France this season because there will be a Breton Congress in St Brieuc around the tenth of September. As it happens, I wanted to inform you about that soon. Our Bretons have sent an invitation to the Welsh that they made me sign, together with La Villemarqué. We want to try to strengthen the bonds between *celtisants* on both sides of the sea.

I send you, for yourself and for Mr James, my new address, which is: *Rue du Ranelagh, nr. 54; Passy, Paris.* I hope it will serve you both to make the trip to Passy, which is now a district of Paris.

My very best wishes to you, and send all my love to the good James family.

H. Martin.]

                    *   *   *   *

NLW, MS. 965E, 235a
Adolphe Pictet to Thomas Stephens

                                        Genevè. 18 Mai 1869
Monsieur,

J'ai reçu la lettre que vous m'avez fait l'honneur de m'adresser en date du 12 Mai,[66] et je ne puis assez vous remercier de l'aimable empressement avec lequel vous avez bien voulu répondre à la

---

[66] This letter does not appear to be extant.

demande de mon ami Henri Martin au sujet des noms de cours d'eau du pays de Galles. La liste que vous m'avez envoyée me sera certainement utile à plusieurs égards, en complétant celle que j'avois extraite déjà de sources diverses. J'aurois désiré seulement que vous eussiez indiqué les positions topographiques, comme par ex : *Crawnon* (=*Crafnant* Lib. Landav. p. 127) tributary to the Usk, Breconshire, the *scraping brook*? et ajouté vos conjectures étymologiques, appuyées, si possible, du caractère réel des cours d'eau, rivière, torrent, ruisseau, rapidité; couleur, encaissement etc, détails, il est vrai, difficiles à réunir à moins d'observations directes.

Le travail que j'ai entrepris, à l'instigation surtout de la commission française de la Topographie des Gaules, [67] comprendra l'ensemble des noms de rivières dans tout le domaine des races celtiques, anciennes et modernes. La comparaison des noms anciens du continent avec ceux de l'Angleterre, de l'Irlande, et de l'Ecosse, est très importante pour leur élucidation étymologique, et c'est pour cela que je désire réunir ces derniers d'une maniéré aussi complète que possible. Je ne voudrais pas abuser de votre obligeance en vous demandant une collection semblable pour le pays de Galles et la Cornouailles; mais vous pouvez peut être m'indiquer quelque topographie bien faites, avec une nomenclature correcte des cours d'eau, comme celle que j'ai trouvée pour le Merionethshire, et Anglesey, dans le Càmbrian Register de 1795, et 1796.[68] Le *Liber Landavensis* n'a fourni un bon nombre des formes anciennes précieuses, et on en trouverait, sans doute, dans ce qui a été publié des *Lives of British Saints*,[69] que je n'ai pas à ma disposition. Le nouvel ouvrage de

---

[67] Pictet became a member of the Commission topographiques des Gaules in 1864.

[68] 'Topography of Merionethshire', *The Cambrian Register, for the Year 1795* (London: E. and T. Williams, 1796), pp. 287–315; 'Topography of Anglesey', *The Cambrian Register, for the Year 1796* (London: E. and T. Williams, 1799), pp. 390–415.

[69] W. J. Rees, *Lives of the Cambro British Saints, of the Fifth and Immediate Succeeding Centuries, from Ancient Welsh and Latin MSS, in the British Museum*

Skene, *Ancient Books of Wales*,[70] m'a été aussi utile sous ce rapport.

Je ne suis encore occupé, pour le moment, qu'à réunir des matériaux dont la masse croissante commence quelque peu à m'effrayer. Quand je serai plus avancé, je vous demanderai la permission de vous consulter sur des points particuliers relatifs aux noms gallois et à leur signification. En attendant, je vous renouvelle mes remerciements pour le secours que vous avez bien voulu m'apporter, et je vous prie d'agréer l'assurance de ma considération la plus distinguée.

Adolphe Pictet

[On the reverse, in Thomas Stephens's handwriting in pencil:]
The Crafnant, and the Crafnell, are both small rivers that fall in to the Usk, a few miles below the town of Brecon, They flow or rather *fall* from the Alpine Region of South Wales. These mountains, go by the various names of Cadair Arthur (Gildas Cambrensis), Bannau Brycheiniog, Ban uwch Denni (in bardic figure) or the Breconshire Beacons. The configuration of the district necessarily causes them to be *scraping* brooks—in rainy seasons they fall precipitously, and carrying before every thing moveable.

[A translation of the above by Nely van Seventer:
Genevè, May 18, 1869
Dear Sir,
I have received the letter which you did me the honour to send, dated the twelfth of May, and I cannot thank you enough for the kind willingness with which you have wished to answer the question of my friend Henri Martin concerning the names of

---

and Elsewhere, with English Translations, and Explanatory Notes (Llandovery: Welsh MSS Society, 1853).

[70] William F. Skene, *The Four Ancient Books of Wales: Containing the Cymric Poems attributed to the Bards of the Sixth Century*, two vols (Edinburgh: Edmonston and Douglas, 1868).

waterways in Wales. The list you send to me will certainly serve me in many respects, completing the one I already assembled from various sources. I would only have wished that you would have indicated the topographical positions, like from example: *Crawnon* (=*Crofnant* Lib. Landv. p. 127) tributary to the Usk, Breconshire, the *scraping book*? and added your own etymological conjectures, supported, if possible, by the real-life character of the waterway, river, torrent, stream; speed, colour, deep embankment, etc.; details that are, in truth, difficult to put together without direct observation.

The work that I have undertaken, encouraged especially by the French commission of the Topography of the Gauls, will include all the names of rivers in the whole area of the Celtic races, ancient and modern. The comparison of ancient names on the continent with those of England, Ireland, and Scotland is very important for their etymological elucidation, and that is why I desire to assemble those last in the most complete way possible. I would not want to abuse your kindness by asking you for a similar collection for Wales and Cornwall, but perhaps you would be able to point me towards some well-made topographies, with a correct nomenclature for waterways, like the ones I have found for Merionethshire and Anglesey in the Cambrian Register of 1795 and 1796. The *Liber Landavensis* has provided me with a good amount of precious ancient forms, and one would find more of these, without a doubt, in that which has been published of the *Lives of the British Saints*, which I do not have at my disposal. Skene's new work, *Ancient Books of Wales*, has also been of use to me in this context.

At the moment I am only occupied with bringing together the materials, whose increasing mass starts to frighten me a bit. When I will have advanced further, I will ask your permission to consult you on particular points in connection with the Welsh names and their meanings. In the meantime, I will renew my thanks for the aid you have been so willing to give me.
Yours sincerely,

Adolphe Pictet.]

Bibliotèque de Genève, MS. fr. 4229, f. 151–152
Thomas Stephens to Adolphe Pictet

Merthyr Tydfil.
May. 27. 1869

Sir

I hasten to reply to your enquiry respecting the brook Crafnant. This first element *Craf* or Crav. enters into the composition of two names, both named in Lib: Landav: ^p^ 127 (and at p.p. 375–6. The verb Cravu in Cymraeg signifies to scratch, or *scrape*, in which latter English word, you will see the Welsh or Kymric letters reproduced or repeated.

These two small rivers
Craf—nant
Craf—nell
fall into the river Usk, the Kymric name of which is wysg = Erse or Gaelic—uisge, a few miles from the town of Brecon, called in Kymric or Cymraeg—Aber-Honddu, from the fall of the river Honddu (dd=dh) into the Usk at that town. Brecon (so called from a man named Brychan) stands nearly in the same relation to the Alpine region of South Wales, as Geneva does to the Sabre. These mountains are the highest in South Wales, being 2862 feet above the level of the sea. They go by various names, as Cader Arthur (Giraldus Cambrensis) Bannau Brycheiniog, Ban Uwch Denni— (A brook so called)—(in bardic figure), and the Breconshire Beacons.

The configuration, and altitude of the Beacons, necessarily cause the Craf-nant, and Craf-nell to be *scraping* brooks. They fall precipitously, and in rainy seasons carry before them every thing moveable that falls in their course.

It is a disputed point among philologists in Wales, whether the old names of rivers are Gaelic or Kymric—such as Wysg, Gwy &c. I adopt the first view; and it is not a little interesting to find in the district of which I am now writing, cases in which the two sections of the Keltic tongue coexist—one overlapping the other. Thus in the Brecon there is a small lake calld *Llyn* Cwm *Llwch*. Here we have evidently two designations for the same thing.

Llwch, probably a Kymric form of Loch sometimes occurs in old Welsh, as in adar Llwch Gwyn, but it never occurs in spoken Welsh. Another instance occurs in the same county—as Maen Llia, where maen is Kymric and Lia Gaelic.

I shall be happy to give ^you^ any assistance in my power, and remain.

       Yours Truly

Mons Pictet.   Thos Stephens

*   *   *   *

NLW, MS. 964E, 6.
Edward Barnwell to Thomas Stephens

Melksham 2 June 1869
My Dear Sir

Mr H. Gaidoz[71] is very anxious to have you as one of his contributors and the honour of your name.[72] He has put me down—by some mistake as I informed him he~~ ~~ I was not a Celtic Scholar although I would gladly take in his review w^h is to be published quarterly—and sent by post to subscription ~~at Rural~~ the

---

[71] Henri Gaidoz (1842–1932) was a French folklorist and Celticist who founded the periodical *Revue Celtique* in 1871.

[72] Stephens's name does not appear as either a contributor or subscriber to the first two volumes of *Revue Celtique* (1870–1875). Gaidoz was indeed, however, interested in having Stephens as a contributor. In 1872 John Peter wrote to R. J. Jones, editor of the *Ymofynydd* that 'a friend of mine in Paris is anxious to see the articles which Mr Stephens of Merthyr wrote, and which are referred to in the current no of the Arch. Cambrensis.' (John Peter to R. J. Jones, Bala, 7 September 1872, Cardiff Central Library, MS 4.208, 157). This interest continued after Stephens's death, with Gaidoz writing to D. Silvan Evans in 1875 to enquire 'Will Stephens' essays be collected and published, as it was done for Th Price? Otherwise, I should be anxious to have for the Revue Celtique some of his unedited Essays, "Discovery of America by Madoc" or "on the Druids" etc.' Henri Gaidoz to D. Silvan Evans, Paris, 8 and 15 June 1875, NLW, MS. Cwrtmawr 900B, 29.

sub. being 1.0.0 per annum. He is however I think more anxious for the litterary support of Celtic Scholars and he has expressed to me his particular wish to have your name. Dr. Guest[73] has just sent in his adherence and promise of assistance

Mr Gaidoz is of the *Sound* school and holds I ~~believe~~ believe some official position and in the French government for the purpose of making *enquiries* into the State of Celtic Knowledge in this country. He was here last year and is coming again this year.

Will you kindly let me have your answer as soon as convenient as I am waiting to report to him my successes in getting you to join him. Mason Williams of Llanfair nr. Harlech has also joined. Do you know who Mr *Peter* of Bala[74] is, and what school he belongs to, for if he is of the wild Bardic Kind, he ought not to be associated with such names as are here given.

> Believe me, my dear Sir
> Yours Truly
> E L Barnwell

*   *   *   *

NLW, MS. 965E, 209
Friedrich Max Müller to Thomas Stephens

28 Feb / 1870

Sir

Accept my best thanks for your interesting note. The coincidences are certainly curious, but unless the historical channel through which such thoughts are supposed to have drifted from East to West is quite evident, I always think that what has naturally sprung up in one country, may spring up again in another country. Still the question deserves far more careful consideration than I can give to it at present, and I think it would

---

[73] Edwin Guest (1800–1880).
[74] John Peter (Ioan Pedr) (1833–1877).

interest many people if you would publish what there is of this
kind of mystic poetry in Welsh
  Believe me, Sir,
    Yours most respectfully
      Max Müller

*   *   *   *

NLW, MS. 964E, 33
Delta Davies[75] to Thomas Stephens

5 Cardiff St. Aberdare
Nov 6. 1874

Hynaws Syr,
Yr ydy'ch, mi wn yn synu fy mod i yn ysgrifenu atoch—
  Y rheswm yw fod genyf gyfaill yn *University* Halle Germany[76]
yn awyddus am ddysgu Llydawaeg, ac ar yr un pryd am ddysgu
Cymraeg. wedi gofyn imi am enwau ysgolheigion Cymraeg goreu
a welwch chwi fod yn dda adael imi eich cyfeirio chwi?
  Mae'n ddyn ieianc gobeithiol ac yn broffesor yn yr ysgol uchod
A welwch chwi fod yn dda nodi imi Cyfran i'w danfon iddo, yn
rhoddi ychydig o hanes neu yn traethu rhyw beth ar y Llydawied
mewn iaith neu arferion neu bob un or ddau (Armoricans
France)—a byddaf yn wir ddiolchgar os gwnewch
  Yr eiddoch yn bur
    Delta Davies
T. Stephens Esq
  Merthyr

---

[75] Possibly the Wesleyan preacher and writer Delta Davies (*d.*1907).

[76] Possibly Hugo Schuchardt (1842–1927) who had become a professor of
Romance Philology at the University of Halle in 1873 and who toured north
Wales in 1875 in order to learn about the Welsh language and culture. See
Hugo Schuchardt, *Romantisches und Keltisches: Gesammelte Aufsätze von Hugo
Schuchardt* (Strassburg: Karl J. Trübner, 1886), esp. pp. 317–86. Available
from the *European Travellers to Wales* website.

[A translation of the above:
Genial Sir,
You are, I know surprised that I am writing to you—

The reason is that I have a colleague in the University of Halle, Germany who is eager to learn Breton, and at the same time to learn Welsh. who has asked me for the names of the best Welsh scholars will you please allow me to refer to you?

He is a promising young man and a professor in the above school

Will you please indicate to me a piece to be sent to him, giving him some history or saying something about the Breton language or customs or both (French Armoricans)—and I will be truly very grateful if you do

Yours sincerely
        Delta Davies]

5

'IT IS A MISFORTUNE THAT WE SO LITTLE VALUE HISTORICAL CRITICISM IN OUR RESEARCHES': REVOLUTIONISING WELSH SCHOLARSHIP

AS WILL be discussed in the next section, Thomas Stephens's best-known scholarly controversy was his pronouncement of Madoc's 'non-discovery' of America at the 1858 Llangollen Eisteddfod. However, thoroughout his short but prolific scholarly career, Stephens's insistence on critical analysis of Welsh literature and history led him to staunchly maintain views which were often at odds with the received, and often romanticised, Welsh bardic historiography. In the opening pages of his last major work, a 1872 essay on 'Coelbren y Beirdd' (the Alphabet of the Bards), Stephens heavily criticised the bardic traditions of the 'Chair of the Bards of Glamorgan'.[1] He asserted these traditions were 'fabrications', 'speculations', and an 'illustration of the extravagances of the Silurian imagination' which appear to have 'rendered the mind of Morganwg incapable of scientific accuracy or of historic truthfullness', and described the bardic traids as 'ficticious things of yesterday'.[2]

As Marion Löffler has noted, Stephens's efforts were part of a 'scientific self-correction' of national historiography.[3] Stephens was already strikingly direct in *Literature of the Kymry*, boldly

---

[1] Stephens had intended to give the subject fuller treatment, but was prevented from doing so by his death three years later. See Thomas Stephens, 'The Chair of Glamorgan', *Archaeology Cambrensis*, Fourth Series, 11 (July 1872), 262.

[2] Stephens, 'An Essay on the Bardic Alphabet Called "Coelbren y Beirdd"', 181–82.

[3] Löffler, 'Failed Founding Fathers', p. 70.

drawing readers' attention to his intentions: 'Reader! Be attentive to what I am about to write ... for the daring spirit of modern criticism is about to lay violent hands upon the old household furniture of venerable tradition'.[4] From the mid-1850s, Stephens's challenge to this 'household furniture' intensified, notably in articles such as 'Studies in British Biography', published in the *Cambrian Journal*, 1854–1857; a series in *Seren Gomer* on the 'Nod Cyfrin', published in 1855–1856; 'Sefyllfa Wareiddiol y Cymry', published in *Y Traethodydd* in 1857; 'The Book of Aberpergwm, Improperly Called the Chronicle of Caradoc', published in *Archaeologia Cambrensis* in 1858; a series of articles on the 'Trioedd Ynys Prydain' in *Y Beirniad* in 1863–1865; and his 1872 essay on 'Coelbren y Beirdd', as well as in shorter letters and reviews in various periodicals.

While Stephens was certainly prominent at the forefront of this new scientific and often iconoclastic criticism, he was not alone, as the letters in this section show.[5] In a review of the entry on 'Druidism' in the *Gwyddionadur; or Enclycopedia Cambrensis*, it was lamented that,

A school has recently sprung up among us, the object of which, apparently, is to depreciate everything of a national character, and to deny all those facts relative to Welsh history and literature which men of learning and research have hitherto considered as sufficiently established. [...] Some, no doubt, take up their pens from a love of notoriety, some are influenced by the spirit of pedantry, not having it in their power to appear learned in any other way, and others again having met with some public slight or disappointment, adopt this course of wreaking their vengeance.[6]

It is hard not to imagine that Stephens's critics ascribed at least

[4] Stephens, *Literature of the Kymry*, p. 216. See also Löffler, 'Failed Founding Fathers', p. 71–2.
[5] See Löffler, 'Failed Founding Fathers', pp. 74–6.
[6] Review of 'Druidism. Second Article in the *Gwyddionadur; or Encyclopedia Cambrensis*. Part XXXII. Denbigh: T. Gee'. *Cambrian Journal*, (Alban Elved 1860), 231–232, 333–40 (231) [Typesetting error in original pagination].

the last of these catagories to him in the wake of the 1858 Eisteddfod, if not others. Other criticism was more personally directed. Several letters appeared in the *Cambrian Journal* entitled 'Stephens *versus* Stephens' highlighting apparent contradictions between Stephens's later writing and *Literature of the Kymry*.[7] Moreover, in a review of 'Sefyllfa Wareiddiol y Cymry' an irreverent writer styling himself 'A Myth' mocked Stephens's meticulous identification of pseudo-historical characters with possible real or mythic archetypes by noting that 'Stephen the martyr lived in the first century; therefore Stephens of Merthyr is a myth—the name a corruption of the former!'[8] Conversely, the letters collected in this section show some of the emotional, social and scholarly support Stephens received. Some were even prepared to go further than he did in rooting out historical myths and misconceptions—David William Nash confessed a belief that Iolo Morganwg had '*tampered* with many documents and *forged* many others',[9] whereas Stephens usually ascribed the anachronisms in Iolo's forgeries to the earlier bards and scribes whose work Iolo purported to have copied.[10]

The majority of the letters in this section concern Stephens's research regarding Hu Gadarn, who was supposed to have led the Welsh to Britain and to have introduced ploughing, cultivation, and the practice of using verses for the purpose of mnemonic preservation. He was also reported to have drawn the Afanc (a water monster) from Llyn Llion, and to have been regarded as a god of

---

[7] See, for instance, Anon. 'Stephens *versus* Stephens', *Cambrian Journal* 2 (Alban Hevin, 1855), 143; [Giraldus Cambrensis], 'Stephens *versus* Stephens', *Cambrian Journal*, Second Series, 1 (Alban Arthan 1858), 364.

[8] [A Myth], 'Civilization of the Cymry', *Cambrian Journal*, IV (1857), 227–29 (228).

[9] David William Nash to Thomas Stephens, Cheltenham, 8 October 1861, NLW, MS. 965E, 215. Emphais in original.

[10] See, for example, Stephens, 'The Laws of Dyvynwal Moelmud', esp. 39–40, 44–59; Idem, 'Prydain ap Aedd Mawr'; Idem., 'The Book of Aberpergwn, Improperly Called the Chronicle of Caradoc', *Archaeologia Cambrensis*, Third Series, XIII (January 1858), 77–96 (95); Idem., 'Coelbren y Beirdd'.

the ancient Welsh, part Noah and part Jesus.[11] In his 'Sefyllfa Wareiddiol y Cymry', Stephens identified Hu as the 'Hercules of the Greeks under another name',[12] but in these letters connections are explored with Hugh le Fort of the French Romances, a Breton devil called Hu Can, and the Irish High King Úgaine Mór. Importantly, in attempting to discover Hu's origins, Stephens drew on research assistance, guidance, and advice not only from Wales, but also from French scholars like Théodore Hersart de la Villemarqué and Henri Martin. This widening of Stephens's research, and of his social and scholarly networks, beyond Offa's Dyke is significant as it illustrates his growing frustration with native Welsh scholarship. As he noted in his article on the Laws of Dyfnwal Moelmud, in his quest 'to waken up the drowsy school of Cambrian critics, it may be well to show that, what they cannot see, is clear enough to the scholars of England and the continent'.[13]

*   *   *   *

---

[11] Williams, *Barddas*, p. 221; Rachel Bromwich, 'Triodd Ynys Prydain; The Myvyrian "Third Series" (II)', *Transactions of the Honourable Society of Cymmrodorion*' (1969) (part 1), 127–56 (129, 139–40). Coward, 'Exiled Trojans or the Sons of Gomer', pp. 174–5.

[12] 'Hercules y Groegiad, dan enw arall'. Stephens, 'Sefyllfa Wareiddiol y Cymry', 233.

[13] Stephens, 'The Laws of Dyvynwal Moelmud', 49.

NLW, MS. 964E, 156
J. Lloyd Jones[14] to Thomas Stephens

St. Davids
March 24 1855

Sir

I hope you will pardon me, a perfect stranger, in thus writing to you, but feel myself compelled to do so, having just returned home; and finding the Cambrian Journal waiting, my first thing was to read your second article on Dyvnwal Moelmud and his laws;[15] I thank you most heartily for them, they are well-timed, sound, and as a whole incontrovertible: am sorry to find an Editorial note of disapprobation accompanying it;[16] is it possible that the second article suits him better? If so; alas for the critical examination of the Welsh Language and Literature, I hope that will not discourage you from pursuing the same path, in dispelling the mist of prejudice and patriotism falsely so called, and placing our historical materials and characters on really terra firma; you will have the thanks of the next race of Celtic Scholars, though you may pass through the fiery ordeal of the present.

Some two years ago I examined these laws for the purpose of writing an essay on the social state of the early Cymry as set forth in them; and am gratified to find that the same triads have been

---

[14] It is unclear who this is. Possibly either John Jones (1786?–1863), a prominent early member of the Cambrian Archaeological Association, or John Jones, Idrisyn (1804–1887).

[15] Stephens, 'The Laws of Dyvynwal Moelmud'.

[16] John Williams (Ab Ithel), the editor of the *Cambrian Journal*, inserted a note following Stephens's article voicing his 'protest against the historical assertion which it contains'. He notes that the journal has received complaints about Stephens's series, apologises to readers 'for the introduction of controvercy' into the journal, and directs readers to a letter by 'Carodoc ap Bran' which contained 'an elaborate and complete refutation of Mr. Stephens' chronological errors'. John Williams [ab Ithel], Editorial Note, *Cambrian Journal*, 6 (February 1855), 59.

marked as you have examined but my conclusion was that they have been composed or rather altered between the eighth and twelfth century, and certainly some of them appear to set forth a state different to the feudal, and especially Celtic, as tr. 61 while others as 66 and 72 &c may justify the conclusion of a Norman influence and knight errantry.

In the meaning which you give to the word *golychwydwr*,[17] I do not agree, it proves the amount of popish influence, and believe it refers to secular priests or monks, have also great doubts that republican principles prevailed but very little in Wales till of late;[18] it was possibly the most loyal part of the country, however these are minor considerations; it is mortifying to find that whilst Schöll, Bopp, Zeuss[19] &c are cultivating our language, and drawing attention to our records and history we ourselves should make them ridiculous to all sound scholars.

Again thanking you and hoping you will forgive my thus trespassing on your time I remain, Sir

Yours very truly
J Lloyd Jones
Judess. Min.

*   *   *   *

---

[17] A religious person or worshiper. Stephens argues that the use of this 'unhistoric name' in the Moelmudian Triads to refer to a Christian priest in place of non-existant druidism was 'really too transparent a fiction to deceive anybody who has eyes to see and a capicty to comprehend'. Stephens, 'Laws of Dyvynwal Moelmud', 44.

[18] Stephens had argued that the liberal, democratic values evident in some of the Moelmudian Triads was evidence of 'a very recent and Cromwellian date'. Ibid., 45.

[19] Probably the German philologists Adolf Schöll (1805–1882), Franz Bopp (1791–1867), and Johann Kaspar Zeuss (1806–1856).

NLW Facs 854
Thomas Stephens to Théodore Hersart de la Villemarqué

Merthyr Tydfil
Nov 20th 1856

My Dear Sir//

I am quite ashamed to think that your letter should have remained so long unanswered; and the only apology I have to offer is that it arrived just as I was preparing to make a tour of Ireland, and judge for myself, respecting its Round Towers and other antiquities, and that my subsequent engagements have left me but very little spare time. During that tour, I may remark in passing, that I found the opinion of Vallancey and O'Brien, as to the Round Towers being "fire worshipping temples" to be pure moonshine, and was convinced that they are Christian erections.[20]

It would have afforded me much pleasure to have gratified the last hours of M. Thierry,[21] with my opinions on the points

---

[20] Throughout the mid-nineteenth cenutry, Irish antiquarians had been engaged with the origins and use of Irish round towers. Charles Vallancy had argued for a pagan origin for them as sun or fire temples, and this had been continued into the nineteenth century by scholars like William Bentham, who argued for Phonecian origins in his *The Gael and the Cymbri* (1834). In 1831, controversy was further sparked when the Royal Irish Academy offered a medal for an essay on the subject. The prize was won by George Petrie, who argued that the towers were Christian structures, while Henry O'Brien, who argued that they were pagan, was awarded a consolation prize. After a heated correspondence, O'Brien published his essay in 1834, while Petrie's essay was published in 1845 as part of his *Ecclesiastical Architecture of Ireland.* Damien Murray, *Romanticism, Nationalism and Irish Antiquarian Studies, 1840–80* (Maynooth: National University of Ireland, 2000), pp. 16–17; G. F. Mitchell, 'Antiquities', in T. Ó Raifeartaigh, *The Royal Irish Academy: A Bicentennial History, 1875–1985* (Dublin: Royal Irish Academy, 1985), pp. 93–165 (pp. 98–99).

[21] Augustin Thierry (1795–1856) was a prominent French historian and liberal. La Villemarque previously mentioned him in a letter dated 14 July. See NLW, MS. 965E, 306a, pp. 121 and 124 above.

suggested. It is quite true that the traces of the Norman Conquest have to a great extent disappeared, especially in Glamorganshire, where the Turbervilles are the only family who now survive; but on the other hand, I am not without an ~~interloping~~ uneasy suspicion that my own name has descended to me from some interloping Fitz Stephen, who took land that did not belong to him in Caermarthenshire.

I had not previously heard of Mr Pictet's edition of the "Cyvrinach";[22] but he has done wrong if he has confounded the old Triads of the Circles with the Prosodial labours of Meurig Dafydd, Llywelyn Sion, and Edward Dafydd. The Old Triads really belong to an old Theosophy, and are more of a mystery than a mystification. I believe myself to possess the key to unlock the mystery, and have a dissertation of about 100 pages on the subject in my new volume.

You are quite correct in your estimate of the passage respecting the Round Table in the Iolo MSS. This came out while the "Lit of the Kymry" was passing through the press, and before I had time to weigh its value. My present estimate of these MSS is implied in the epithet "slipshod" [23]

As to the date of the battle of Cattraeth, I arrive at it thus. You missed it by overlooking that "Cadvannan" is a proper name. Several heroes figured at Cattraeth who had previously been at the battle of Mannan in 584. For instance in verse we read,—

"Rae ergit Catvannan catwyt," which I translate,

He was preserved from the blows of Mannan fight. The only battle after, that answers the requirements of the case is that of 603. Allusions to Catvannan occur in two other places. In all, you will I think admit, that your version is less natural than that above given.

---

[22] Adolphe Pictet, *Le Mystère des Bardes de l'Île de Bretagne ou la Doctrine des Bardes Gallois du Moyen Age* (Genève: Joël Cherbuliez, 1856).

[23] See NLW, MS, 965E, Letter 306a, pp. 121 and 125 above. Stephens used the same adjective to describe the Iolo Manuscripts in the second of his 'Studies in British Biography'. Stephens, 'Laws of Dyvynwal Moelmud', 47.

Having thus disposed of your queries, I am ~~disposed~~ inclined to trouble you for a little information in return.

Hu Gadarn figures prominently in the *later* traditions or *speculations* of the bards; but he does not appear in our writings until the 13ᵗʰ century, and then his name first occurs, I think, in the Welsh translation ^from the Latin,^ of the Romance of Charlemagne. The passage runs thus,

"I have a heulrod [sun cap][24] of the skin of a fish; with that on my head I will stand before Hu, when he is dining; and I will eat with him, and I will drink, without any notice being taken of me."

What I desire is the original of this passage, ^either in Latin or Old French^; and it will be of service to me, if you can supply it. Any supplementary information in the shape of illustrative comment will also be acceptable. I think the name Hu must have come to us from without, probably from Provence; and shall be glad to have your assistance in tracing its origin.

I am sorry that I cannot afford you any assistance in tracing the history of the Round Table; none of our documents bearing on this subject can lay claim to any great antiquity; but they are unanimous in attributing its origin to Brittany; and the unity [illegible] self-abnegation of this testimony ought to have some weight. There is some acute criticism on the origin of the "San Greal" in Herbert's Cyclops Christianus, which is the work of a very learned, ^and^ acute, but whimsical writer.

Believe me Yours truly
Thos Stephens
M. le Compte de Villemarque

P.S. I believe that the Story of Charlemagne was translated from "the Romance" or Lingua Franca into Latin; and the Welsh translation professes to be made from the latter. It may therefore be necessary to compare the Latin with its original.

*   *   *   *

---

[24] Square brackets in original.

NLW, MS. 965E, 307
Théodore Hersart de la Villemarqué to Thomas Stephens

Aux Eaux de Néris a 29 aout 1857
Monsieur & cher Confrère,
N'ayant point exécuté mon voyage au Pays du Galles, et ayant au contraire pris ma route, cet été, vers le midi où je suis venu prendre les eaux, je suis privé du plaisir de faire votre connaissance, et à mon grand regret. Mais jespère été plus heureux une autre fois.

En passant par Paris jai fait les recherches qui vous m'avez prié de faire, aux manuscrits de la Bibliothèque impériale dans le roman de Charlemagne: malheureusement votre indication n'était pas assez précise, il m'eut fallu au moin une page du texte gallois à comparer avec l'original français, et vous ne m'avez donné qu'une phrase, sans m'indique approximativement dans quelle partie du roman elle se trouve. Jai donc cherché, comme l'on dit, une aiguille dans une charretée de foin. Si vous avez l'obligeance de préciser un peu plus, je ferai avec plaisir des nouvelles recherches.

En attendant je vous soumettrai une hypothèse: Jai remarqué dans un manuscrit du collège de Jesus intitulé *Lucidar* et que jai décrit dans une *Notice* récente que je vous ai envoyée, le nom gallois *Hu* qu'on y donne comme l'équivalent du nom français *Hughes*. L'auteur gallois de la traduction du roman de Charlemagne n'aura t-il pas de même traduit par *Hu-gadarn*, le nom de *Hughes-le-fort*, un de nos preux les plus illustres? Vous en jugerez.

Je ne partage pas toutefois entièrement votre opinion en sujet de Hu. Il se peut, comme vous l'avez constaté, qu'il ne paraisse pas dans vos bardes avant le XIIIe siècle, mais s'en suit il que ce ne soit pas un caractère Kymrique ou anciens breton, et que nos ancêtres communs, je discens des temps héroïques, ne le connaissent point? Je serais téméraire de l'affirmer, et plus téméraire de le croire d'origine provençale. La preuve qu'il a une origine Kymrique c'est qu'il figure dans la légende armoricaine de St Hervé où on le représente comme le génie des vieilles superstitions payennes luttant contre le christianisme naissant. Cette légende a été rédigée aumoins au XIe siècle, d'après les traditions populaires de l'époque. Je viens d'en donner une traduction nouvelle où jai fondu les souvenirs encore vivants qui éclairent si bien les anciens vieils manuscrits: Si vous la désirez, je vous l'adresserai aussitôt qu'elle aura été imprimée.

Avez-vous publié vous même le livre que vous m'annoncez, où vous avez cent pages, sur le *Mystère des bards*, et où vous en avez donné la clé? Soyez assez bon pour me dire chez quel libraire d'Angleterre je pourrai me le procurer. Tout ouvrage de vous est une bonne fortune pour le public breton soit de l'ile soit du continent. Existe t-il quelqu'autre livre nouveau sur les vieux sujets que nous aimons?

Comme Président de l'*Association Bretonne*, jai la primeur des articles publiés dans le Revues galloises qu'on nous adresse et je m'en félicite. Votre étude sur les *cromlechau* m'a fort instruit & intéressé.[25]

Mais je n'ai point encore vu ma nomination dans vos revues, comme un des Vice-présidents du *Cambrian Institut*; je n'ai même rien, d'autre nouvelle de cette honneur que par vous-même y aurait-il eu quelque lettre égarée?

Je vous remercie de votre critique aussi juste que polie du passage du *Gododin* relatif á Catvannan. Mais sur quelle autorité placez-vous le combat de *Mannan* en 584? Je pense que vous en avez quelqu' une bien solide pour donner une date aussi précise, et je serais on ne peut plus reconnaissant si vous avez l'obligeance de me la faire connaître, vous l'aurez sans doute due à quelque ancien ouvrage que je n'aurai pas en sous la main; ou peut être y serez vous arrivé par le rapprochement des textes que ne connais pas.

Je serai chez moi en Bretagne dans dix jours, et au mois de décembre de retour à Paris où je demeure maintenant rue des Beaux arts no 17. Toutes les recherches que vous aurez à y faire dans nos manuscrits, je les ferai volontiers de nouveau, je vous le

---

[25] Thomas Stephens, 'On the Names of Cromlechau', *Archaeologia Cambrensis*, Third Series, 6 (April 1856), 99–109.

répète. Agréez, Monsieur, l'assurance de ma considération distinguée.

Le Vte Hersart De la Villemarqué

[A contemporary translation of the above under the same number. This translation contains many crossings out and amendments, likely by Stephens, and is presented here with these revisions incorporated:

Mr Thos Stephens
   Merthyr Tydfil
      South Wales, England.
   The Waters of Nesis: Aug. 29th 1857
Sir and Dear Confrere.
Not having executed my journey to Wales, and having on the contrary taken my route this Summer to the South, where I have come to take the waters, I am deprived of the pleasure of your acquaintance, and to my great regret. But I hope to be more fortunate another time.

In passing thro' Paris I made the researches which you prayed me to make in the MSS of the Imperial Library, in the romance of Charlemagne: unfortunately your indication was not sufficiently precise: it would take me at least a page of the Welsh text to compare with the original French, and you have not given me but one phrase, without indicating to me approximately in what part of the romance, it is found. I might have searched, as we say, for a needle in a bottle? of hay. If you will have the goodness to be more specific, I will with pleasure make new researches.

In the mean time I submit to you an hypothesis. I remarked in a MS in Jesus College entitled *Lucidar*, and which I described in any a recent *Notice* which I sent to you, that the Welsh name Hu was given as the equivalent of the French name Hughes (The person named was Hughes or Hugues de Saint-Victor of Paris) Has not The Welsh author of the translation of the Romances of Charlemagne in the same way translated by Hugh Gadarn the name of *Hughes le Fort*, one of our most illustrious (Knights) worthies? you will judge.

However I do not partake altogether of your opinions on the subject of Hu. It may be as you have stated that he does not appear among your Bards before the 13th century; but does it follow, that it is not a Kymric or ancient British Character, and that our common ancestor, I mean those of the heroic time, did not know it

It would be rash to affirm, and still more rash to believe the Provencal origin (I had suggested that the name came from the Breton or Provencal). The proof of that it has a Kymric origin is that it figures in the Armorican Legend of St Herve, where he is represented as the Genius of the ancient pagan superstitions, contending against rising Christianity This legend was written at least in the XIth century after popular traditions of the period. I am going to give a new translation when I can embodied the remembrance still living which explain so (well?) in ancient manuscripts details. If you desire it, I will address (?) it to you immediately it is printed.

Have you yourself published the book which you have announced to me, where you have those page respecting the Mystere des Bards, and of which you have given the key? Be so good as to tell me of what English bookseller I can procure it. This work of yours is boon to the British Public, both of the island and the continent.

Exists there any other new work on the ancient subjects which we love?

As President of the Breton association I have the first reading of the Welsh Reviews, which are addressed to me; and to my felicity. Your study on the Cromlechau was to me most instructive and interesting.

But I have not yet seen my nomination in the reviews as one of the Vice Presidents of the Cambrian Institute. Nor have I received any other news of this honour but from you yourself. May it be that a letter is lost?

I thank you for your just and polite critique in the passage of the Gododin relating to Catvannan. But on what authority do you place the battle of Mannan in 584? I think you have a very solid ground for giving a date so precise; and I shall be still more grateful if you will oblige me by making it known. You owe it no doubt some ancient work which I have not at hands, or perhaps you have arrived at it by a comparison of texts unknown to me.

I shall be at home to Bretagne in 10 days, and in the month of December I return to Paris, and where I reside now at Rue de Beaux Arts No 1. All the researches which you wish to be made in our manuscripts, I will feel pleasure in making anew if you desire. Accept &c &c

Le Cte Hersart De la Villemarqué]

*   *   *   *

NLW Facs 854
Thomas Stephens to Théodore Hersart de la Villemarqué

Merthyr Tydfil
Nov 9 1857

My Dear Sir:

I beg to thank you for your "Notice" of our Ancient MSS, which ~~are~~ is very acceptable as containing in a collective form an account of our oldest documents, so that a rational judgement may now be formed respecting their antiquity and historical and philological value. I refer to it often, and find it very serviceable. Both that and Pictet's little book on the *Cyvrinach*, which your remarks ~~led~~ made known to me, and which I made known to the Editor, have been favourably reviewed in the *Cambrian Journal*.[26]

---

[26] Anon., Review of 'Notices des Principaux Manuscrits des Anciens Bretons, avec fac-simile, lues a l'Institut (séances des 2 et 30 Novembre, 1855). Par Th. Hersart de la Villemarqué, M.C. de l'Academie de Berlin. Paris: Imprimerie Impériale. 1856', *The Cambrian Journal*. 13 (March 1857), 79–80; Anon., Review of 'Le Mystere des Bardes de l'Ile de Bretagne on la Doctrine des Bardes Gaules du Moyen Age sur Dieu, la vie future et la Transmigration des Maes Text original, Traduction et Commentaire par Adolphe Pictet. Geneve: Joel Cherbuliez, Libraire-Editeur. Paris. Même Maison, Rue de la Monnaie, 10. 1856', *The Cambrian Journal*, 14 (June 1857), 158–60.

As to the authority for the date of Catvannan, it must have been an oversight on my part, that it was not given. It is now subjoined:–

D.LXXXI. Bellum Manan, in quo victor erat Aodhan Mac Gawran.

AD 582. Bellum Manan per Aodan

> *Annales Ultonensis* (Annals of Ulster, in Ireland)

581. The Battle of Man, ^(Prelium Mannense)^ in which Aedan son of Gabhran was victorious

582 The same words

> Annals of Tigernach (Irish)

Dr Todd of Dublin[27] remarks that "double entries of this kind are very common in our (i.e. Irish) Annals, shewing that the compiler had different authorities before him".

584 Bellum contra Euboniam. (Isle of Man)

> Annales Cambriæ

You will of course observe a slight discrepancy in the Chronology; but in old chronicles that is not much of account; for they often adopted different systems of chronology, and thus frequently and regularly differ. Bede in two of his works has two systems, with a difference of 2 years between them; and thus it is often found that the Welsh annals are ^a^ year behind the Irish, and ^the^ Saxon Chronicle a year or two after the Welsh. But with a view to fix the date of the Gododin, it is not material whether we place this battle in 582 or 584. You will probably recollect that the Gododin expressly connects Aedan with the battle of Mannan, i.e. the Isle of Man.

Ac Adan Catuannan cochre veirch,

Aedan of the (blood-stained) ruddy steeds of Mannan,

I am sorry to have given you so much trouble to search for the passage in the Romance of Charlemagne; but I rejoice that my attention has been fixed upon it. Neither of us appears to have aware that this romance had been printed by Fr Michel,[28] and

---

[27] James Henthorn Todd (1805–1869).

[28] Francisque Michel, *Charlemagne: An Anglo-Norman Poem of the Twelfth Century* (London: William Pickering, 1836). Stephens wrote to Michel for

^that^ this was the original of our Welsh translation. I have found the passage sought; and am much inclined to adopt your suggestion that Hugun le Fort is in some way to be connected with our Hu Gadarn. Nevertheless there are great difficulties in the way of accounting how Hugun le fort could have become reputed first colonist of Britain; and I shall be very glad to see your life of St Herve, in the hope it might show throw some light on this subject.

The Bardic mystery is exciting much attention here at present. Your will perceive that the *Editor* of the *Camb Journal*[29] has committed ^himself^ to very absurd views; and Archdeacon Williams[30] has ~~declared the worship of~~ shown an inclination to seek for very unfounded correspondences with the metaphysical views of our Sir W. Hamilton.[31] We have also a small prophet named "Iewan Myfyr" ^an illiterate man,^ who professes to be the sole depository of Bardo-Mystic knowledge![32] I have not yet published my views; for that would be injudicious at present. The MSS of the Iolo family have been sold to Lady Hall; and the *Editor* of the *Camb Journal* says they contain *unpublished* documents on *Bardism*. It is proposed to collect these and to publish them shortly.[33] Until then it will be unwise to rush into print; but you will see an outline of the views I am likely to put forward, in the *Traethodydd*, of which I send you the two last numbers.[34] It will

---

further information, who replied that while he found the question interesting, he was completely ignorant of the the details about which Stephens was enquiring. See Francisque Michel to Thomas Stephens, Oxford, 22 November 1857, NLW, MS. 965E, 203.

[29] John Williams (Ab Ithel) (1811–1862).

[30] John Williams (1792–1858).

[31] Possibly a reference to John Williams's letter in the *Cambrian Journal* on 'Cyfrinach y Beirdd', *The Cambrian Journal*, 15 (Sep 1857), 224–27. This view is discussed and criticised specifically and at some length in Stephens's 'Sefyllfa Wareiddiol y Cymry', 316–19.

[32] Evan Davies (Myfyr Morganwg) (1801–1888).

[33] Williams, *Barddas*.

[34] Stephens sent the first two instalments of his article on 'Sefyllfa Wareiddiol

also be necessary to have definite views respecting Hu Gadarn; and if you can give me any information respecting Hugun le fort, or indicate where it may be found, I shall be obliged, for as yet I know nothing further than that he appears in the romance of Charlemagne.

Your name has regularly appeared in the *Camb* Journal, as one of the Vice Presidents of the Institute, but I fear that owing to postal difficulties the Journals have not been sent to you. However I have written to the publisher, and trust there will be no further cause of complaint.

I remain My Dear Sir
Yours Faithfully
Thos Stephens
Le Compte H de Villemarque

*   *   *   *

NLW, MS, 965E, 306b
Théodore Hersart de la Villemarqué to Thomas Stephens

Château de Keransker, près Quimperlé, Finistere
le 3 aout 1858.

Cher Monsieur,

Depuis le mois de novembre 1857, je me promettais de vous écrire pour vous remercier des deux nos qui vous m'avez adressés du *Traethodydd* et sans adresser ^moi-même^ les renseignements que vous avez bien voulu me demander sur Hu gadarn: j'esperais que le livre que jai sous presse, intitulé *La Légende celtique*[35] serait livré au public beaucoup plus tôt et j'avais le projet de vous l'envoyer pour répondre à votre question, mais cet ouvrage tardant à paraitre, je' ne puis remettre plus longtemps la réponse & les remerciements que je vous dois. Vos

---

y Cymry', *Y Traethodydd*, 13 (1857), 230–40, 297–323.
[35] Le Vicomte Hersart De La Villemarqué, *La Légende celtique, en Irelande, en Cambrie et en Bretagne, suivie des Textes originaux Irelandais, Gallois et Bretons, rares ou inédits* (Paris : A. Durand, 1859).

deux articles sur les *Kymris* m'ont fort interessé, je suis de votre avis sur bien des points, et jai vu avec plaisir que M. Nash[36] vous a lu et a profité de plusieurs de vos observations: comme vous il *doute* et "c'est le commencement de la sagesse," mais il ne faudrait pas douter éternellement, après avoir commencé de la sorte notre Descartes a *affirmé*; la critique négative est bonne pour déblayer le terrain de la science, mais une fois le champ nétoyé, il faut bâtir. Je voudrais une bonne histoire du Pays de Galles, et vous l'écriviez mieux que personne. Je le disais il y a peu de temps à mes confrères de l'institut de France, où jai été reçue le 21 mai dernier, et où on commence à s'occuper avec interet des choses celtiques.

Pour en venir au point sur le'quel, je vous dois une réponse, C'est à dire à *Hu Gadarn*, voici ce que jai trouvé à son sujet, dans la *Portefeuille des Blancs Manterey*, (Bibliothèque impériale), no 38, légende manuscrite Saint Hervé, composé 'au XIe Siècle , p. 857 et 858) St Hervé trouve un démon déguisé en moine et lui demande qui il est: le démon répond: "Ego Hu canus nomine et Hybernia huc veni faber ferrarius, liguarius, atique cemertarius, nanta quo'que peritus, et omnia opera componere physice postum minibus.

Hervé lui répond quil ne le croit pas, et il adjure au nom de la Trinité de d'avouer qui il est: le diable alors lui dit: et ego quidem unus sum ex immundis spiritibus ideo artem veni ut monachos deciperem qualibet fallacia quibus Superabundat hic spiritibum patria et il précipite dans la mer du haut d'un rocher qu'on appelle en breton roch-Hu-Kan, et à propos, l'auteur de la légende s'écrie aponte: "O quam ingens tumultus tunc resultavit in pelagus cum projectus fuit dæmon Hucanns a quo *rupes Hucani* nominatus quae in aquas supervienit, et ibique diversis specibus perdire compicitur!

Le dialogue entre Saint Hervé et le diable est un peu différent dans la tradition populaire que j'ai suivie dans *la Légende Celtique* (3e partie): le voie tel que je l'ai recueilli de la bouche même de nos paysans

---

[36] David William Nash (d. *c*.1876–7).

"Quel est ton nom? lui demanda Hervé
—Je suis maitre charpentier, Seigneur
—Ton nom? te dis-je, reprend le Saint.
—Seigneur, je suis maçon, serrurier, capable de tous les métiers
—Ton nom! pour la troisième fois, je t'adjure de me dire ton nom au nom du Dieu Vivant!
—Hu-Kan! Hu-Kan! Hu-Kan! s'écrie le démon; et il se précipite, la tête en avant, du haut d'un rocher dans la mer."
J'ajoute cette réflexion:
"les superstitions druidiques s'évanouissaient ainsi devant Hervé après lui avoir rèsisté un moment et l'avoir voulu tromper sous différents déguisements: cet Hu-Kan, c'est à dire *Hu-le-Génie* n'est autre que le Dieu *Hu-Kadarn* des traditions cambriennes"

Je pense que vous sera aussi de mon avis. Nous pourrions causer de toutes les questions qui nous occupent si vous veniez en Bretagne: plusieurs de vos compatriotes, fesant partie de notre Association bretonne, et membres de l'Association Cambria nous annoncent leur arrivée à Quimper pour le 3 octobre prochain où ils se proposent d'assister à notre XVe congrès breton; je serais bien aisé de vous voir vous joindre à eux, et très heureux de vous ramener de Quimper chez moi, après le congrès Vous verrez avec cette le programme des questions proposées et qu'on y traitera: vous verrez qu'il le y en a plusieurs à votre adresse.

Pourriez-vous me dire si la grammaire d'Edeyrn tafawd aur a été imprimée dernièrement, comme on me l'assure, et qui la publiée?[37] Le Livre de M Adolphe Pictet est tombé en France, dans le plus complet discrédit, je vois que votre article du Traethodydd

---

[37] John Williams, Ab Ithel (ed. and trans.), *Dosparth Edeyrn Davod Aur; or The Ancient Welsh Grammar, Which Was Compiled by Royal Command in the Thirteenth Century by Edyrn the Golden Tongued, To Which is Added Y Pum Llyfr Kerddwriaeth, Or the Rules of Welsh Poetry, Originally Compiled by Davydd Ddu Athraw, in the Fourteenth, and Subsequently Enlarged by Simwnt Vychan, in the Sixteenth Century* (Llandovery: William Rees, 1856).

est de nature à produire un bon effet sur les personnes de votre pays qui pourraient attacher quelque importance à ce livre.

Votre tout devoué

Vcte Hersart De la Villemarqué
Membre de l'Institut

[A partial contemporary translation of the above under the same number, probably by Stephens:

Chateau de Keransker
nr Quimperle, Finisterre
the 3rd Augt. 1858

Dear Sir

Since the month of November 1857, I have promised myself to write to you, to thank you for the two No's which you addressed to me, of the *Traethodydd*, and to address you myself the information which you have been good enough to demand of me about Hu Gadarn. I hope that the book which I am printing, entitled *The Celtic Legends*, would be published much sooner, and I had intended to send it to you, in reply to your questions, but the book was delayed in preparation, that I *did not?* remit for a long time the response and the thanks which I owed? you. Your two articles on the Kymry interested me strongly: I am of your opinion on all the points; and I have seen, that M. Nash has read you, and profitted by most of your observations. Like you he doubts, and "it is the commencement of knowledge", but he should not doubt eternally. After having commenced in this way, our Des Cartes *affirmed*: the Negitive Critique is good to serve the domain of science; but a faith in the Shadowy field it fails to build.

I promise a good History of Wales, and you are the person to write it.

I said this   time   to my confreres of the Institute of France, on visiting them the 21st of last month, and they begin to occupy themselves with interest in Celtic Affairs.

To go to the point on which I have to give you an answer, i.e. Hu Gadarn. Behold, I found on this subject, in the *Portfolio of White Monks* (Imperial Library) No 38 a MS legend of Saint Herve, composed in the XIth century, pp 857 and 858. St Herve finds a *demon* disguised as a monk, and demands of him what he is. The Demon replies.—

"I am Hu-Can by name, come here from Ireland, a blacksmith, a carpenter, and cementer(?), skilful also in fluids, and all walled work I am able to put together."

Herve replied, that he did not believe him, and adjured him in the name of the Trinity to avow who he was.

The devil then said to him, "I truly, am one of the unclean spirits: for that cause therefore, I came as a monk deceiving whoever would, with fallacies, in which this country abounds." And he precipitated himself into the Sea   off a rock called in Breton Roch-Hu-Kan

of the legend writes,—"O what fiery tumult thou resulted in the Sea into which the Demon Hu-Canns was precipitated, from which they have given the name of the Hill of Hucanns

{A translation of the remainder of the letter by Nely van Seventer:

The dialogue between Saint Hervé and the devil is a bit different in the folk tradition that I have followed in *La Légende Celtique* (third part): here it is in the way I have recorded it from the very mouth of our peasants.

"What is your name? Hervé asked

—I am a master carpenter, Lord

—Your name? I tell you, the saint continued.

—Lord, I am a mason; a locksmith, I can do any craft

—Your name! For the third time, I command you to tell me you name, in the name of the Living God!

—Hu-Kan! Hu-Kan! Exclaimed the demon, and head forward, he hurls himself from the summit of a rock into the sea."

I add this thought:

"The druidic superstitions thus vanished before Saint Hervé, after having resisted for some time, and having wanted to deceive him under different disguises: this Hu-Kan, that is to say *Hu-the-Genie,* is no other than the god Hu-Kadarn from the Cambric traditions."

I think you would agree with me. We might chat about all the questions that occupy us, if you would come to Brittany: several of your compatriots, who are members of our Breton Association, and members of the Association Cambria, have informed us about their arrival in Quimper next October the third, where they intend to be present at our fifteenth Breton congress: it would give me great pleasure to see you joining them, and I would be very happy to bring you back from Quimper to my home, after the congress. You will hereby find the programme of the proposed questions that will be dealt with there: you see that there are several that are relevant to you.

Could you tell me whether the grammar of Edeyrn tafawd aur has been printed lately, as I have been assured, and who published it? The book of Mr Adolphe Pictet has in France fallen into the most complete discredit, I see that your article from the Traethodydd is of such a nature that it might have a good effect on the people in your country who might attach some importance to that book.

Yours faithfully.

Vcte Hersart De la Villemarqué
Membre de l'Institut}]

*   *   *   *

NLW, MS. 964E, 147
Harry Longueville Jones to Thomas Stephens

Mr T Stephens. Merthyr Tydfil

9 Norfolk Crescent
Bath. Mar 16/59

Cambrian Archaeological Association
[printed letterhead]

My dear Sir

I send you by this post specimens of the MS. Ystoria Chyarlys.—It is in handwriting of the 15th century & almost all the contents of the Llyfr Coch [&c] The calligraphy is excellent: hardly any contractions—and after a few minutes practice, legible enough. It extends on 25 ~~pages of~~ columns I have transcribed the two first columns & also the last: I have extracted some passages in which mention of *Hu Gadarn* is made: specifying which is the *first* of these passages. It is nothing more than the well known romance tale published by M. Michel—as far as I can make out.

In the same volume there is a *Buchedd Charlemain,*—the Incipit and Explicit of which I also send: and I doubt whether in point of *literary* (I do mean archeological merit) this be not by far the more valuable of the two.

I could transcribe the whole MS. with the [greatest faculty] had I the time: but it would require 10 or 12 hours. To photograph it would cost £5.

I do not know of anybody in Oxford that could transcribe it. If transcription is ultimately decided on the best way will be for *me* to do it myself ^this next spring^: & it will also be by far the *cheapest* in as much as I shall consider the pleasure of doing it a full equivalent for the trouble.

I found in the *Reliquiae Lhuydianae* enough to fill the Arch. Camb. for the next *five* or *six* years!—and am going to make use of it for that purpose—all new: all unknown!

I remain My dear Sir

Yours vry Truly

H Longueville Jones

*   *   *   *

NLW, Cwrtmawr MS. 919B, 4[38]
Thomas Stephens to William W. E. Wynne

Merthyr Tydfil
Feb 6th 1860

Sir

In common with most Welshmen of an antiquarian turn of mind, I have learnt with real pleasure that the Hengwrt MSS. have come into your hands; and I trust you will emulate the fame of

---

[38] This letter is a copy.

Robert Vaughan their first collector, by publishing some of the most valuable of them. Especially should your attention be directed to _The Greal_ omitted by Lady Charlotte Guest, so she informed me, because she could not get permission to have it copied.[39] I believe it is only a translation of Christian De Troyes French romance; but as it has obtained much celebrity, and as only two MSS. of the Welsh translation now exist, the other at Gloddaith, you would render an acceptable service to our literary countrymen, and earn enduring honour for your ^own^ good name, by completing the series of Mabinogion. Any literary assistance that I can give will be cheerfully placed at your service

Commending that suggestion to your respectful consideration, I have one or two other matters that I wish to speak of. Among the Hengwrt MSS. are several Welsh versions of Carlovingian Romans, such as Nos. 3, 5, and 36, in Aneurin Owen's Catalogue, published originally in the Transactions of the Cymmrodorion, and now in the last number of the Cambrian Journal.[40] These, however, are ^the^ common romances of the Pseudo-Turpin. But No. 46 is a different, less known, and more interesting one; and one that is the more remarkable as containing the first reference to Hu Gadarn, usually made to be a Kymric hero-god, but there represented as Emperor of Constantinople, ~~I have promised to edit~~ ^and^ ~~translate~~ and ^the^ contemporary of Charlemagne! I have promised to edit and translate it for the Archæologia Cambrensis, and shall be glad to obtain a copy. It extends over about 26 folio columns in the Red Book of Hengest; and though the Hengwrt MS. volume is said ^to be^ 1½ inches thick the bulk must be composed of the Cywyddau or Poems which form the latter part of it. Michel the French antiquary has published the French original which occupies 36

---

[39] Wynne replied that 'Sir Robert Vaughan lent the Greal to Mr. Aneurin Owen to copy for L.y Charlotte Guest. Before it was completed he died, & his son was to have gone on with it, but it was returned before he did so.' W. W. E. Wynne to Thomas Stephens, House of Commons, 14 February 1860, NLW, MS. 8543C.

[40] Aneurin Owen, 'The Hengwrt MSS.', _Cambrian Journal_ (Alban Arthan 1859), 276–296.

duodecimo pages.

Under No^s. 7 and 41 I read of "Laws of Dyfnwal"; these I presume are only the fragments published by Mr. Owen, in the Venedotian Code of the Laws of Howel; but I should esteem it a favour to be positively informed. In No. 158, in a list of the Kings of Ireland: do Aedh mac Neil, and Domnail mac Aedh appear among the number?

Lastly the MSS. of Guthyn Owain connect themselves with our Madoc Legend. He is quoted by Dr. Powell to the effect that Madoc went a *second time to America*, with ten ships.[41] Now I suspect that Guthyn says nothing about a *second voyage*, nor mentions America, but simply that Madoc went *to sea* with 10 ~~ten~~ ships. This statement is only known from Powell's citation, and does not exist in the Basingwerk Chronicle, as I have ascertained. It is therefore probable that it occurs in one of the two MSS. at Hen-gwrt, viz. No. 22. The Calendar of Guthyn Owain. Here it would probably occur about the year 1169, when Owen Gwynedd died. 113. volume of ^Old^ Pedigrees by Guthyn Owain. Here it would probably occur in the pedigree of Owain Gwynedd.[42] If you would be kind enough to think of these queries, when you have a leisure hour, you would ensure the gratitude of your obedient servant

Thos. Stephens

W. W. E. Wynne, Esq.

It is almost a pity to send this bit of paper blank all the way to Merionethshire, so I will ask one other favour. The word *Morwerydd* has a bearing on the Madoc question. "Madoc went across *Morwerydd*:" the word within the last 20 years has come to mean the Atlantic; but Dr. Davies and the old Lexicists say it

---

[41] David Powel, *The Historie of Cambria, Now Called Wales: A Part of the Most Famous Yland of Brytaine, written in the Brytish language about Two Hundreth Yeares Past: Translated into English by H. Lhoyd Gentleman: Corrected, Augmented, and Continued out of Records and Best Approoued Authors* ([London: Rafe Newberie and Henrie Denham, 1584]) (Reprinted London: John Harding, 1811), p. 167.

[42] It appears that Stephens did not find the original wording. Stephens, *Madoc*, p. 24.

was the Irish Sea. Will you oblige me in looking up the word in the old Dictionaries numbered 277?

*   *   *   *

NLW, MS. 965E, 349 (2)[43]
Morris Williams (Nicander) to Thomas Stephens

Llanrhyddlad Rectory,
Holyhead, Aug. 31. 1860

Dear Sir,

I never was a believer in the discovery of America by Madog: your remarks seem quite decisive of the point. It is a misfortune that we so little value historical criticism in our researches. Too much prejudice and too little knowledge have, on the other hand, puffed us up to take credit for many things that really do not belong to us. How often, for instance, have the words of Tacitus been applied to the Cymry—"Cimbri, parva nume civitas, sed Gloria ingens." Tacitus here makes not the remotest allusion to the Welsh, who in his time were by no means a "parva civitas": he is in fact speaking of a tribe of Germans.

I remember being much struck with your identification of *Aedd Mawr* with the Roman general *Aëtius*.[44] There seems to me to be more common sense in this view than in that of Dr Meyer, who suggests that the *Ædui* of Gaul were so called from a god *Aed* whom they worshipped, and whom he identifies with the *Aedd mawr* of the Triads! These Ædui, he thinks, gave this Island the name of *Aeddon* or *Eiddin*, which is perpetuated in the word *Edin*burgh.

Most of our Scholars, in endeavouring to grasp at distant shadows, disregard, and therefore miss the substance that is nearer home, and really available for our true history. What a

---

[43] This letter was printed in the second edition of *Literature of the Kymry*, p. xlvii.

[44] Thomas Stephens, 'Dyvynwal Moelmud', 169.

havoc Niebuhr[45] would have made of our traditions, and what materials he would have found for Welsh history where one would have least expected to find any.

It is amusing to see how some actually good scholars receive all our crudest traditions as sound articles of historic faith, and defend them as such with all zeal and earnestness.

> I remain,
>> Dear Sir,
>>> Truly yours
>>> M. Williams

*   *   *   *

NLW, MS. 965E, 215
David William Nash to Thomas Stephens

Brandon Villa   Cheltenham
                                                                Octr. 8. 1861.

My dear Sir

I am making use of your 'Studies in British Biography' in a work I am now writing on the Historical Triads & the Bardic Traditions[46] and I shall be very much obliged to you if you will furnish me with the continuation of the genealogies given by you 'from Gutyn Owain and others' Cambrian Journal vol 4. p. 256. *From Dyfnwal Moel Mud down to Beli* Beli Mawr. I want to see how it is that the pedigree of Gruffyd ab Cynan omits Dyfnwal Moel Mud and goes straight down to Beli Mawr without passing through Dyfnwal.

I am quite aware that you have said every thing I can say on these subjects, but I shall put them differently and they will come differently from an Englishman.

My real belief is that Edward Williams *tampered* with many documents and *forged* many others, but of course it is difficult to

---

[45] The German historian Barthold Georg Niebuhr (1776–1831).

[46] It is possible that this work was abandoned and never published. See Nash's letter to Stephens dated 20 October 1861, pp. 182–83 below.

prove it.

I cannot express my astonishment at the course pursued by the Editor of the Cambrian Journal. Druidism & nothing but Druidism seem to be his motto & the wonderful system pursued of stating the most ludicrous fables as positive facts, and then ignoring every thing and every body on the other side of the question. The Rev. J Williams ab Ithel is certainly an able man, & it is wonderful how he can continue to shut his eyes to reason and common sense. I think of bringing out my book before the publication of the *Barddas* by the Welsh MS. Society though I run the risk of ignorance of many documents which will be there cited. Still 'ex pede Herculem' we have enough in print to show their line of action, & I propose to attack the Bardic school at once. If I might so far venture to trouble you I should be very glad of your counsel in the matter and am

Yours very truly
D. W. Nash

Thos Stephens Esq

*   *   *   *

NLW, MS. 965E, 214a
David William Nash to Thomas Stephens

Brandon Villa Cheltenham Oct. 16. 1861

My dear Sir

I cannot say how much I am obliged to you for your most kind and disinterested conduct towards me. I believe there are few members of the republic of letters who would take the chivalrous part you have, in warning me of the pitfalls before me, and communicating your own important discoveries before publication.

With regard to Dyfnwal Moel Mud I have placed him just before the commencement of the Christian era, about the time of Beli Mawr, whom I think the same with Belinus. I look at Dyfnwal as a genuine historical character. I have no doubt you are right, but I shall not tread on your new authority unless you should desire that I should do so.

With regard to Hu Gadarn, your discovery will change the face of Welsh traditional literature. I shall be most happy to share the expense of transcription of the document. That which you have so kindly communicated will cause me to soften down many of my expressions, and to treat the subject more carefully than I otherwise should have done. But unless the MSS of the Red Book is older than Iolo Goch, the source of the tradition still remains, as to the name. In this I have not been able to do any thing, though I have the source of the Tafrobani[47] part of the legend.

When I had got so far as the analysis of the "three natural pillars" I found that there were still Bardic traditions and the Llywelyn Sion documents, (to which latter circle I believe the third series of Triads belongs) in which the Prydain legend was supported. It was necessary therefore to ascertain what authority was to ^be^ assigned to them. I therefore took to the Barddas.[48]

The cosmogony, theosophy & symbolism, are all in print, in sufficient amount to furnish full materials for analysis.

The symbolism is clearly modern & its sources may be traced. The cosmogony &c is ancient in form but may well have been written in the 18: century, & there is internal evidence that some part probably was so.

The external history of the documents may be made pretty clear. I am still of opinion that there is fraud somewhere, but after your observations I shall be more careful in expressing my opinions. The cosmogony is certainly very curious, and what seems to me strange is, that it was clearly known to Rowlands, Mona Antiqua[49] that such views existed, though every one else appeared quite ignorant on the subject when first broached by

---

[47] 'Deffrobani', the land from which Hu Gadarn supposedly led the Cymry to Britain.

[48] This is not a reference to Ab Ithel's *Barddas*, as it was not published until the following year.

[49] Henry Rowlands, *Mona Antiqua Restaurata: An Archaeological Discourse on the Antiquities, Natural and Historical, of the Isle of Anglesey, the Ancient Seat of the British Druids* (Dublin: Robert Owen, 1723).

Dr. Owen Pughe from E. Williams' instructions.

I had gone pretty well through all this before receiving your letter, and had thought of writing an essay on the Druidism of the 19: century separately from the Triadic history, and publishing it first, to clear the way as it were. But since reading your letter two or three times over, a "horrid doubt" has entered my mind. In the lines of Iolo Goch is this,

A bywyd oll o'r bydd oedd

Is this rightly translated, "And the life of all the world" If so compare the lines of Rhys Brydydd "Bychanau o'r bychenid &c". Is it possible that this can have reference to the Pythagorean doctrine of the Cosmogony in Barddas, the soul of the world, & the origin of all things in the Monad in which 'the life' this Divine energy existed?

Will you turn this over in your mind: because if it were so, the authenticity of the Bardic documents would be established up to the 14: century.

Now if Hu Gadarn was really a name for the Deity in the 14: century and Hu=IUO or IAO[50] we cannot well avoid the conclusion that there was still earlier a secret society holding their pantheistic doctrines, and I think it would take us up to the writings of Johannes Scotus Eriugena[51] in the 9: century.

If Iolo Goch obtained the name of Hu Gadarn from a popular romance how could he have applied it as he does? On the other hand if the romance got the name from Welsh sources, how can it be that it never appears in the popular literature of Wales? I confess I am greatly puzzled. That the name in the 14th–15th century was connected with some religious heresy is clear from the words of Sion Kent. I thought from some expressions of Iolo that it was a kind of Unitarianism or Arianism. But even while I am writing I can see that I shall have to consider the whole subject over again from the beginning. Suppose after all there

---

[50] Iesus Alpha Omega, the secret name of God. See Williams, *Iolo Manuscripts*, note to pp. 690–91.

[51] John Scottus Eriugena was a ninth-century Irish theologian and philosopher.

should be something in the alleged mysticism contained in the earliest poems. It was only last night I was reading Davies' Celtic Researches[52] over again, & I was struck by some things which it seems to me I had overlooked when I wrote 'Taliesin'. Your letter this morning has made me pause and think again. With many thanks to you for your kindness.

Believe me
To remain
Yours very truly
D. W. Nash

P.S. A week or two ago I sent for the part of the Gwyddoniadur[53] containing the article reviewed in Cambrian Journal Sept. 1860.[54] Since then I have had a letter from Mr R. J. Pryse Denbigh[55] on things in general, but doubt if he has gone below the surface.

I have just been reading the remarks on you in the Saturday Review of Oct. 12.[56] That about Madoc is excellent.

---

[52] Davies, *Celtic Researches* (1804).

[53] Parry, *Y Gwyddoniadur Cymreig*. The third volume (CYN–DUW) was published in 1861.

[54] Review of 'Druidism. Second Article in the *Gwyddionadur; or Encyclopedia Cambrensis*'. This article, attributed to William Roberts (Nevydd), adopted many of the arguments utilized by Stephens in his 'Studies in British Biography' and 'Sefyllfa Wareiddiol y Cymry' and was heavily criticized in the review.

[55] Robert John Prys (Gweirydd ap Rhys) (1807–1889).

[56] 'But all honour be to Mr. Stephens of Merthyr, a Welshmen of the Welshmen, who lately stood on the stone [Arthur's Stone on the Gower] and affirmed that certain Triads were no older than the sixteenth century. Happily he was surrounded by a strong band of able-bodied antiquarians of various nations, or a raging host of Druids, Bards, and Ovates might have been expected to rise from the earth or drop from the clouds and tear the heretic in pieces. Mr. Stephens, be it observed, is a true martyr. Some Eisteddfod or other offered a prize for the best essay on Prince Madoc's settlement in America. Nobody doubted that Mr. Stephens' essay was the best, but he was refused the prize because he proved incontestably that Prince Madoc never did settle in America.' [Anon.], 'Gower', *Saturday Review*, 311: 12 (12 October 1861), 375–76 (375).

NLW, MS. 965E, 214c
David William Nash to Thomas Stephens

Brandon Villa Cheltenham
Oct 20. 1861.

My dear Sir

I am very much obliged to you for sending me the Traethodydd.[57] I have read the article & am now abstracting it which takes me some time as so many of the words are quite new to me. I must say that its perusal has humbled me a good deal, as I see how you have forestalled me at every step. That matter of the Archdeacon's Ap' is which I certainly thought a masterstroke, you had printed in Sept. 1857—while my book was in the press as you will see by the date of my preface.

I have been a great reader of the Cabbala, & possess the Cabbala Demendata of Knorr von Rosenroth 3 vols—^ and also Franck's La Cabbala^ but I thought that the Cabbalistic sources in Barddas were indirect, and though I looked at the table of the ten Sephirot the form of the /|\ did not strike me.[58] The quotation from Isaiah is of the greatest importance in unravelling the question, though I begin to doubt very much whether I shall be able to do much with it.

I have sent for the Charlemagne romances, & Life of Turpin[59] to see what they contain. I observe in the "Sefyllfa" that you think Druidism remained as a living faith in the North down to the battle of Arderydd in the 6: century.[60] This is no doubt very probable, and would lead to the belief that a good deal of the old creed may have remained in the popular superstitions and been worked up afterwards in the Mabinogion.

---

[57] Stephens, 'Sefyllfa Wareiddiol y Cymry'. This is the same series of articles which Stephens sent to La Villemarqué with his letter dated 9 November 1857, p. 167 above.

[58] This is discussed in Stephens's 'Sefyllfa Wareiddiol y Cymry', 320–21.

[59] This refers to the eighth-century Archbishop of Reims, not the eighteenth-century Essex highwayman.

[60] Stephens, 'Sefyllfa Wareiddiol y Cymry', 303.

I think it is a pity you do not at once bring out a comprehensive work on the whole subject. You have already an European reputation and what you say will be taken as authority on the Continent. In the mean time you get forestalled by little and little, though I really believe there is no one but yourself competent to treat the whole subject. It is no use to write in Welsh, it is lost to the literary world in general.

I do not think I shall go on with either of my essays, as I see now there is a great deal more to be done than I had any idea of, before I read your paper.

That story of Olwin—the kindred 'events' was used by Monk Lewis in his Romantic Tales.[61] It is all very curious and I hope you will publish it

With many thanks I remain

　　Yours very truly

　　　　D. W. Nash

I shall return 'Traethodydd' tomorrow.

Thomas Stephens Esq

*　　*　　*　　*

NLW, MS. 964E, 191[62]

Henri Martin to Thomas Stephens

Paris, Sept 24 1862

Dear Sir,

I found to London the books there you was so kind to send me, and that i accept with much pleasure and gratitude. I am glad to possess the collection of *Salmon*, work into which the good old man was putting valuable part of himself.

---

[61] M. G. Lewis, *Romantic Tales*, four vols (London: N. Shury, 1808). Mathew Lewis (1775–1815) was often referred to as 'Monk' Lewis, owing to the success of his novel *The Monk: A Romance* (London: J. Bell, 1796).

[62] This letter was written on black-bordered paper, likely indicating that the writer was in mourning.

Since my visit to Merthyr,[63] I made an most interesting travel in Ireland: I was acquainted with the learned Dr. Todd, of Trinity College, Dr Petrie[64] which wrote the beautiful book on the *round towers*, and Mr Clibborn,[65] of Irish academy, i was thus in means to labouring easily in both the libraries and celtic museum. I was moreover visiting the main monuments of antiquity to New Grange, Monasterboyce, ~~and~~ Glendalough, &c. I was obtaining complete proofs on merely Christian origin of the round towers but also confirmation of my feeling towards Druidical and primitive antiquity at oghams, as for ~~the~~ both the *alphabets* quoted by Zeuss in Grammatica Celtica as Celtic (from the MSS. of ^the^ Bodleyan library), they are really, as you think, Scandinavian; because they are founded in cave of an great Danish *tumulus* in Orkneys isles; which inscriptions are translated.

The round towers are, as to building, entirely christian; but the symbols and ornaments of the christian irish age remains mixed ~~known~~ with the druidical features until the franco-norman invasion; everywhere, the *greek* cross inscribed in druidical circle; everywhere, the ancient features and ornaments, which are founded in mystic cave of New Grange, and which ^are^ appearing in pagan celtic armours and ornaments likewise continue to show one's self in the christian age. As for religious traditions, since the clouds gathering by the forgeries of Macpherson[66] are dissipated, the intime connection between Gaëls and Cymrys appear perfectly evident among the former remains in mythological appearance that, among the others, took one philosophical character: the ground, the basis, it is the same. Everywhere, the transmigration of souls, the fall in inferior existences, as punition; as [illegible]; the ascension until superior

---

[63] Martin met Stephens in Merthyr in 1861. See pp. 108 and 137 above.

[64] George Petrie (1790–1866).

[65] Edward Clibborn was an Irish antiquariy and archaeologist who served as assistant librarian for the Royal Irish Academy from 1839.

[66] This is a reference to the Ossianic poetry of James Macpherson (1736–1796), the authenticity of which was debated heatedly from the 1760s.

world, whence the blessed shall not going down again, *&c by free own will.*

The *dreadful* question of mysterious *hu Gadarn* me turns more and more complicating: I saw everywhere appearing in Irish annals a some *Ugaine Mor*, a great conqueror and monarch, ~~the~~ whose ~~the~~ domination extends from *Eiriann* until Spain and Italy, and which was living about six centuries before J. C. most remarkable coincidence with the herodite's date as for the departure of Cimmerians from Black sea. Otherwise, none allusion to the Orient in this irish tradition. - Ugaine Mor, the great gaëlic King, hu the God, husband of Ceridwen, the ^british^ devil hu can, hu Gadarn, the leader of Cymryc tribes and your hugan Le Fort, how many people to grant together, ~~and~~ or to separate in order to assign to every one ~~the~~ his place! I confess that the relation between Ugaine Mor and hu Gadarn ~~the~~ me prepossess. Ugaine Mor is an old personage and tradition.

Believe me
    Dear Sir
    Yours very truly
    H Martin

P.S. Will you present my amiable remembrances to the excellent James Family; i was much to regret the absence of our friend Mr James at the time of my travel

*   *   *   *

NLW, MS. 964E, 70
Daniel Silvan Evans to Thomas Stephens

Llanymawddwy
Viâ Shrewsbury
Nov. 25, 1863.

Dear Sir

Pardon my apparent neglect to answer your interesting communication of the 12th inst. I have of late been more than ordinarily busy, especially in connexion with brick and mortar. I have now however partly washed my hands.

My connexion with the *Brython* has long ceased, but I have duly forwarded your letter to the office, accompanied with a request that a proof should be sent to you.

Your discovery of the source of the Myth of Hu Gadarn is most important, and will no doubt cause many to stand aghast. Pray when do you intend publishing the whole story from the Llyfr Coch?

The confession of Iolo Morganwg (Brython No. 39, p. 43) respecting Hu Gadarn is rather more than we could have expected from him.[67] How do you account for the position occupieds by Hu in *Barddas*, p 220?[68]

The Triads, apparently, cannot be looked upon but as the embodiment of the floating legends and traditions of the age in which they were composed.

I cannot find any allusion to *Tre-Dindywydd* in the Brython, No. 39, p. 20. There is an old fort called Din Drywydd or Din Drewydd on the boundaries of the Parishes of Mellteyrn and Bryncroes in Lleyn; and I believe there are other places so called in other parts of Wales. I do not know where to look for the *Dindywyt* of the Gododin, st. 48. Please to give me a correct reference to the passage in the Brython.

Talking of the Gododin, have you any thing about that poem? Some of the stanzas strike me as being much older than the

---

[67] See [Moeddyn], 'Barn Iolo Morganwg am Hu Gadarn', *Y Brython*, 5: 39 (December 1862), 43: 'O bob anhawsder a welir yn yr hen lyfrau, nid oes un mwy na deall pwy, ym mha le'n byw, ac ym mha oes, oedd Hu Gadarn. Tebygid wrth a welir mewn rhai fanau mai un o enwau Duw oedd Hu Gadarn. Wrth a geir mewn manau ereill, ymddengys mai Dyn ydoedd, a'r cyntaf a ddysgodd i genedl y Cymry lafurlaw tir.' ('Of every difficulty arising in the old books, there is none greater than understanding who was Hu Gadarn, in what place he lived, and in what age. Typically, as can be seen in some places, Hu Gadarn was one of the names of God. According to other places, he was a man, and the first to teach the Welsh to work the land').

[68] 'Hu the Mighty,—Jesus the Son of God,—the least in respect of His worldly greatness whilst in the flesh, and the greatest in heaven of all visible majesties.' Ab Ithel, *Barddas*, p. 221, English translation, p. 220.

others; some are very difficult and almost unintelligible, while others are comparatively plain and easy.

Can you help me to trace the pedigree the "Marchog Crwydrad," which I am publishing by instalments in the Brython? The work has the appearance of being a translation. The MS. from I transcribed it appears to belong to the early part of the 17th century. About one half of the whole has already appeared.

Believe me
Yours faithfully
D. Silvan Evans
T. Stephens Esq.

* * * *

NLW, MS. 965E, 281
William Forbes Skene to Thomas Stephens.

20 Inverleith Row,
Edinburgh
[printed letterhead]

2d Novr 1864

Dear Sir

I have just had the pleasure to receive your letter of the 27th octr I was at Peniarth for a few days in September but I left on the 23d September and have not been there since. I need not say that if I had received your letter at Peniarth I should have had much pleasure in making the enquiries you wish. I did not see the Greal when I was there as I was occupied the whole time with other MSS.

What you mention of Hu Gadarn is very curious and well deserves being worked out. It would be curious to see whether he can be identified as the same person with some other name in other copies of the Ystoria. I suppose the copy at Oxford is in the Red book of Hergest and I shall look for it the next time I am at Trewen Hall. The text I adopted for the Gododdin is that in the MS which belonged to Carnhuanawc[69] succv to Sir Thos Phillipps.[70] I adopted it because I consider it the oldest known text but on collating with it, I found the text printed by ab Ithel on the whole very correct. The only variations were a word here or there and the stanzas mention by ab Ithel 92, 93, 94, 95, 96, 97 are in a diff[t] hand & appear to be subsequent additions to the poem

I am Dear Sir
Yours faithfully
William F Skene

---

[69] Thomas Price (Carnhuanawc) (1787–1848).

[70] Thomas Phillipps (1792–1872) of Middle Hill, Worcestershire. In 1852 Stephens wrote to Phillipps, who in reply informed him that 'You may have heard that I wished to establish my Library in Wales. Had I been able to do so, I looked forward to the hope of being able to secure *you* as the Librarian.' Thomas Phillipps to Thomas Stephens, Middle Hill, 29 August 1852, NLW, MS. 965E, Letter 233a.

6

'THERE IS NOTHING TO BE TAKEN FOR GRANTED IN THE MADOGIAN QUESTION': DISPROVING THE MADOC MYTH

THE most infamous controversy in which Stephens was engaged, over whether or not America was discovered by the twelfth-century Welsh prince, Madoc ap Owen Gwynedd, began at the Llangollen Eisteddfod of 21–24 September 1858. Billed as the first 'national' Eisteddfod, the event was largely organised by the Rev. John Williams (Ab Ithel) and was characterised by grandeur and pageantry but also controversy, including accusations of nepotism over the number of prizes carried off by members of Ab Ithel's family.[1] A prize was offered for the 'best essay on the Discovery of America in the Twelfth Century by Prince Madoc ap Owen Gwynedd' and Stephens argued in a well-researched essay that far from discovering a new continent, Madoc had stayed home and died in Wales. The adjudicators, D. Silvan Evans, Thomas James (Llallawg), and Evan Davies (Myfyr Morganwg) were divided over whether Stephens's essay was worthy of the prize, or, indeed, eligible for it at all. Evans felt strongly that the question should be treated as an open one and that Stephens had both proved his side and done so better than the other, pro-Madoc competitors.[2] Myfyr, on the other hand, not only thought the Madoc story, 'one of the chief jewels hanging upon the breast of our mother-race … so that we are not to suffer her to be divested of it, until its rejection show proof of clear and positive facts to annul the claim', but also suggested that Stephens's essay was not on the proposed topic, analogizing that if the topic had

---

[1] Löffler, *The Literary and Historical Legacy of Iolo Morganwg*, pp. 55–58.
[2] Reynolds, 'Editor's Preface', pp. iv–viii.

been Christ's ascension into heaven, the prize would not be awarded for blasphemy! Notwithstanding, he advised splitting the prize between Stephens and the best pro-Madoc essay, a piece by 'Wild Man of the Woods'.[3] Llallawg declined to make a decision. The organisers stepped in and, deciding that Stephens's essay was off-topic, denied him the prize, which was not awarded to any of the competitors.[4]

This led to 'A Scene', as it was described in the *Cardiff and Merthyr Guardian*, in which Stephen rose to speak but was prevented by a brass band. The noise of the crowd, however, overcame the band, and Stephens was allowed to have his say. He argued that 'he had before denied and would continue to deny that an Eisteddfod was to be an arena for special pleading, but rather for the promulgation of truth' and that 'he would still continue to urge strongly and persistently every merit honestly pertaining to the history or national character of the Kymry …; but he thought it lowered them as a people, to be arguing claims which they could not prove'.[5] The committee attempted to backtrack, stating that their decision was not meant to be final, but as time went on the controversy only festered and worsened. Legal action was even occasionally suggested, particularly when it emerged that the essay submitted by Wild Man of the Woods was written in Ab Ithel's handwriting, although Ab Ithel claimed he had only transcribed it for the competitor. Later he admitted that he had written it, although he claimed only to have acted as amanuensis to the true author.[6]

The question of Madoc's (non)discovery of America occupied Stephens's research for years afterwards. The submitted essay, as it currently exists, is heavily amended, with pages and entire

---

[3] Myfyr Morganwg to Thomas Stephens, Pontypridd, 14 October 1858, NLW, MS. 962C, Letters 117, 121. Stephens's translation.

[4] Reynolds 'Editor's Preface', p. vii.

[5] 'A Scene' *Cardiff and Merthyr Guardian, Glamorgan, Monmouth, and Brecon Gazette*, 2 October 1858, 6, accessed via *Welsh Newspapers Online*. This argument formed a major theme in his 1857 'Sefyllfa Wareiddiol y Cymry'.

[6] Reynolds, 'Editor's Preface', pp. x–xiii.

sections added, removed, and replaced throughout.[7] Read alongside Stephens's correspondence on the Madoc question, it provides an unique insight into the evolution of Stephens's thought from eisteddfod essay to posthumously published book, as well as research methods and systems of knowledge exchange in nineteenth-century Wales, England, and the United States. Indeed, Stephens's correspondence on the Madoc question has largely been separated from the main body of his letters into two volumes—one focusing on the adjudication and the other focusing on research—perhaps by Stephens himself.[8]

The Llangollen Eisteddfod and the summary in *Y Brython* which followed were not the end of Stephens's research on the subject; on the contrary they sparked a period of remarkably intensive research. Much of this involved checking the sources and citations of Wild Man of the Woods's essay. In order to do this, Stephens wrote to fellow scholars as well as researchers and staff at the British Library and Museum to locate books, articles, and accounts. This research began even before the dust of Llan-gollen had settled, and did not wait for the publication of Wild Man of the Woods's essay in Ab Ithel's own *Cambrian Journal* in the summer and fall of 1859.[9] The letters in this section show the lengths to which Stephens went to gather information and the various research strands which he perused. He worked to identify, locate, contextualise, and analyse early modern Welsh

---

[7] Manuscript of Stephens's 'Madoc: An Essay on the Discovery of Amercia by Madoc ap Owen Gwynedd in the Twelfth Century', NLW, MS. 961 C.

[8] NLW, MS. 962–3 C. Letters sent to Thomas Stephens regarding the Madoc controversy and later research.

[9] [John Williams (Ab Ithel)], 'An Essay of the Discovery of America in the Twelfth Century by Prince Madoc ap Owen Gwynedd', *Cambrian Journal* (Alban Hevin and Alban Elvid 1859), 90–106, 161–193. In addition to using his journal as a medium for his own work, Williams also took the opportunity to rally readers in support of his position, inserting a Editor's Note asking them to 'follow the example of the author of this essay, and kindly furnish us with such additional matter as will make the evidence, in favour of the claims of Madoc to the discovery of America, as complete as possible'. (90)

and English accounts of Madoc's alleged voyage and the legendary Welsh Native American tribe which it spawned, writing to researchers as well as friends. The latter notably included several Quakers from Neath whom Stephens had presumably known since childhood; in writing to them he raises queries about possible discussions of Madoc in connection with the emigration of Welsh Friends to Pennsylvania. Stephens also investigated the history, ethnography, and historical geography of Native American tribes, working on the question from a transnational and trans-Atlantic perspective. Unlike Madoc, Stephens's letters even reached North America, as he wrote to James Hadley of Yale about Madoc, and through him was in contact with noted American historian, linguist, surveyor, and founding member of the American Ethnological Society, John Russel Bartlett, who had also investigated the Madoc question. Stephens's research into the non-discovery of America was one of the most infamous projects in his short but brilliant career. The correspondence attached to it demonstrates many of the salient themes which marks Stephens's scholarly correspondence as a whole. The letters show his meticulous attention to detail, willingness to challenge received knowledge, a wide range of respected amateur and professional researchers called upon to offer specialist knowledge, and a willingness to look outside of Wales in order to investigate Welsh questions. Above all, they demonstrate a vibrant and robust exchange of knowledge through reciprocal social and scholarly networks.

*   *   *   *

NLW, MS. 962C, 63[10]
Daniel Silvan Evans to Thomas Stephens

Llangïan, Pwllheli
Dec. 8, 1858

My dear Sir

I send by the same post the document of which the enclosed is a copy, to Carn Ingli,[11] with a note requesting him to communicate the same to his colleague Ab Ithel.[12]

I believe a witness to the certificate is unnecessary.

If this adjudication will not avail as a legal instrument it cannot but prove of some ^importance^ before the tribunal of public opinion.

You should not lose sight of the fact that Myfyr[13] virtually acknowledged that your essay was upon the subject when he wished to divide the prize between you and the "Wild Man".[14]

I am much obliged to you for the "Star". French talks of my "invincible prepossessions".[15] He is right enough; I *have* "invincible prepossessions"; but unfortunately for *him* in this affair, those "prepossessions" are in favour of truth, and opposed to wild theories. Was it he, I wonder, that wrote under the signature "Pwy" about "*Columbus's*" letters to *William Pitt*, Prime Minister of England"! the "History of Wales by that acute researcher Hakluyt"! and other topics equally interesting.

I now enjoy tolerable health, but I am very weak, and the least exertion is enough to upset me. Very unaccountably my late illness has considerably affected my handwriting. It was bad

---

[10] This letter was written on black-bordered paper, likely indicating that the writer was in mourning.

[11] Joseph Hughes (Carn Ingli) (1803–1863).

[12] John Williams (Ab Ithel) (1811–1862).

[13] Evan Davies (Myfyr Morganwg) (1801–1888).

[14] Ab Ithel. See NLW, MS. 964E, Letter 68b, p. 197 below.

[15] Several letters criticizing Stephens and his supporters signed 'R. H. French' appeared in the *Star of Gwent* late in 1858, available via *Welsh Newspapers Online*.

enough at all times, but it is now considerably worse.

Zeuss' Gramatica Celtica[16] I have not seen, nor Latham's Edition of Prichard.[17] I am well acquainted with Prichard's own edition, and having this, I cannot persuade myself to give 16/- for Latham's, though Latham is a favourite writer of mine. Zeuss is dear. But I must have both these works someday or other. Gee's conduct towards my poor Dictionary has annoyed me sadly.[18] But still I intend publishing a *Gramadeg Cymraeg* for the use of Welshmen at some future period.

I hope you will soon be able to "report progress" with regard to the Madoc affair, and that you will make a public example of the small cabal of Llangollen.

 Believe me
  Yours faithfully
   D. Silvan Evans
T. Stephens, Esq. }

* * * *

---

[16] J. C. Zeuss, *Grammatica Celtica* (Leipzig: Weidmannos, 1853). Thomas Stephens read and took extensive notes from this work. NLW, MS. 922C.

[17] James Cowles Prichard, *The Eastern Origin of the Celtic Nations Proved by a Comparison of their Dialects with the Sanscrit, Greek, Latin, and Teutonic Languages: Forming a Supplement to Researches into the Physical History of Mankind*, ed. by R. G. Latham (London: Houlston and Wright, 1857).

[18] Thomas Gee (1815–1898) published Evans's *An English and Welsh Dictionary*, the first volume of which appeared in 1852, and the second in 1858. The two men had several ongoing disagreements over the presentation and use of Evans's work in the period. This comment probably refers to Evans's accusations that Gee had severely altered the second volume ('Tusk'–'Z') and not allowed Evans a chance to amend the proofs before printing. Thomas Gwynn Jones, *Cofiant Thomas Gee* (Dinbych: Gee a'i Fab, 1913), pp. 113–19. Thomas Parry, 'Daniel Silvan Evans, 1818–1903', *Trafodion Anrhydeddus Gymdeithas y Cymmrodorion* (1981), 109–185 (116).

NLW, Cwrtmawr MS. 919B, 2
Thomas Stephens to Daniel Silvan Evans

Merthyr Tydfil

March 11ᵗʰ 1859

My Dear Sir

I am happy to be able to forward you the second part of the "Madogwys" by this post; but under present circumstances, ~~where~~ I shall not be able to send you the third part for some time; and it would be of comparatively inferior interest, it ^need^ not be much regretted

I have to apologize for not having answered your enquiry respecting Bruce Knight's pamphlet.[19] I do not happen to have it; nor is there, that I am aware of, a single copy in Merthyr.

The statement respecting the Pennillion must I think be an error; I am not aware of any such pamphlet published in Merthyr, but will enquire. You are of course aware that a good many were published in the Camb-Briton; and there was a prize for 900 awarded to "Thos Mills, Llanidloes," at Rhuddlan Eisteddfod.

I had promised Clarke of Ruthin to assist in editing Taliesin;[20] but on finding Ab Ithel concerned in it, I have written to withdraw my name.

The Llangollen Essay has been returned to me; and if I can make arrangements with ^the^ *Arch* Cambrensis folks it shall be published; but this intention must be kept secret—in order to keep the lash over Ab Ithel's head a little longer, not that I care for the money, but that the public mind may be thoroughly

---

[19] This query does not appear in Evans's extant letters to Stephens.

[20] *Taliesin* was a Welsh-language journal founded by John Williams (ab Ithel) and published by Isaac Clarke of Ruthin. Clarke had approached Stephens on 15 February about taking on the role of joint editor. Isaac Clarke to Thomas Stephens, Ruthin, 15 February 1849, NLW, MS. 964E, 26. See also James Kenward, *Ab Ithel: An Account of the Life and Writings of the Rev. John Williams Ab Ithel, M.S., B.B.D., Late Rector of Llanymowddwy, Merioneth* (Tenby: R. Mason, 1871), p. 165.

satisfied of his meanness. The publication of the Essay will justify your judgment, and show that the Essay was not unworthy of the subject

Yours truly

Thos Stephens

*   *   *   *

NLW, MS. 964E, 68b
Daniel Silvan Evans to Thomas Stephens

Llangïan, Pwllheli

March 30, 1859

My dear Sir

I enclose a copy of *Crochan's* letter to Governor Dinwiddie.[21] The name of the writer, which occurs three times is spelt *Crochan* (the Welsh word for *pot*) in my copy, which is apparently in the handwriting of Ieuan Brydydd Hir.[22]

I was not aware that any portion of the letter had been printed. Ab Ithel in his essay quotes a portion of it as being a MS. in the British Museum.

The Governor of Canada in 1753 must have been a French official. I have no account whatever to give you of Dinwiddie. Might he not be the Governor of New England, or some other British Colony in North America?

My copy, as you will perceive, is ~~taken~~ stated to have been taken from another copy sent by "J. Philips" to Dr. Worthington.[23] This "J. Phillips" I take to be Dr. James Phillips, rector of Llangoedmor by Cardigan,[24] a friend and correspondent of Edward

---

[21] See Stephens, *Madoc*, pp. 67–69.

[22] Evan Evans (Ieuan Fardd or Ieuan Brydydd Hir) (1731–1788).

[23] Probably William Worthington (1704–1778), a Welsh cleric and author of several theological texts. See *Dictionary of Welsh Biography*, s.v. 'Worthington, William'.

[24] James Phillips (1703–1783) was a Welsh cleric and antiquarian who was rector of Llangoedmor from 1738/9. He spent time at Blaen-pant where he

Richard,[25] and most of the Welsh literati of that day.

Does the original really exist in the British Museum? There is nothing to be taken for granted in the Madogian question. A friend of mine is just now engaged in copying different Welsh documents at the Museum. Could you furnish any reference which he could find out whether this document exists there or not? The pretended original *may* be a myth. Does the letter look like the composition of an Englishman?

Who was George Crochan? A query respecting him as ^well as^ respecting Governor Dinwiddie in *Notes & Queries* would very probably elicit something worth knowing about them.

I am very glad that your Essay is likely to be published. In the introduction I hope you will give the public at large a summary of Ab Ithel's history with regard to the Madoc Essay, and that you will find it not inconvenient to let people know that he is the author of the Essay signed "Wild Man of the Woods"—for it is undoubtedly his, although he had the temerity to deny the fact.

In your list of believers in the Madogian Discovery you have omitted to mention old Charles Edwards, author of "Hanes y Ffydd." His opinion is of course of no great importance, but it forms a link in the chain. He says thus:—"Yn amser y blinderau hyn mentrodd Madog, un o feibion Owen, tywysog Gwynedd, i geisio gwlad arall ar amcan hyd y Môr Mawr tua machlud haul: a chwedi gweled gwedydd hyfryd heb drigolion, dychwelodd adref, a llanwodd ddeg o longau â'r cyfryw o'i genedl ag ydoedd chwannog i fyned lle caent heddwch: a thybir iddynt wladychu ym Mecsico (1170). O herwydd pan ddatguddiwyd yr America i'r Europeaid yn yr oes ddiweddaf aeth heibio, cafwyd yno eiriau

---

made use of the library of Owen Bringstoke for antiquarian research about which he corresponded with the English antiquarian Samuel Pegge as well as Evan Evans (Ieuan Fardd) and Edward Richard of Ystradmeurig. *Dictionary of Welsh Biography*, s.v. 'Phillips, James'.

[25] Edward Richard (1714–1777) was a Welsh schoolmaster, scholar, and poet who kept a school at Ystradmeurig, Cardiganshire, from 1735 or 1736 and was noted for his pastoral poetry. *Dictionary of Welsh Biography*, s.v. 'Richard, Edward'.

Cymreig: canys pan ymddidd^an^ant ynghŷd, dywedant wrth eu gilydd, Gwrando, ac y mae yno aderyn brith a chraig a alwant Pengwyn, ac ynys a elwir Corroeso, a Phen Briton; ac afon elwir Gwyndor".[26]
(Hanes y Ffydd, cng. Caerfyrddin, 1856, t. 205).[27] The first edition of "Hanes y Ffydd" appeared in 1671.[28]
    Yours very faithfully
      D. Silvan Evans

*   *   *   *

NLW, MS. 965E, 350a
Robert Williams to Thomas Stephens

Rhydycroesau, Oswestry.
    June 24. 1859.
Dear Sir/
    I have been looking everywhere that I can think of for the origin of Humphrey Llwyd's assertion about Madog,[29] but

---

[26] In the time of these adversities, Madog, one of the sons of Owen, prince of Gwynedd, trying for another land ventured purposefully the length of the Great Sea to the sunset: and having seen beautiful lands without inhabitants, he returned home, and filled ten ships with such of his people as were eager to go with him to where they could have peace: and it is supposed they established a colony in Mexico (1170). Because when America was discovered to the Europeans in the age which has recently passed, they had Welsh words there, including when they conversed together, they said to one another, Gwrando ['listen'], and there are a speckled bird and a stone there which they call Pengwyn ['white head'], and an island which is called Corroeso ['welcome'], and Pen Briton ['Briton's Head']; and a river called Gwyndor ['white water'].

[27] Charles Edwards, *Y Ffydd Ddiffuant: sef, Hanes y Ffydd Gristionogol a'i Rhinwedd*, gol. gan William Edmunds (Caerfyrddin: William Spurrell, 1856).

[28] It was published in 1667.

[29] Stephens' conclusion was that 'the sole author of Llwyd's narrative was Llwyd himself'. Stephens, *Madoc*, p 183.

without any success. You should know that Guttyn Owen[30] was the author of a valuable Chronicle called Llyfr Basyng, but I learned from a letter of Aneurin Owen's that this is only a transcript of the Welsh Chronicles as preserved in the British Museum. Guttyn Owen's portion is only a continuation by him from the year 1332 to 1461—"but unfortunately ~~of~~ so meagre as to be of no interest, the whole continuation being comprised in 8 pages"—I fancy that this work however contains the assertion about Madog's emigration. I have none of Guttyn Owens poetry. I send you a copy of my new prospectus—I only want the subscribers necessary (to cover *half* the expense of printing) before putting it into the press, but I fear that I must wait a long time
    Yours truly
      Rev^e Williams

*   *   *   *

NLW, MS. 963C, 7
John Morgan to Thomas Stephens

London
Aug 3rd /59

Dear Sir
    I fear you will be but ill satisfied with my endeavours at the Museum—but at the very earliest possible opportunities I commenced the search, the result of which I now send.
    As to Jocelyn's "History of Virginia."—I have carefully searched the Museum Catalogue—Watts's Bibliotheca Britannica[31]—Alibone's Dictionary of English Literature[32]—and

---

[30] Gutun Owain was a fifteenth-century Welsh poet, transcriber of manuscripts, and genealogist. See *Dictionary of Welsh Biography*, s.v. 'Gutun Owain or Gruffudd ap Huw ab Owain'.

[31] Robert Watt, *Bibliotheca Britannica; or a General Index to British and Foreign Literature*, four vols (Edinburgh: Archibald Constable and Company, 1824).

[32] Samuel Austin Allibone, *Critical Dictionary of English Literature and British*

Trubner's Guide to American Literature[33]—but no such work or name can I find.[34] And I cannot find any reference to it in notes, &c. of other and subsequent histories.

In the Turkish Spy, vol. viii, pp. 160–161,[35] there is an account of Madoc—but not a word as to its original. Not a word about its being copied from Captain Jocelyne. Truly, in parts of the narration, there are the usual signs of quotation, and that is all. The edition I could get was the 26th. Dr. Williams refers to this ^account^, p. 12, note.

As to the Hakluit. Vol. 3, page 1,[36] contains a quotation *acknowledged* in the heading to be from Dr. Powel's History of Wales.[37] Unfortunately the only copy I can find of this is in black letter. But the first reference to David Ingram I find in the account of Gilbert's Voyages, "For it appeareth by the relation of a countryman of ours—namely David Ingram (who travelled in those countries xi, months ^and more^) that the savages generally for the most part, are at continual war with their next adjoining neighbours, and especially the cannibals." (vol. 3, p. 169)[38]

---

and American Authors, three vols (Philadelphia: J. B. Lippencott & Co., 1854–1871).

[33] Nicholas Trübner, *Trübner's Bibliographical Guide to American Literature* (London: Trübner and Co., 1859).

[34] 'The work alluded to as "Jocelyn's History of Virginia" was probably one of the curious publications of John Josselyn, who paid a visit to New England in 1638-9, and another in 1663-71. He published his impressions of the country in two works, viz.: "New England's Rarities Discovered," 8vo. 1672, 1674, 1675; and "An Account of Two Voyages to New England," 12mo. 1674.' Stephens, *Madoc*, p. 135.

[35] This letter is quoted in Stephens, *Madoc*, pp. 133–35.

[36] Richard Hakluyt, *The Principal Navigations, Voiages and Discoveries of the English Nation, Made by Sea or Overland*, three vols (London: G. Bishop, R. Newberie & R. Barker, 1598–1600) (first, one vol. edn, 1582).

[37] Powel, *The Historie of Cambria, Now Called Wales*.

[38] [Sir George Peckham], *A Trve Reporte, of the Late Discoueries, and Possession, Taken in the Right of the Crowne of Englande, of the Newfound Landes: By that Valiaunt and Worthye Gentleman, Sir Humfrey Gilbert Knight* (London: I.C. for Iohn Hinde, 1583).

In the same account, (p. 173) it is said that among these people, who are the descendants of Madog, the word "Pengwin" is used for Land and for a fowl with a white head. Also that "Gwynethes" is the name of a fruit there. To which is added, "Moreover, there are other divers Welsh words at this day in use, as David Ingram aforesaid reporteth in his relations."

Any other reference to David Ingram, tho' his name occurs in this connection several times, I cannot find.

I could not get the "Cambrian Journal."

I shall leave London on Monday. I am now getting well, and shall be able to do anything further, if you write me by Saturday morning. It will not be the least trouble to me, for just now I have nothing else to do, unless I write an article or two for the "Faner".

My belief is that no such work as "Jocelyne"'s exists—that Ab Ithel has not seen it—but a reference to the name.

However, if you can set me on the scent any further, it will be to my own satisfaction to find out the truth of the matter.

I am, dear Sir
Very resply yours
John Morgan

T. Stephens, Esq.

*   *   *   *

NLW, MS. 963C, 15
John Morgan to Thomas Stephens

Dyffryn, via Carnarvon
August 10th / 59

Dear Sir

Your second letter found me here. Had I anticipated it on Friday, I might easily have stayed a few hours longer in London.

I found in the Museum several allusions to Capt. Smith; but did not see his work,[39] nor his name in the Catalogue. But I cannot

---

[39] John Smith, *The Generall Historie of Virginia, New-England, and the Summer Isles with the Names of the Adventurers, Planters, and Governours from their*

say that I searched much after it, inasmuch as my object was to find Jocelyn.

As to "those countries," in which (Hakluit 3, 169) David Ingram is said to have travelled xi months, my impression is that Mexico is referred to. I am pretty certain that Virginia is not. The doubt in my mind is as to North America. My memory of late is too treacherous to be relied upon.

In referring, as you do, from Gilbert's account, that Ingram published or wrote an account of his travels, I made a fair search after the work, but could find no further trace.

I am very sorry that I cannot satisfy the queries. Still, upon the whole, I do think there is fair ground to call upon Ab Ithel to furnish his readers with a more satisfactory account of his authorities.

I have some recollection of hearing that Jones of Bethesda formerly was appointed curate, or something, of Penydaran. If he is still there, I would be much obliged if you could without trouble, send me his address.

I remain, dear Sir
Yours Faithfully
John Morgan

T. Stephens, Esq.

*　　*　　*　　*

First Beginning An: 1584 to this Present 1624. With the Procedings of those Severall Colonies and the Accidents that Befell them in all their Journyes and Discoveries. Also the Maps and Descriptions of all those Countryes, their Commodities, People, Government, Customes, and Religion yet Knowne. Divided into Six Bookes (London: I.D. and I.H., 1624).

NLW, MS. 965E, 262
Isaac Redwood to Thomas Stephens

Cae wern near Neath 4/5mo[40] 1860
My dear friend
 I send for thy perusal a book on the settlements of Friends in America giving correct dates of the period of those Settlements. I believe there is no ground for the idea that Wm Penn[41] ever issued an Address to the Welsh Friends, holding out to them the prospect of finding in America, a Colony of *Welsh* Indians. The existence of such a Colony appears to be one of those fascinating but long existing illusions, fostered by National Vanity, but altogether, unsupported by facts. It *has* been, and *will continue to be*, the dream of the Poet, regardless of historic truth, seeking only "to Point a Moral, or Adorn a Tale"[42]. I believe all history is more or less made up of fable. Tyler has proved in his "Harry of Monmouth",[43] that so far from that Prince, being the boon companion of profligates, and the dissipated youth descended by *Poets* and *Historians*, he was diligent, and attentive in the discharge of all the important duties, which devolved upon him. Well might Horace Walpole[44] give to the world his "Historic Doubts" and had he extended those doubts to every reign since the Conquest, by a careful examination of the Public Records, he would have conferred upon his country an invaluable benefit. I saw thy excellent father about a fortnight since, I thought him looking

---

[40] July
[41] William Penn (1644–1718), Quaker leader and founder of Pennsylvania.
[42] Samuel Johnson, *The Vanity of Human Wishes: The Tenth Satire of Juvenal, Imitated* (London: R. Dodsley, 1749), line 222.
[43] J. Endell Tyler, *Henry of Monmouth, or Memoirs of the Life of Character of Henry the Fifth, as Prince of Wales and King of England*, two vols (London: Richard Bentley, 1838).
[44] Horace Walpole (1717–1797) was an English Member of Parliament, antiquarian, art historian and writer. He is best known for his home, Strawberry Hill, London, with its distinctive Gothic style, and his novel *The Castle Otranto* (London: Tho. Lownds, 1764).

well, though with him as with me, "Time rolls his ceaseless course".[45] He told me he had not heard from thee for some time. To him might truly be applied that line of Pope's, An honest man's the noblest work of God."[46]

Thy sincere friend
I Redwood

*   *   *   *

NLW, MS. 963C, 31
W. Walker Wilkins[47] to Thomas Stephens

London. 31 Dec. 1861

Dear Sir,

By referring to Dr John William's Enquiry (1791) I have been able to trace Morgan Evans' letter.

It appeared in the Gent's Mag. for March 1740 (i.e. Vol. x. p. 140); to wh periodical it was communicated by Theophilus Evans,[48] Vicar of St Davids; Brecon. If you wish a transcript of it, I shall have much pleasure in forwarding you one.

The article in wh Jones' strange composition appears is entitled

"The Crown of England's Title to America prior to that of Spain"; hence the reason of the title not being mentioned in the Genl Index.

---

[45] Walter Scott, *The Lady of the Lake. A Poem* (Edinburgh: James Ballantyne and Co., 1810), Third canto, Verse 1, Line 1.

[46] Alexander Pope, *An Essay on Man, Being the First Book of Ethic Epistles. To Henry St. John, L Bolingbroke* (London: John Wright for Lawton Gilliver, 1734), Epistle IV, Line 248.

[47] The author of *Political Ballads of the Seventeenth and Eighteenth Centuries*, two vols (London: Longman, Green, Longman, and Roberts, 1860).

[48] Theophilus Evans (1693–1767).

The Rev. T. Evans states that it ^was^ communicated to Dr Plott[49] among others, but does not add that the last named gentm had it before the Royal Society.

In order not to lose this evening's post, I have written in great haste.

Dear Sir

Yr Obligd & ob ser

W Walker Wilkins

T. Stephens Esq

*   *   *   *

NLW, MS. 963C, 35

W. Walker Wilkins to Thomas Stephens

18 Stampshire Grove, Camden Rd.

London. N. W.

30 Decr 1862

Dear Sir,

Many thanks for yr prompt & courteous reply to my former note. The story of the balance sheet is, as I concluded, an apocryphal one.[50] My friend Mr Smiles,[51] (the biographer of Mr Stephenson) informed me that he had only met with it in Roebuck's political brochure: and where the garrulous member for Sheffield got it must remain (I fear) a ?

In answer to yr question:

1. The Gent's Mag. originally appeared in the year *1731*; & I do

---

[49] Robert Plot (*c*.1640–1696).

[50] Wilkins had previously written to Stephens concerning 'an anecdote of "Lady Charlotte Guest & her balance sheet" (of Dowlais Works) which was as strongly marred with improbability as impertinence; nevertheless the story, like all other the most improbable stories, was repeated usque ad nauseaum,' desiring Stephens to let him know if it 'originally appeared in some Welsh publication—& if so, in *what* & *where*?' W. Walker Wilkins to Thomas Stephens, London, 17 December 1862, NLW, MS. 965E, 330.

[51] Samuel Smiles (1812–1904).

not find on referring either to Vol. 40, or to the Genl Index, which is very complete, any notice whatever of the imaginary Welsh Indians earlier than the year 1791 (or in Vol. 61), when the late Dr Owen Pughe revived the Madawgwys controversy.

2. There are a dozen papers at least by Dr Robert Plott, the topographer &c, contained in the Philosophical Transactions of the Roy Socy, but not one of them relates to the above subject. Nor can I discover that the Dr ever published a separate treatise upon it.

3. I have searched for the Indian tribes you mention in all the maps from 1589–1710 inclusive, which are preserved in the Liby of the Brit. Museum, & in vain. I have found in one or two of them "Indian Town" inscribed in the angle of Cape Hatteras; & in the county of Rappahanock, a little to the east of "the falls" on the last mentioned river, a tribe called the *Doogs*.

I have also consulted the works of Mackenny (*Memories of Indians*),[52] Wheeler (*Hist of N. Carolina*),[53] Lawson (*Voyages to C.*),[54] & Schoolcraft (The *Mississippi*),[55] & can find in neither of them any mention of "Doeg" or of "Nanticokes". Lawson refers

---

[52] Thomas L. McKenney, *Memoirs, Official and Personal; with Sketches of Travels Among the Northern and Southern Indians; Embracing a War Excursion, and Descriptions of Scenes along the Western Borders*, two vols (New York: Paine and Burgess, 1846).

[53] John H. Wheeler, *Historical Sketches of North Carolina, From 1854 to 1851. Compiled from Original Records, Official Documents, and Traditional Statements*, two vols (Philadelphia: Lippencott, Grambo and Co., 1851).

[54] John Lawson, *A New Voyage to Carolina; Containing the Exact Description and Natural History of that Country: Together with the Present State thereof. and A Journal Of a Thousand Miles, Travel'd thro' Several Nations of INDIANS. Giving a Particular Account of their Customs, Manners, &c.* (London: [James Knapton], 1709).

[55] Possibly, Henry R. Schoolcraft, *Travels in the Central Portions of the Mississippi Valley: Comprising Observations on its Mineral Geography, Internal Resources, and Aboriginal Population* (New York: Collins and Hannay, 1825), although Schoolcraft, an ethnographer and explorer who discovered the Mississippi River's source, published several works on his explorations of that river undertaken in 1821 and 1832.

incidentally to a tribe of Hatteras Indians, whose ancestors were white people, & could "talk in a book"; the truth of which (he adds) is confirmed by gray eyes being among these Indians & no others. These people were manifestly the descendants of the colonists sent thither by Raligh in 1587, & who were absorbed or spirited away by the native population within three years afterwards, & not heard of more. Perhaps this fact gave rise to the elaborated statements contained in old Hakluyts pages concerning the involuntary emigration of Prince Madoc & his companions—? The line between truth & fiction was not very critically defined in the 16th century

Being a Cymro myself I take a lively interest in every thing pertaining to the past history & present welfare of the Principality; & I beg, therefore, in the event of your wishing the confirmation of any book, or statement concerning the old country you will not hesitate to command my humble services. I visit the Reading Room of the Brit. Museum generally twice or thrice a week, & possess moreover a large literary connection, so that I experience little difficulty in arriving by the *shortest* route at the fountain-head of information.

Within the past few weeks enquiries have been made thro' the medium of Notes & Queries for some promised work on the Welsh as White Indians by Bartlett, author of *Americanisms*, who, it is said, is in a position to finally close the controversy respecting them.[56] Credat Judæus!

I beg to subscribe myself, dear sir,
        Yr obliged & obt servt
            W. Walker Wilkins
Thos Stephens esq

P.S. In the *Analectic Magazine* (Philadelphia) Vol. ii. 410 is an account of the Paduca or Maduca Indians, or as the writer contends *Madouckwir*, or Madock Men. He subscribes himself "D. J." — which smells very like *Jones*!

---

[56] The work of John R. Bartlett (1805–1886) concerning Madoc is discussed below in James Hadley to Thomas Stephens, New Haven, Connecticut, 4 October 1865, NLW, MS. 963C, 59. See pp. 220–21 below.

NLW, MS. 963C, 47
W. Walker Wilkins to Thomas Stephens

London 2 Jany 1863
Dear Sir, The Brit museum is closed from the 1st to the 8th inst inclusive: when it reopens I will gladly verify for you the map or maps on which the situation of the tribe of Doogs is indicated.

On reference to Mackenney & Halls' sumptuous *History of the Indian Tribes*, 3 Vols fol., which was published under the auspices of the U.S. government,[57] I find (in vol. iii. pp. 1–6, footnote) a list of 272 names of tribes which are (the authors say) mentioned in the early narrations & histories of the Indians. That list includes the *Tuscaroras* & the *Conoyeas or Nantihokes*, but neither the Doegs nor Doogs. The latter, judging from the locality they occupied, were an offshoot no doubt of the great Tuscarora tribe; which, it appears removed bodily from North Carolina, in the year 1717, & united themselves with the Five Nations in the Lake Districts. Whether the Doags accompanied them or not I cannot say, ^according to Morgan Jones' letter they were certainly dependent upon them.^ This migration of the Tuscarora Tribe is a noteworthy fact, because it precludes the possibility of supporting any argument on the descent of that or any other Indian Tribe from a Welsh stock, occupying the same country, & visited subsequently to the above date.

Mackenny & Hall make no mention of ~~these~~ Welsh Indians, nor do they lead their readers to suppose that one tribe was superior to another in a social or intellectual respect. Of the aboriginal inhabitants of the great American continent they remark: "They were stationary, looking upon life as a scene of physical excursion, without improving or attempting to improve, with the exception of the half-civilized empires of Mexico & Peru, the condition & improvement of which we are satisfied were grossly

---

[57] Thomas McKenney and James Hall, *History of the Indian Tribes of North America, with Biographical Sketches and Anecdotes of the Principal Chiefs*, three vols (Vol. 1: Philadelphia: E. C. Biddle, 1836) (Vol. 2–3: Philadelphia: D. Rice and J. G. Clark, 1842–44).

exaggerated by the early adventurers, all the primitive inhabitants, from the straits of Magellan to the Hudson's Bay, were in
this state of helpless ignorance & imbecility. Whether they
inhabited the mild & genial climates, were burned by the vertical
sun of the tropics, or by a still harder fate were condemned to the
bleak & still regions of the north, all were equally stationary &
improvident. Ages passed by & made no impression upon them.
The experience of the past, & the aspiration of the future, were
alike unheeded. Their existence was confined to the present. We
confess our inability to explain this enigma, & we leave it without
further observation." (vol. iii p. 12)

These remarks be it remembered are made by gentlemen who
passed many years in traversing the American continent, & in
collecting from the aborigines themselves their traditions &c.
"Their previous history & progress are utterly lost—lost in that
long interval of darkness which preceded authentic history
amongst all nations—it rests, & probably will ever rest, upon the
Indians". Our authors are further of opinion that no Indian
tradition is of any value whatever that extends for a period
further back than 50 years

The letter communicated to the Gent's Mag. (Vol. x. p. 104) by
Theophilus Evans is dated from New York, 10 March 1685/6 & is
subscribed "Morgan Jones, the son of John Jones of Basaleg, near
New-port, in the county of Monmouth."

When the Museum reopens I will get the Quarter rate settled
for you. In the interim, Ble me,[58]

Dear Sir,
Faithfully yrs
W. Walker Wilkins

Thos Stephens

P.S. I am told there is a very curious notice of the Welsh Indians
in old Sir Thos Herberts Travels (1630)[59] do you know of it?

---

[58] Likely an abbreviated form of 'Believe me'; Wilkins signs at least one other
letter to Stephens with a different abbreviated form of the same phrase. See
Wilkins to Stephens, London, 12 June 1863, NLW, MS. 965E, Letter 311.
[59] Thomas Herbert, *Some Yeares travels into Divers Parts of Asia and Afrique*

NLW, MS. 963C, 51
W. Walker Wilkins to Thomas Stephens

London. 10 Jany 1863
Dear Sir,
      Since the reopening of the Brit Museum on the 8th inst, I have succeeded in spotting the several Indian Tribes in which you are interested.
      1. The Doegs or Doogs. According to Thornton's Maps & Charts of Nth America, fol. 1704, this tribe was located on the narrow strip of territory between the Potomac & Rappahonnock, a little to the eastward of the falls on the last mentioned river. The district now forms part of King George County
      2. The *Tuscaroras*. Back at the time & long subsequently to the colonizing of N. Carolina by Europeans this powerful tribe occupied the seaboard of that state. About the year 1717, the Tuscaroras conspired against the whites, & butchered in cold blood several hundreds of them. A retaliatory war ensued, in which the savages got worsted, losing more than 1000 of their warriors, the survivors were compelled to abandon for ever their old country, & repaired to the "Five Nations," which received them into their confederacy. With the consent, it is to be presumed, of the local authorities, the Tuscaroras established themselves upon the Virginian boundary; that is, between the heads of rivers Fluvanna & Rivanna, & were hemmed in by the Blue Ridge or South Mountains (*Vide* Jeffery's American Atlas. fol. 1775) In modern atlases this district is designated Albemarle County.
      3. The *Canoyeas* or *Nantihokes*. These were settled in Maryland, occupying the Districts to the east of Chesapeake Bay

---

Describing Especially the Two Famous Empires, the Persian, and the Great Mogull: Weaved with the History of these Later Times as also, many Rich and Spatious Kingdomes in the Orientall India, and Other Parts of Asia; Together with the Adjacent Iles. Severally Relating the Religion, Language, Qualities, Customes, Habit, Descent, Fashions, and Other Observations Touching Them. With a Revivall of the First Discoverer of America. Revised and Enlarged by the Author (London: R. B, 1638), which is cited in Stephens, *Madoc*, p. 34.

(now known as Dorchester County). Jeff. Am. Atlas. *ut supra*.

The date of the quaker Loyd's letter—8: 14: 3/4—I have submitted to the editorial staff of "Notes & Queries", with whom I cooperate, & they conjecture that it means the 14 Sep. 1694 (et. I.).

I cannot make out to what country David Ingram belonged. He was an enterprising voyager at the close of the 16th & beginning of the 17th centuries, & is incidentally mentioned by D Harris, the naval historian, in conjunction with one Miles Philips. He appears on one occasion to have fallen into the clutches of the Spaniards, & to have been carried by them over a considerable part of the American continent. On getting enlarged, he was the first to acquaint his countrymen of the prodigious extent, &c, &c of the countries thro' which he was carried. He was subsequently one of those who attempted to discover the Northwest passage, of which attempt (says Harris) he wrote the best account.

In Michalson's *Journal of Natl Philosop. &c* (Vol xii. 181) is a paper entitled "Observations Conjectures relative to the supposed Welsh Indians in the Western parts of Nth America Republished from the "Kentucky Palladium", with additional remarks & conjectures by the editor of the Philosl. Medl. & Physl. Journal".

This paper contains an account of the adventures of one Maurice Griffith, a native of Wales, who was captured by a party of Shawnee Indians, on the head of Roanoke river (Virginia), & detained by them in their own country. Whilst their prisoner Griffith accompanied five of their number to explore the sources of the Missouri, where, according to his account, he met with a tribe of white Indians speaking the Welsh Language. But no doubt you are better acquainted than myself with the particulars of this man's story. It is related by one Harvey Toulmin. The american editors are somewhat sceptical of the matter.

Literary men two centuries ago were like a flock of sheep; where one made a gap all the rest *instinctively* followed thro it.

Hakluyt, Purchas,[60] Harris,[61] Pinkerton,[62] & the whole squad of naval writers, not excepting the *historian* Monson,[63] repeated each other usque ad nausium—To read one is to read the whole of them, as I know by weary experience. I cannot discover in them anything *new* for you. Being engaged at present upon an extended memoir of Sir Francis Drake, I have familiarized myself tolerably well with their pages.

Of Broughton[64] & Davy,[65] to whom you refer in your note of the 3rd inst, I neither know nor can make out anything. Who were they?

---

[60] Samuel Purchas, *Haklvytvs Posthumus or Pvrchas his Pilgrimes. Contayning a History of the World, in Sea Voyages & Lande Trauells, by Englishmen & Others* (London: Henrie Fetherstone, 1625).

[61] Stephens notes that 'Dr Harris, the naval historian, names [David] Ingram in connection with one Miles Phillips', in his *Madoc*, p. 34. He was informed of this reference by W. Walker Wilkins in a letter dated 10 January 1863, London, NLW, MS. 963C, Letter 51.

[62] John Pinkerton, *A General Collection of the Best and Most Interesting Voyages and Travels in all parts of the World*, seventeen vols (London: Hurst, Rees, and Orme, 1808–1814).

[63] Possibly, William Monson, *A True and Exact Account of the Wars with Spain, in the Reign of Q Elizabeth, (of Famous Memory.) Being the Particualrs of What Happened between the English and Spanish Fleets, from the Years 1585 to 1602. Shewing, The Expeditions, Attempts, Flights, Designs, Escapes, Successes, Errors, &c. on Both Sides. With the Names of Her Majesty's Ships and Commanders in Every Fleet. Being the Pattern and Warning to Future Ages* (London: W. Crooke, 1782). Sir William Monson's papers were printed by the Naval Department in the early twentieth century. Michael Oppenheim (ed.), *The Naval Tracts of Sir W. Monson*, five vols (London: Navy Records Society, 1902–1904).

[64] William Robert Broughton, *A Voyage of Discovery to the North Pacific Ocean: In which the Coast of Asia, from the Lat. Of 35° North to the Lat. Of 52° North, the Island of Insu* (Commonly Known under the Name of the Land of Jesso), *The North, South, and East Coasts of Japan, the Lieuchieux and the Adjacent Isles, as well as the Coast of Corea, have been Examined and Surveyed* (London: T Cadell and W. Davies, 1804).

[65] Likely a reference to John Davey, who was supposed to have identified a language he heard being spoken by a Native American tribe as similar to Welsh. See Stephens, *Madoc*, p. 51.

Kohl's new work on the Discovery of America has not yet appeared,[66] or at all events has not yet found its way into the Museum. It related, I am informed, more to the hydrography than to the ethnography of the Western hemisphere.

I remain, Dear Sir
    Vy faithfully yrs,
        W. Walker Wilkins
Thos Stephens Esq
P.S. I have been twice thro "Roebuck's Hist of the Whig Ministry,[67] & cannot find in it the Guest anecdote.

*   *   *   *

NLW, MS. 965E, 314c
Thomas Watts to Thomas Stephens

British Museum
Feb. 9th 1863

Dear Sir/
    I am, as you suppose, the writer of the article on Welsh Literature in Knight's English Cyclopædia,[68] an article the obvious imperfections of which can only be excused by the hurry in which it was written. As long however as it remains the only general account of the subject it may be defended on the well-known principle that a percentage in the pound is better than nothing.

---

[66] J. G. Kohl, *Geschichte der Entdeckung Amerika's von Columbus bis Franklin* (Bremen: Heinrich Strack, 1861); Idem, *A Popular History of the Discovery of America, from Columbus to Franklin*, trans. by R. R. Noel, two vols (London: Chapman and Hall, 1862).

[67] John Arthur Roebuck, *History of the Whig Ministry of 1830, to the Passing of the Reform Bill*, two vols (London: John W. Parker and Son, 1852).

[68] This was republished privately in London in 1861 as an essay entitled *Sketch of the History of the Welsh Language and Literature*.

Enclosed you will find the collation of the article you requested in the Gentlemans Magazine. The Rev. T. Evans says in his letter to the Editor "I shall first quote a letter from Mr Morgan Jones, Chaplain to the Plantations of South Carolina, sent to Dr. Thomas Lloyd of Pennsylvania, by whom it was transmitted to Charles Lloyd of Dol-y-fran in Montgomeryshire Esq. and afterwards communicated to Dr. Robert Plott by the hands of Mr Edward Lluid A.M. keeper of the Ashmolean Museum in Oxford. It is as follows." And then follows the narrative as you will find it, differing in many respects from the copy printed by Owen in the British Remains, but enclosed within inverted commas as if a close transcript from the original. Evans then proceeds "I shall next make some remarks on the above Letter. It appears by this narrative that the author Mr Morgan Jones was probably unacquainted with the history of his own country. He was surpriz'd (and well he might) to hear the Doeg Indians talk the British Language, and concludes (and indeed very justly) that they must be descended from the Old Britons, but when and how, our Author seems to be at a loss. But the Welsh History (first wrote by Caradoc Abbot of Llancarvan and since published by Dr Powell) sets the whole matter in a clear light and unravels the mystery. For it informs us that in the year 1170 Madoc ap Owen Gwyneth" &c &c &c Evans speaks of Mexico as probably the country to which Madoc sailed "since there Prince Madoc was bury'd as his Epitaph since found there does make evident beyond all contradiction.

"Madoc wyf mwy dic ei wedd"
&c &c &c

"It is indeed the common Opinion that in the course of a few Generations Madoc and his Men incorporated with the Nations and made one People with them, whence proceed the various British words that the Europeans found among the Mexico Indians such as Pen-Gwyn, Groeso, Gwenddwr, Bara, Tad, Mam, Buwch, Clugiar, Llwynoc, Coch y dwr, with many more received in Sir Thomas Herberts Travels p. 222. But by this Narrative, it is evident that they keep as yet a distinct People, at least in the year 1660 when our Author was amongst them. For Mr Jones says he not only conversed with them about the ordinary Affairs of Life but preached to them three Times a Week in the British Language, and that they usually consulted him when anything appeared different in the same Language, which evidently demonstrates that they still preserve their original Language, and are still a Colony or People unmixed," The remainder of Evans's letter is an argument in favour of the prior right of the English to the discovery of America which "oure Statesmen would fain have persuaded Queen Elizabeth to insist on" &c &c which is I dare say already known to you.

Evans does not mention where he got his copy of Jones's report and in the Philosophical Transaction I find nothing on the subject. I have referred to the general index of the first seventy volumes of the Phil. Trans. by Maty but among the various papers contributed by Dr Plott there is none on this. ~~subject~~

My delay in answering your letter has proceeded from no remissness on my part but is the effect of my position at the Museum. Any literary inquiries that you wish to be made at this library can be much more readily and conveniently made by a reader who has admission here than by one of the officers. For some hours of the day I am engaged in the centre of the magnificent Reading Room under circumstances which render any such occupation as collection impossible, and even when I retire to my room I am liable to continual interruptions which seldom leave me undisturbed many minutes. I am delighted to have been able, under these difficulties, to render any assistance to your valuable researches and ~~remain~~ am

Sir
Yours very truly
Thomas Watts

Thomas Stephens Esq.

*   *   *   *

NLW, MS. 965E, 263
Jonathan Rees to Thomas Stephens

Neath 1m[69] 20 1863

Respected Friend
    Thos Stephens
    I fancy thou wilt be following an ignis fatuus[70] in trying to find
any document of Mr Penn respecting the Welch—Wm Penn
appears to have issued a statement of the ~~state~~ of some of the
productions &c vol 1—pp 377 and at pp 299 he gives the frame
work of his government
    Many friends were induced to go from Radnorshire and
should think from Montgomeryshire and Merionethshire most of
them earning a scanty subsistence for themselves and families on
the poor soil of Wales, some going and much bettering themselves induced others to go also that there was a district formed
called North Wales in Pennsylvania—A friend of Eskergoch on
the side of Plinllimon named Jn⁰ Goodwin his father and some of
the family having gone he was disposed also to go but felt an
intimation on his mind that it was right for him to remain with
the belief that he should have all things needful he was a valuable
minister amongst friends lived to a good old age and found the
premon verified that ~~th~~ those who seek first the kingdom of
Heaven all things necessary will be added—I think as well to put
thee on thy guard against Thos Rees' statement as to the number
of Friends in Wales about 1715 also about the time of writing his
book on Welch nonconformity[71] in which he has very much
maligned our early friends. He has stated the number of friends
at the time of his writing to be from 6 to 700 whereas I am nearly
sure they do not exceed 125 and about 1715 he states them at

---

[69] March
[70] Literally 'foolish fire'. A spirit which leads travellers astray similar to a will-
o'-the-wisp.
[71] Thomas Rees, *History of Protestant Nonconformity in Wales from its Rise to
the Present Time* (London: John Snow, 1861). This was the seminal text of
nineteenth-century Welsh nonconformist historiography.

three thousand when I believe three hundred would be a nearer approximation to the truth—I consider he has been led into error by considering those who attended the Yearly meetings were members of our society, but by a recent inspection into the records of the Y[72] meetings I am more confirmed ^in my view^ We have only 1 member in Pembrokeshire about 90 in Glamorganshire and Monmouthshire a very few in Radnorshire and Denbighshire and not one in either of the other 8 counties. I send herewith 2 volumes of Clarkson's Penn[73] and a work respecting Ja^s Logan[74]—It is much to be regretted that such a nobly minded man ^as WP^ should be ungenerously treated by the world and also these early settlers whom he used so honourably I ~~would lend thee them~~—And Macaulay I fear from sheer spite to friends has tried to blacken his character but I think it will fall back upon him to his shame.[75]

Altho' I do not like Hepworth Dixon's[76] manner of sketching Penn's religious character which he cannot appreciate I will also lend that and hope if it does not clear up the myth that racks upon thy mind, it may otherwise prove entertaining and instructive at

---

[72] Yearly

[73] Thomas Clarkson, *Memoirs of the Private and Public Life of William Penn*, two vols (Philadelphia: Richard Taylor and Co., 1813).

[74] James Logan (1674–1751) was Quaker, scholar, and colonial official in Pennsylvania. The work referred to is likely, Winston Armistead, *James Logan; A Distinguished Scholar and Christian Legislator; Founder of the Loganian Library at Philadelphia; Secretary of the Province of Pennsylvania; Chief Justice; Commissioner of Property; and (as President of the Council) for Two Years Governor of the Province including Several of his Letters and those of his Correspondents, Many of which are now Printed from the Original MSS. Collated and Arranged for the Purpose* (London: Charles Gilpin, 1851).

[75] Thomas B. Macaulay, *The History of England: From the Accession of James II*, five vols (1848). See W. E. Forester, *William Penn and Thomas B. Macaulay: Being brief Observations on the Charges made in Mr. Macaulay's History of England, against the Character of William Penn* (London: Charles Gilpin, 1849).

[76] William Hepworth Dixon, *William Penn: An Historical Biography*. With an Extra Chapter on 'The Macaulay Charges' (London: Chapman and Hall, 1851).

page 397 thou may see that W Penn thinks the Indians descended from the Jews.

I have written a poor scrawl—When thou hast finished with the three books shall be pleased to have them back

From neither of the books wilt thou have a right appreciation of W P as a religious character

Respectfully thy friend

Jonr Rees

I intend sending the books by the afternoon train of tomorrow

*   *   *   *

NLW, MS. 963C, 59
James Hadley to Thomas Stephens

Yale College, New Haven, Conn^t. Oct. 4, 1865.

Thomas Stephens, Esq.

My dear Sir,

The bundle of books from Low & Co. reached me safely two days ago.[77] Mr Jones had succeeded in obtaining for me a copy of Rowlands' Grammar; according to your direction, therefore, I shall place your copy in our College Library. But the "Literature of the Kymry" has been found for some years in the College Library, where I have often consulted it, and always with much interest and pleasure. Having now a copy of my own, I shall hope to become more fully and familiarly acquainted with it. It is rare

---

[77] In 1861, John D. Jones of Yale Theological Seminary, formerly of Bala, north Wales, had written to Stephens about his research on Welsh literature, books which he was attempting to obtain for Hadley, a professor of Greek at Yale, and the possibility of Stephens receiving an honorary MA from Yale. Stephens was requested to procure 'a copy of Dafydd Ap Gwilym's poems together with Revd Thos Rowland's Grammar of the Welsh Language' and directed to 'send them to my care here, whether thro' one of the Ocean Expresses, or thro' one of the London publishers to one of the New York Publishers, addressed to me, together with the price &c'. John D. Jones to Thomas Stephens, New Haven, CT, 30 November 1861, NLW, MS. 964E, 159.

to find a writer, treating of his country's literature, whose patriotic feeling while it gives a glow to his treatment, is not allowed to blind his critical judgment; and especially in the field of Celtic antiquities, it is rare to find a writer of Celtic birth who knows how to exercise that judicious skepticism which historic truth demands. I shall be glad to have such a writer always at hand in my own study, and may be led perhaps to give more attention to subjects of which I have been hitherto, it must be owned, more an *amateur* than a *connoisseur*. I must thank you also for the "Gorchestion"[78] with its specimens of the middle period of Welsh poetic literature. In regard to Dafydd ab Gwilym, I have often wondered that the Cambrian literati should let it be so difficult to obtain the works of a poet whom outsiders at least will be apt to regard as the great ornament of Cambrian poetry, admiring his simplicity and naturalness more than the cloudy splendors and sublimities of Cynddelw and Gwalchmai. May we not hope that some competent editor will ere long undertake the task, and give to the world an edition of Dafydd ab Gwilym, as thorough and exact (though not, I trust, so expensive) as that of the Mabinogion by Lady Charlotte Guest. It would be desirable to find in such an edition that full and precise information in regard to the manuscripts on which it should be founded, which adds so much to the value of Lady Guest's book. Such information is of the highest importance, not only as bearing on the purity of the text, but as a guide and help to inquiries into the history of the language; and the want of it strikes me as a very serious defect in the Myvyrian Archaeology,[79] both in its original form and in the recent republication. In regard to most of the pieces you in that great collection, the reader knows nothing as to the manuscripts on which they are founded—what their condition as respects carefulness and legibility—what their age, how near to that of the

---

[78] Rhys Jones, *Gorchestion Beirdd Cymru: neu Flodau Godidowgrwydd Awen. Wedi eu Lloffa, a'u Dethol, allan o Waith rhai o'r Awduriaid Ardderchoccaf, a fu erioed yn yr Iaith Gymraeg* (Amwythig: Stafford Prys, 1773). This work was edited, added to, and republished in 1864 by Robert Ellis (Cynddelw).

[79] Jones, Williams, and Owen, *The Myvyrian Archaiology of Wales.*

author, and what the probability therefore of their representing him with exactness—whether the printed text follows one of them, or is made by combining several, and, in the latter case, on what principles they are combined together.

Your letter of July 29th was received about the first of September. On reading it, I had little doubt that I should be able to find in our College Library any thing which Mr Bartlett might have published in relation to the supposed discovery of America by Prince Madoc. I was not able, however, for some time to commence the search; and when at length I set about it, failed to discover what I sought for. Indeed I was led to doubt whether Mr Bartlett had published anything on the subject. Thinking it best, therefore, to seek information at headquarters, I wrote a letter of inquiry to Mr Bartlett himself, who resides in Providence, Rhode Island, and received from him a reply, which I transcribe entire.

"Providence, Sept. 30, 1865. My dear Sir. I have your letter of the 28th instant, making enquiry about an examination by me of the question of the discovery of America by the Welsh in the 12th century by an expedition under Prince Madoc.

Many years ago I examined this question very thoroughly, and wrote out the results, which I sent to the Estesfodd [sic],[80] a Welsh National Society in Wales. I wrote to the Secretary that he could find my MS. at Wiley and Putnam's, American Booksellers in London. I received no reply to my letter, and about two years after, finding the MS. had not been called for, it was returned to me.   In 1851 or '52 I loaned my MS. to the Rev. Dr. Hawks of New York; but after repeated efforts to get it back, was unsuccessful until within a few months, and then obtained but a portion of it. Some five or six years ago I sent a Welsh gentleman, connected with a Welsh newspaper or magazine, for the MS., who obtained a portion of it; but neither he nor the Doctor advised me of it at the time, and I cannot now tell the gentleman's name, although I have made every effort to find it out.   Thus you see a fatality has thus far attended my MS., and that a portion is gone. But this does not discourage me, with what I already have, I shall

---

[80] 'Sic' in original.

be able to discover what is wanting, and intend, the coming winter, to go over the whole subject once more, and if my life is spared, to publish my Essay.   In one respect it is well that my essay was not given to the world when it was written; for I had adopted certain views in regard to the so-called "Welsh Indians" which have been materially changed by my three years' journeys in the interior of the country while Commissioner on the U.S. and Mexican Boundary Survey.   Yours very truly, John R. Bartlett.

Should Mr Bartlett carry out the intention here expressed, I will send you at once a copy of his essay. I shall look for it with much interest; for with every disposition to accept a Welsh discovery of this continent, I have not been able thus far to see that there was much force in the evidences for such a discovery. The contemporary testimonies in regard to Madoc prove little more than he was distinguished among Welsh chiefs for his love of a seafaring life and that he sought distant settlements by sea. The later tradition, as given by Powell, is so remote from the time of Madoc, and so liable to be colored by the subsequent discovery and colonization of America in the 15th and 16th centuries, that it seems impossible to rely upon it with any confidence. It is difficult, moreover, to believe that, if Madoc ^had brought back^ the report of a double voyage of 3000 miles across the open sea, an announcement so unprecedented and stupendous would not have left a more distinct impression on the annals or literature of the time; just as the much less astounding visit of the Scandinavians to America in the 10th and 11th centuries are established by unquestionable documentary evidence. The lack of evidence thus far might, however, be compensated by finding in America clear traces of old Welsh settlement, action, or influence. But all the traces of this kind which I have seen alleged seem to me ^either^ uncertified or inconclusive; thus the proofs of ^early^ European influence which Mr Catlin found among the Mandans,[81]

---

[81] Probably George Catlin, *Letters and Notes on the Manners, Customs, and Condition of the North American Indians*, two vols (London: published for the author, 1842) which deals with the subject and was utilized by Stephens. However, it may also refer Catlin's later work, Idem, *Catlin's North American Indian Portfolio. Hunting Scenes and Amusements of the Rocky Mountains and*

appear too vague and equivocal to be relied on as proofs of any doubtful proposition. These things, I say, not as the result of any special investigation, but only to show how the question presents itself to my own mind, and why I shall be glad to see any new light thrown upon it by Mr Bartlett.[82]

Our Friend, Mr Jones, after pursuing his studies, theological and philosophical, in this place for some two years or more, left us little more than a year ago, and went to Virginia in one of the last regiments raised here for the war.[83] He held the post of chaplain. Since the war closed in the sudden and complete collapse of the slave-holding Confederacy, I have heard nothing from him. If he is alive and well, it is likely that he will at least pay us a visit before very long.

I cannot close without again expressing my sense of obligation for the books, of so much interest and value, which you have sent me, and my regret that I cannot do more to reciprocate the favor. I need not say that it will always give me pleasure to hear from you, and that if I can do any thing to serve you, I hope you will not fail to let me know it.

Believe me, with much respect,
Yours very truly
James Hadley

Thomas Stephens, Esq.
   Merthyr Tydfil, South Wales,
      Great Britain.

Prairies of America. From Drawings and Notes of the Author, Made during Eight Years' Travel amongst Forty-eight of the Wildest and Most Remote Tribes of Savages in North America (London: Geo. Catlin, 1844).

[82] 'The subject appears to have also occupied the attention of our cousins across the Atlantic. Mr. John Russell Bartlett, the Secretary of the American Ethnological Society, in the winter of 1841, at New York, stated that he had been investigating the subject, and that he was in possession of affidavits and other documents, to attest the truth of the Cambrian tradition, and of the existence of Welsh Indians. His work has not, I believe, yet seen the light; but if the affidavits were those of the Rev. Morgan Jones and Colonel Crochan, they will be found in the present Essay." Stephens, *Madoc*, p. 86.

[83] The American Civil War, 1861–1865.

RETROSPECTIVE

IN HIS three-part essay on 'The Story of Prince Madog's Discovery of America' published in the *Red Dragon* a decade after Thomas Stephens's death,[1] Edward Owen noted that as Iolo Morganwg was 'endowed with indefatigable energy, burning with a patriotism that was ever at the white heat of enthusiasm, and possessed with the idea that whatever redoubled to the glory of Cambria must be accepted and supported with implicit faith and unwavering devotion' it was 'no wonder he exercised such power over his contemporaries as to warp their judgement and take captive their common sense'.[2] As the controversies in which Stephens was embroiled show, Owen could well have extended this influence to many of the prominent figures of nineteenth-century Wales. However, he also notes that Iolo's 'influence upon the minds of his countrymen is only now losing its hold through the advance of a more scientific and critical method' of scholarship and draws attention to the debt owed by modern Welsh scholars to Thomas Stephens for his 'steadfast opposition through much evil report to the wild speculations and monstrous assumptions of the Morganwg school, and to his firm purpose of proving all things and holding to those alone which he believed to be true'.[3] It is fair to say that Owen's essay owes much to Stephen's scholarship, clearly acknowledged in the closing portion of the work in which he laments that Stephen's full, reworked essay on Madoc had not yet been published.

Stephen's highly critical and scientific approach has been seen as a precursor to the more sustained and lasting dismissal of

---

[1] Edward Owen, 'The Story of Prince Madoc's Discovery of America', *Red Dragon*, 8 (1885), 546–60; Idem., 'The Story of Prince Madoc's Discovery of America, II', *Red Dragon*, 9 (1886), 172–83; Idem., 'The Story of Prince Madoc's Discovery of America, III', *Red Dragon*, 9 (1886), 342–53.

[2] Owen, 'Story of Prince Madoc's Discovery of America, II', 181–82.

[3] Ibid., 182.

mythic, romantic historiography in Wales which would follow over a generation later—Prys Morgan has even credited the Madogian scandal at Llangollen with 'destroy[ing] the credibility of Welsh Romantic scholarship'.[4] As Marion Löffler has shown, from the turn of the twentieth century the dominance of the bardic myths and legendry championed by the successors of Iolo Morganwg against which Stephens had set himself began to erode under the pressure of professional and critical historiography, culminating in Griffith John Williams's exposure of Iolo as the author of poems attributed to Dafydd ap Gwilym and Rhys Goch ap Rhicert.[5] In 1896, Sir John Morris-Jones dismantled the historic foundations of the Gorsedd of the Bards of the Isle of Britain in a lengthy essay published in instalments in the journal *Cymru*, believing that it was 'high time for the nation more clearly to understand the truth' of the institution's history and the 'fiction and fraud on which its assertions are based'.[6] Morris-Jones built conspicuously on the groundwork which Stephens had laid in the mid-1850s, and Stephens's articles are referenced throughout the series. In 1911, Morris-Jones published a summary of his essay in his new journal *Y Beirniad* ('The Critic') in which he acknowledged Stephens's contribution strikingly by using Stephens's own words for the climax of his argument:

> One thing, however, is certain: that the new druidism is fraud and deceit, devised to prop up lies concerning poetic metres and bardic traditions. I cannot do better than to cite the words of the critic and historian Thomas Stephens from the *Archaeologia Cambrensis*. 1872. p. 182:

---

[4] Morgan, 'Mid Victorian Wales and Its Crisis of Identity' in Laurence Brockliss and David Eastwood (eds), *A Union of Multiple Identities: The British Isles, c.1750–c.1850* (Manchester: Manchester University Press, 1997), 95–109 (p. 98).

[5] Löffler, *The Literary and Historical Legacy of Iolo Morganwg*, pp. 137–46.

[6] John Morris-Jones, 'Gorsedd Beirdd Ynys Prydain', *Cymru*, 10 (1896), 21–29, 133–40, 153–61, 197–204; 293–99 (21): 'mi gredaf ei bod hi yn hwyr bryd i'r wlad ddeall yn eglurach wir hanes yr Orsedd, a'r ffug a'r twyll yr seilir ei honiadau arnynt'.

'The Chair of Glamorgan has falsified the history of bardism, corrupted the genealogies of Glamorgan, vitiated the chronicles of Gwent and Morgannwg, and given such currency to "a falsehood, a delusion, and a snare," that the author of the *Celtic Researches* was almost the only Welshman sagacious enough to detect the forgery, strong-minded enough to resist its seductions, and honest enough to expose its real character.'[7]

Just as Stephens looked back to Edward 'Celtic' Davies as a vital voice against the siren's call of history based on flattering legendry rather than sound scholarship, this new generation of scholars acknowledged Stephens's voice in the mid-nineteenth century debate over the character of Welsh history and literature.

Neil Evans has noted that increasingly in nineteenth-century historiography 'Myth was no longer enough. Footnotes and a critical approach to sources were also necessary'.[8] This shift did not occur overnight, requiring lengthy and impassioned debate across the mid- to late-nineteenth century in order to balance the cultural need to retain cherished myths and legends integral to national identity against the rigours imposed by modern scholarship and the respectability it afforded.[9] As Löffler has noted, Stephen set the parameters for this process,[10] challenging cultural institutions and beliefs through establishing boundaries between fact and fantasy. From his critique of the old guard in his

---

[7] 'Un peth, fodd bynnag, sydd sicr: mai twill a hoced yw'r dderwyddiaeth newydd, wedi ei dyfesio i atgell celwyddau am fesurai cerdd a thraddodiadau'r beirdd. Nid allaf wneuthur yn well na dyfynnu geiriau'r beirniad a'r hanesydd Thomas Stephens o'r *Arch. Camb.* 1872, td. 182'. The quoted material by Stephens is in English. Idem., 'Derwyddiaeth Gorsedd y Beirdd', *Y Beirniad*, I (1911), 66–72 (71–72).

[8] Neil Evans, 'Finding a New Story: The Search for a Usable Past in Wales, 1869–1930', *Transactions of the Honourable Society of Cymmrodorion*, New Series, 10 (2004), 144–62 (145).

[9] See Evans, 'Finding a New Story'; Morgan, 'Early Victorian Wales and its Crisis of Identity', pp. 97–98.

[10] Löffler, 'Failed Founding Fathers', p. 70.

early letters in the *Cambrian*,[11] to his 'laying violent hands upon the old household furniture of venerable tradition' in *Literature of the Kymry*,[12] to his systematic disproof of invented traditions and contemporary promotion of provable Welsh contributions to history, Stephens's scholarly career constantly provoked debate over the nature and meaning of the Welsh past.

The letters collected in this anthology record the development of that career, but, with their focus on the importance of scholarly networks of knowledge exchange to it, they also show that Stephens was not a lone voice of reason in the face of romantic credulity. From letters offering guidance and encouragement for his early career and in his various controversies, to letters which solicit his help and advice on various matters, they show Stephens as a prominent participant within a wider scholarly republic of letters. This republic was international in nature, showing the growing importance of international, collaborative, comparative approaches to the past which Stephens and others increasingly pursued. Still, Stephens's contribution in challenging the romantic orthodoxy of his day was justly held as an exemplar by many the scholars who followed. As the letters collected here show, his international scholarly reputation was built on the gathering and exchange of knowledge, and the social and scholarly support, of a wide range of writers from Wales, Britain, Europe, and the wider world.

---

11 See Löffler and Rhys, 'Thomas Stephens and the Abergavenny Cymreigyddion'; Eadem, 'Thomas Stephens a llythyru cyhoeddus yng Nghymru Oes Victoria'.

12 Stephens, *Literature of the Kymry*, p. 207.

APPENDICES

APPENDIX A:
NOTABLE CORRESPONDENTS

THE following is a list of some of the notable people who appear in this volume as the writers or addressees of letters collected in this volume.

Edward Lowry Barnwell (1813–1887) was a Welsh antiquarian and schoolmaster. He was heavily involved with the Cambrian Archaeological Association, serving as its secretary from 1854 to 1875, and periodically as editor of *Archaeologia Cambrensis*, as well as contributing many papers and articles to the journal.[1]

Richard Rolt Brash (1817–1876) was an Irish architect and antiquarian. His profession as an architect led to an interest in ecclesiastical architecture and archaeology, on which subjects he published several works. As his letters to Stephens show, Brash was a frequent contributor to *Archaeologia Cambrenisis* and an attendee of Cambrian Archaeological Association meetings as well as contributing to other journals in Ireland and Britain such as the *Proceedings of the Royal Irish Academy*, *Proceedings of the Antiquaries of Scotland* and, especially, the *Journal of the Kilkenny Archaeological Society*. In addition to his many articles, he also published *The Ecclesiastical Architecture of Ireland to the Close of the Twelfth Century* (1875) and his extensive notes on ogham inscriptions was edited posthumously and published as *The Ogham Inscribed Monuments of the Gaedhil in the British Isles* (1879).[2]

George Thomas Clark (1809–1898) was a London-born engineer and antiquary. He was largely responsible for the

---

[1] *Dictionary of Welsh Biography*, s.v. 'Barnwell, Edward Lowry'.

[2] Anon. 'Three Memorable Cork Archaeologists', *Journal of the Cork Historical and Archaeological Society*, 6: 45 (1900), 32–47 (39–42).

running of Dowlais Ironworks, near Merthyr Tydfil, from 1852–1897. Clark was an avid antiquarian who took a great interest in the history of south Wales, particularly medieval castles. He was active in the Cambrian Archaeological Association and in 1843 he helped to found the Royal Archaeological Institute. He also had a great interest in social issues including health and education, and served as an investigator, and later a commissioner, of the General Board of Health.[3]

Walter Davies (Gwallter Mechain) (1761–1849) was a prominent Welsh poet, historian, litterateur, antiquarian, and cleric of Llanrhaeadr-ym-Mochnant from 1837. One of 'yr hen bersoniaid llengar', he was closely associated with the London-based Gwyneddigion Society, and was heavily involved with burgeoning local eisteddfodau. He published works on a wide range of subjects including *Rhyddid: Traethawd a Ennillodd Ariandlws y Gwyneddigion* (1791), *Diwygiad neu Ddinystr* (1798), which was a translation of a work by T. Bowdler, and a *General View of the Agriculture and Domestic Economy of North Wales* (1813) as well as editing the poetry of Huw Morris and Lewis Glyn Cothi (with John Jones (Tegid)).[4]

Alfred Erny (b.1838) was a French author who travelled to Wales in 1862 with the French historian, Henri Martin. An account of their tour of Wales was published as Alfred Erny, 'Voyage dans le pays de Galles', *Le Tour de Monde*, 15: 1 (1867), 257–88.[5]

Daniel Silvan Evans (1818–1903) was a notable Welsh cleric, editor, translator and lexicographer. He was an editor of *Archaeologia Cambrensis* and was appointed examiner in Welsh at St David's College Lampeter in 1873 and as professor of Welsh at University College Aberystwyth in 1875. In 1897 he was

---

[3] *Dictionary of Welsh Biography*, s.v. Clark, George Thomas. See Brian Ll. James (ed.), *G. T. Clark: Scholar Ironmaster in the Victorian Age* (Cardiff, University of Wales Press, 1998).

[4] *Dictionary of Welsh Biography*, s.v. 'Davies, Walter (Gwallter Mechain)'.

[5] See also Williams, 'La construction du Moyen Âge dans les récits de voyage français portant sur le pays de Galles, ou'.

elected to a three-year fellowship of £100 a year at Jesus College, Oxford, and in 1901 was given a D.Litt by the University of Wales. His notable editorial work included two editions of Ellis Wynne's *Y Bardd Cwsg* (1853, 1865), Lewis Morris's *Celtic Remains* (1878), three volumes of the works of Walter Davies (Gwallter Mechain) (1866–1869), and the second edition of Stephens's *Literature of the Kymry* (1876). He also published a work on Welsh orthography entitled *Llythyraeth yr Iaith Gymraeg* (1856), and the first four volumes of his dictionary *Geiriadur Cymraeg* (1887–1896).[6]

Henry Griffiths (1812–1892) was a Welsh Independent minister and educationalist. From 1842–1853 he was the senior tutor of Brecon Independent College. He was a firm supporter of the voluntarist cause in education, served as the secretary of the voluntarist college at Brecon and in 1848 published a pamphlet on *Education in Wales*.[7]

Charlotte Guest (later Schreiber) (1812–1895), is perhaps best known as the translator of the collection of medieval Welsh prose tales, *The Mabinogion* (1838–49), into English. She married the Welsh Ironmaster of Dowlais Ironworks and MP for Merthyr Tydfil, John Josiah Guest, in 1833 and later took over the management of the works upon his death in 1852. She championed education, establishing a notable and progressive school at the works. Her interest in Welsh history and literature began soon after her arrival in Wales in the 1830s, when she became involved in the Abergavenny Cymreigyddion Society and developed notable relationships with Thomas Price (Carnhuanawc), John Jones (Tegid), and Lady Augusta Hall of Llanover. In April 1855, she married Charles Schreiber, whom she had employed as a tutor for her eldest son Ivor. The Schreibers spent much of their time away from Wales collecting ceramics, and from this period her involvement with Welsh affairs diminished greatly.[8]

---

[6] *Dictionary of Welsh Biography*, s.v. 'Evans, Daniel Silvan'.

[7] Ibid., s.v. 'Griffiths, Henry'.

[8] Ibid., s.v. 'Guest (Schreiber) Lady Charlotte Elizabeth Bertie'. See Guest and

Daniel Henry Haigh (1819–1879) was an English anti-
quarian and notable Roman Catholic. His antiquarian interests
included numismatics, Anglo-Saxon history and antiquities,
Assyrian history, and biblical archaeology. He published essays
in various antiquarian journals as well as works including *An
Essay on the Numismatic History of the Ancient History of the
Angles* (1845), *The Conquest of Britain by the Saxons* (1861), and
*The Anglo-Saxon Sagas: an Examination of their Value as Aids to
History* (1861).[9]

**Augusta Hall (née Waddington) (Gwenynen Gwent, Lady
Llanover) (1802–1896)** was a Welsh cultural patron and
advocate, perhaps best known for her invention of the Welsh
national costume. She was heavily involved with the Abergavenny Cymreigyddion Society, and it was through her that
many of that society's connections with European scholars were
forged. She was, for instance, sister-in-law to Christian Carl Josias
von Bunsen. She also encouraged and assisted other scholars,
including Maria Jane Williams and Daniel Silvan Evans, even
financing publications. In 1853, Lady Hall and her husband Sir
Benjamin Hall purchased Iolo Morganwg's manuscripts from the
widow of Taliesin ab Iolo. These were preserved at Llanover Hall
for the benefit of Welsh scholars.[10]

Harry Longueville Jones (1806–1807) was a Welsh cleric
and antiquarian. He studied at Cambridge and was ordained as a
deacon in 1829 and as a priest in 1831. In 1834 he married and
moved to Paris, where he lived until 1846 when he settled at
Beaumaris, Anglesey. In 1846, he was appointed an inspector of
church schools for Wales, a position he held until 1864. Jones was
elected a fellow of the Society of Antiquaries in 1841, and in 1846
he, along with John Williams (ab Ithel) began the journal

John, *Lady Charlotte Guest*.

[9] *Oxford Dictionary of National Biography*, s.v. 'Haigh, Daniel Henry'.

[10] Prys Morgan, 'Lady Llanover (1802–1896), 'Gwenynen Gwent'', *Transaction
of the Honourable Society of Cymmrodorion*, New Series, 13 (2007), 94–107;
Dictionary of Welsh Biography, s.v. 'Hall, Augusta, Lady Llanover ("Gwenynen
Gwent")'.

Archaeologia Cambrensis, which led to the founding of the Cambrian Archaeological Association in 1847. Differences between Williams's bardic approach to Welsh antiquities and Jones's more scientific scholarship and views led to Williams's departure in 1853, but Jones remained editor of the journal until his death, often at personal financial loss.[11]

William Basil Jones (Tickell) (1822-1897) was a Welsh cleric and antiquarian and Bishop of St Davids from 1874. He was heavily involved with the Cambrian Archaeological Association, attending every meeting from 1849–1854. He served as one of the secretaries from 1848–1851, as joint editor of *Archaeologia Cambrensis* in 1854, and as president in 1875 and 1878. His major works include *Vestiges of the Gael in Gwynedd* (1851) and *The History and Antiquities of St Davids* (with E. A. Freeman, 1852–57).[12]

Théodore Claude Henri, vicomte Hersart de la Villemarqué (1815-1895) was a Breton scholar, best known for his collection of Breton folk-songs, *Barzaz-Breiz* (1839). The songs in this collection were heavily adapted by La Villemarqué and displayed as illustrative of the history of Brittany from the age of the druids to the present, coloured by the author's Romantic views of that history. He also had a wider interest in the Breton, Welsh, and 'Celtic' past, including in Arthurian legends. Indeed, Mary-Ann Constantine has described him as 'a positive magnet for all things faux-antique', and his Romantic sensibilities and less-than-meticulous use of sources makes his correspondence with Stephens of particular interest. La Villemarqué also corresponded with other Welsh scholars, notably Thomas Price (Carnhuanawc), and visited Wales in 1837–1838 where he was made a Bard of the Isle of Britain at the

---

[11] *Dictionary of Welsh Biography*, s.v. 'Jones, Harry Longueville'; *Oxford Dictionary of National Biography*, s.v. 'Jones, Harry Longueville'.

[12] *Dictionary of Welsh Biography*, s.v. 'Jones, William Basil'; *Oxford Dictionary of National Biography*, s.v. 'Jones, (William) Basil'.

1837 Abergavenny Cymreigyddion Society Eisteddfod and stayed with both the Halls and the Guests.[13]

Mary Pendrill Llewelyn (née Mary Catherine Rhys) (1811–1874), was a Welsh translator and writer best known for her translations of Welsh hymns, particularly those of William Williams, Pantycelyn. Her husband, the Revd R. Pendrill Llewelyn, was vicar of Llangynwyd, near Maes-teg, Glamorgan.[14]

Henri Martin (1810–1883) was a French historian best-known for his fifteen-volume *Histoire de France* (1833–1836) and six-volume *Histoire de France depuis 1789 husqu'à nos jours* (1878–1883). Martin was also a liberal and nationalist republican politician, particularly active during the Third Republic, his historiographical approach mirroring his idealisation of the French character as demonstrated in French history. In his historical research he was especially interested in the ancient Celts, particularly the Gauls and the Druidic religion, regarding them as embodying the ideals of liberty, equality, and fraternity which marked French republicanism. Within this, supposedly Celtic concepts of the immortality and reincarnation of the soul were particularly integral to his ideals of Gallic liberty. His often less-than-scientific approach to the Celtic past makes his correspondence with Thomas Stephens related to the history of bardism and druidism of particular interest.[15]

Carl Meyer (*c.*1801–*c.*1884) was a German scholar and librarian. In 1842, Meyer won a prize at the Abergavenny Cymreigyddion Society Eisteddfod, set and sponsored by Christian von Bunsen, on the place of Welsh among the Celtic Languages and the relationship of Celtic languages to Indo-European languages, adjudged by James Cowles Prichard, a translation of which by Jane Williams (Ysgafell) was published in

---

[13] Mary-Ann Constantine, '"Impertinent Structures": A Breton's Adventures in Neo-Gothic Wales', *Studies in Travel Writing*, 18:2 (2014), 134–147 (quote from p. 136).

[14] *Dictionary of Welsh Biography*, s.v. 'Llewelyn, Mary Pendrill'.

[15] Charles Rearick, 'Henry Martin: From Druidic Traditions to Republican Politics', *Journal of Contemporary History*, 7: 3/4 (July–October 1972), 53–64.

the *Cambrian Journal* in 1854. Meyer toured Wales in 1843–1845 in order to study Welsh language and culture, visiting prominent Welsh scholars and cultural figures such as William Rees, John Jones (Tegid), Thomas Price (Carnhuanawc), W. J. Rees (Casgob), Walter Davies (Gwallter Mechain), Bishop Connop Thirlwall and Lady Augusta Hall. In 1846 he was appointed the German Secretary and Librarian to Albert, the Prince Consort, in which position he accepted Thomas Stephens's *Literature of the Kymry* on behalf of the Prince. He seems to have been dismissed from this position in 1850 and returned to Germany in the early 1850s.[16]

Friedrich Max Müller (1823–1900) was a German-English philologist based in Oxford. In 1844, Müller studied in Berlin under Franz Bopp and the philosopher Friedrich Schelling, before moving to Paris where he undertook a major work — the first printed edition of the *Rig Veda*. In 1846, he moved to England, where he became acquainted with Christian von Bunsen and Horace Hayman Wilson who persuaded the East India Company to print his *Rig Veda* (1849–1874). In 1851 he secured a position at Oxford as the deputy Taylorian Professor of Modern European languages, and full professor in 1854. The chair of comparative philology was created specifically for him in 1868. Müller was a leading figure in the fields of Vedic studies, comparative philology, and comparative mythology, wherein he advocated ideas of the 'disease of language' and 'solar mythology', clashing notably with British anthropologists and folklorists such as E. B. Tylor and Andrew Lang. His works included *Chips from a German Workshop* (1867–75) and *Contributions to the Science of Mythology* (1897).[17]

---

[16] Marion Löffler, 'Bunsen, Müller a Meyer: Tri Almaenwr, y Gymraeg, Y Frenhines a'r Ymerodraeth', *Y Traethodydd*, Ionawr 2018, 19–32, esp 21–23.

[17] *Oxford Dictionary of National Biography*, s.v. 'Müller, Friedrich Max'; Richard M. Dorson, 'The Eclipse of Solar Mythology', *The Journal of American Folklore*, 68: 270 (October–December 1955), 393–416; Guiseppe Cocchiara, *The History of Folklore in Europe*, trans. by John N. McDaniel (Philadelphia: Institute for the Study of Human Issues, 1981), pp. 277–95.

David William Nash (d. *c.*1876–7) was a Cheltenham-based writer on Welsh literature, history, and antiquities. He was a member of the Cambrian Institute, 1858–1864, and was elected a Fellow of the Society of Antiquaries in 1864. In additions to contributions made to the *Cambrian Journal*, he published several works, the most notable of which were his *On the Antiquity of the Egyptian Calendar* (1845), *Taliesin, or the Bards and Druids of Britain* (1858), and *On the Battle of Cattraeth and the Gododin of Aneurin* (1861).[18]

Eugene O'Curry (Eoghan Ó Comhraí) (1794–1862) was an Irish scholar. From 1835–1842 he worked with John O'Donovan on the topographical and historical section of the Irish ordinance survey. Around the same time he was engaged in making copies of important manuscripts for the Royal Irish Academy and from 1842 he was employed on the initiative of James Henthorn Todd and Charles Graves to catalogue the Irish manuscripts held there. O'Curry was made a member of the Royal Irish Academy in 1853 and became professor of Irish history and archaeology at the Catholic University in Dublin in 1854. From 1852, he worked with O'Donovan on the publication of all known Irish law texts, with O'Curry focusing on texts in the British Museum and Bodleian Library. *The Ancient Laws and Institutes of Ireland* was published after both men's deaths between 1865 and 1901.[19]

John O'Donovan (Seán Ó Donnabháin) (1806–1881) was an Irish scholar. From 1830, he worked on the Irish Ordinance Survey as an orthographer and etymologist in order to arrive at a standard English orthography of Irish place names, acquiring a great knowledge of Irish language, antiquities, history, folklore, and manuscripts, and becoming acquainted with other anti-quarians such as George Petrie and Eugene O'Curry. In 1836, he also worked at Trinity College Dublin, cataloguing manuscripts. O'Donovan is best known for his transcriptions, translations, and editions of Irish manuscripts, including *The Banquet of Dun na*

---

[18] *Dictionary of Welsh Biography*, s.v. 'Nash, David William'.
[19] *Dictionary of Irish Biography*, s.v. 'O'Curry (Curry, Ó Comhraí), Eugene (Eoghan)'.

nGedh and the Battle of Magh Rath (1842), *Leabhar na gceart or the Book of Rights* (1847), and *Annála Rioghachta Éireann: Annals of the Kingdom of Ireland, by the Four Masters* (1848–1851). He also published a *Grammar of the Irish Language* in 1845. From 1852 he, along with Eugene O'Curry, was appointed by the British government to publish all known Irish law texts. *The Ancient Laws and Institutes of Ireland* was published after both men's deaths between 1865 and 1901. In 1848, O'Donovan was awarded the Cunnington medal for his work by the Royal Irish Academy. From 1849 he was appointed Professor of Celtic Languages at Queens College, Belfast, he was given an honorary LLD by Dublin University in 1850 and in 1856 became a member of the Preussische Akademie der Wissenschaften, Berlin, on the recommendation of Jakob Grimm.[20]

Aneurin Owen (1792–1851) was a Welsh scholar and historian, and the son of William Owen Pughe (1759–1835). From 1825, he edited the laws of Hywel Dda, which appeared in 1841 as *Ancient Laws and Institutes of Wales*. He also compiled a list of the Welsh manuscripts of north Wales, which was printed by the Cymmrodorion Society in 1843, and edited the *Brut y Tywysogion*, which was published posthumously.[21]

Adolphe Pictet (1799–1875) was a Swiss comparative linguist, philologist, and Celticist, best known for his investigations of the relationships between Celtic and other Indo-European languages. His works include, *De l'affinité des langues celtiques avec le sanscrit* (1837), *Essai sur quelques inscriptions en langue gauloise* (1859), and *Les origines indo-européennes, ou les Aryas primitifs* (1859–1963).[22]

Thomas Price (Carnhuanawc) (1787–1848) was a notable Welsh historian, antiquarian and Vicar of Llanfihangel Cwm-du, Breconshire. One of *'yr hen bersoniaid llengar'*, he was heavily involved with the Abergavenny Cymreigyddion Society, had a

---

[20] Ibid., s.v. 'O'Donovan (Ó Donnabháin), John (Seán)'.
[21] *Dictionary of Welsh Biography*, s.v. Owen, Aneurin.
[22] *Lexikon der Schweiz*, s.v. 'Pictet, Adolphe'.

keen interest in the connection between Welsh and Breton, and championed the Welsh language.[23]

John Bruce Pryce (1784–1872), brother of William Bruce Knight (1785–1845) and father to the politician Henry Austin Bruce (1815–1895), was a Welsh antiquarian.[24]

Isaac Redwood (1792–1873) was a prominent Quaker tanner in Neath. Notably, he and his brothers were friendly with Iolo Morganwg, supported him financially in his final years, and served as trustees of his will.[25] According to a manuscript biography of Stephens,

> during his school days at Neath he was a frequent visitor a the house of Mr. Redwood a Quaker, and in years after he used to recall with gratitude the kindness he received from him and from whom he used to say that he had learnt the value of plain yeas and no. [...] It is very likely that the early impressions derived from his visits to this Quaker gentleman influenced his after life, for reticence of speech and manner was a distinct feature of his character.[26]

Jonathan Rees (*d.*1869) was a prominent Quaker and member of Neath society, whom D. Rhys Phillips described as a 'fearless advocate of civil and religious liberty'. He was the brother of Evan Rees, the Quaker writer and first Corresponding Secretary of the Peace Society. Jonathan published *Memoirs of Evan Rees, consisting chiefly of Extracts from his Letters* in 1853.[27]

William Rees (1808–1873) was a notable Welsh printer and publisher from Ton near Llandovery. In 1829 he and his uncle, D. R. Rees, began a press at Llandovery which soon became one of the most notable in Wales, publishing Charlotte Guest's *Mabinogion* (1848–49), Robert Williams's *Eminent Welshmen*

---

[23] *Dictionary of Welsh Biography*, s.v. 'Price, Thomas (Carnhuanawc)'.

[24] Ibid., s.v. 'Bruce, Henry Austin'.

[25] D. Rhys Phillips, *History of the Vale of Neath*, p. 445; Geraint H. Jenkins, Ffion Mair Jones, and David Ceri Jones, *The Correspondence of Iolo Morganwg*, three vols (Cardiff: University of Wales Press, 2007), III: p. 798.

[26] NLW, MS. 966C, p. 3

[27] Phillips, *History of the Vale of Neath*, pp. 446–47.

(1852), and *The Literary Remains of the Rev. Thomas Price, Carnhuanawc* (1854–55), in addition to Stephens's *Literature of the Kymry*.[28]

William Rushton was Professor of History and English Literature at Queen's College, Cork and an active member of the Cambrian Institute.

Albert Schulz (San Marte) (1802–1893) was a German Arthurian scholar and medievalist. In 1841, Schulz won a prize at an Abergavenny Cymreigyddion Society Eisteddfod for 'The Influence of Welsh Tradition upon the Literature of Germany, France, and Scandinavia' which was translated into English and published the same year. His interest in Welsh, as well as Arthur, led him to publish several other related works, notably *Nennius und Gildas* (1844), *Gottfried von Monmouth Histori Regum Britanniae* (1853) and *Die Sagen von Merlin* (1853). He also translated Stephens's *Literature of the Kymry* into German and published it as *Geschichte der wälschen Literatur vom XII bis zum XIV Jahrhundert* (1864).[29]

Charlotte Schreiber (1812–1895), see Charlotte Guest.

William Forbes Skene (1809–1892) was a major Scottish historian and Celticist. His major works included editions of *The Highlands of Scotland, their Origin, History, and Antiquities* (1837), *Chronicles of the Picts and Scots* (1867), *The Four Ancient Books of Wales* (1868), John of Fordun's *Cronica gentis Scotorum* (1871–2), and his *magnum opus*, *Celtic Scotland: A History of Ancient Alban* (1876–1880).[30]

Ebenezer Thomas (Eben Fardd) (1802–1863) was a Welsh schoolmaster and poet, considered one of the leading poets of the nineteenth century. He participated in eisteddfodau throughout his life, both as a competitor and an adjudicator, and also took an

---

[28] *Dictionary of Welsh Biography*, s.v. 'Rees, William'.

[29] *Allgemeine Deutsche Biographie*, s.v. Schulz, Albert'; Edith Gruber, 'King Arthur and the Privy Councillor: Albert Schulz as a Cultural Mediator Between the Literary Fields of Nineteenth-century Wales and Germany', unpublished PhD thesis, Bangor University, 2013.

[30] *Oxford Dictionary of National Biography*, s.v 'Skene, William Forbes'.

interest in the local antiquarianism of Clynnog on the Llŷn peninsula.[31]

James Henthorn Todd (1805–1869) was an Irish librarian, cleric, scholar and antiquarian. Todd was the assistant librarian at Trinity College Dublin from 1831 and the librarian from 1851. He was appointed regius professor of Hebrew in 1849 and a senior fellow in 1850. Elected a member of the Royal Irish Academy in 1833, Todd took an active part, becoming a member of the council in 1837 and serving as secretary from 1847 to 1855 and president from 1856 to 1861. He contributed over fifty papers on a variety of subjects to the *Proceedings of the Royal Irish Academy*. His publications included *The Book of Obits and Martyrology of Christ Church* (1844), *St Patrick, Apostle of Ireland* (1864), *The Book of Vaudois* (1865), and *Cogadh Gaedhel re Gallaibh: The War of the Gaedhil with the Gaill* (1867).[32]

Thomas Wakeman (1778–1868) was a Monmouthshire-based antiquarian and Justice of the Peace who collected extensive notes on Monmouthshire antiquities and contributed frequent articles and essays to Monmouthshire-based antiquarian journals as well as *Archaeologia Cambrensis*.[33]

Thomas Watts (1811–1869) was an English librarian. From 1838 he worked as an assistant at the library of the British Museum, where he was responsible for the acquisition of foreign titles and the organisation of books. Watts spoke many languages including western European languages (including Welsh), Slavonic languages, Hungarian, and several eastern Asian languages. He was appointed assistant keeper in 1856 and in 1857 became the first superintendent of the new reading room. He also published articles and essays in a variety of periodicals and reference works throughout his life.[34]

William Robert Wills Wilde (1815–1876) was an Irish surgeon, archaeologist, antiquarian, biographer, naturalist,

---

[31] *Dictionary of Welsh Biography*, s.v. 'Thomas, Ebenezer'.
[32] *Dictionary of Irish Biography*, s.v. 'Todd, James Henthorn'.
[33] 'Obituary', *Archaeologia Cambrensis*, Third Series, 55 (July 1868), 340–41.
[34] *Oxford Dictionary of National Biography*, s.v. 'Watts, Thomas'.

statistician, topographer, and folklorist. After studying eye and ear surgery in London, Vienna, and Berlin, he set up his practice in Dublin, which included a dispensary for poor patients in a converted stable. In 1845 he took over the editorship of the *Dublin Journal of Medical Science*, and in 1846 began the *Dublin Quarterly Journal of Medical Science*. In 1853 he became oculist in ordinary to Queen Victoria in Ireland. His interest in folklore having been stimulated when he was a child (he published *Irish Popular Superstitions* in 1852) he was elected a member of the Royal Irish Academy in 1839, devoting much of his time to antiquarian interests, including excursions, and completing the catalogue of the Royal Irish Academy's Irish antiquities which had been begun by George Petrie. He was assistant commissioner for the 1841 and 1851 censuses. It was in connection with his work on these censuses that he undertook research on the history of disease and famine in Ireland, which is the subject of much of his correspondence with Stephens. He was bestowed the Order of the Polar Star by Carl XV of Sweden in 1862, a knighthood in 1864 for his work on the Irish censuses, and the Cunnington gold medal in 1873. Among his publications are *A Narrative of a Voyage to Madeira, Teneriffe, and along the Shores of the Mediterranean* (1839), *The Beauties of the Boyne* (1849), *Practical Observations on Aural Surgery* (1853), *Lough Corrib, its Shores and Islands* (1867), and *Memoir of Gabriel Béranger* (1880) as well as countless contributions to medical, antiquarian, and biographical journals. He was the father of the playwright, poet, and prose writer Oscar Wilde, and the husband of the poet, nationalist and folklorist Lady Jane Wilde (Speranza).[35]

William Walker Wilkins was the author of *Political Ballads of the Seventeenth and Eighteenth Centuries*, two vols. (London: Longman, Green, Longman, and Roberts, 1860).

Jane Williams (Ysgafell) (1806–1885) was a Welsh writer and historian. Before moving to London in 1856, Ysgafell lived at Neuadd Felen, near Talgarth, Breconshire where she became associated with Lady Augusta Hall of Llanover and other noted

---

[35] *Dictionary of Irish Biography*, s.v. 'Wilde, Sir William Robert Wills'.

Welsh historians, antiquarians, and writers. Among her best known works are *Miscellaneous Poems* (1824), *Artegall; or Remarks on the Reports of the Commissioners of Inquiry into the State of Education in Wales* (1848), *The Autobiography of Elizabeth Davis: A Balaclava Nurse* (1857), *The Literary Remains of the Rev. Thomas Price, Carnhuanawc* (1854–55), *The Literary Women of England* (1861), *Celtic Fables, Fairy Tales and Legends Versified* (1862), and her *History of Wales Derived from Authentic Sources* (1869).[36]

John Williams (1792–1858) was a cleric, schoolmaster, and classical scholar. He was Archdeacon of Cardigan from 1833 and the first warden of Llandovery College 1848–1853.[37]

Maria Jane Williams (Llinos) (c.1795–1873) was a noted folk-collector and folk-musician, perhaps best known for her *Ancient National Airs of Gwent and Morganwg* (1844), which won a prize at an Abergavenny Cymreigyddion Society Eisteddfod in 1838. She was involved with that society and worked in cooperation with several other notable scholars, including the musician John Parry (Bardd Alaw), the Irish folklorists Thomas Crofton Croker and Thomas Price (Carnhuanawc).[38]

Morris Williams (Nicander) (1809–1874) was a Welsh cleric, poet, and writer. He matriculated at Jesus College, Oxford, in 1832 and received a B.A. and M.A. from that college in 1835 and 1838 respectively. He served several parishes in north Wales and was one of the pioneers of the Oxford Movement in the Diocese of Bangor. He was a frequent competitor at eisteddfodau and contributor to Welsh periodicals. He also assisted in the revision of the Welsh version of the Book of Common Prayer and translated Aesop's Fables into Welsh.[39]

---

[36] *Dictionary of Welsh Biography*, s.v. 'Williams, James'.

[37] Ibid., s.v. 'Williams, John'.

[38] Ibid., s.v. 'Williams, Maria Jane'. See also Daniel Huws, 'Introduction' to Maria Jane Williams, *Ancient National Airs of Gwent and Morganwg*, ed. by Daniel Huws ([N. P.]: The Welsh Folk-Song Society, 1994), pp. xxv–xxxviii, esp. pp. xxv–xxviii.

[39] *Dictionary of Welsh Biography*, s.v. 'Williams, Morris (Nicander)'.

William Watkin Edward Wynne (1801–1880) was a Welsh politician and antiquarian. He was MP for Merionethshire from 1852–1865 and High Sheriff of that county in 1867. From 1859, he became the custodian of the Hengwrt manuscripts, which he inherited from Sir Robert Williams Vaughan, allowing Welsh scholars access to, and providing advice about, these valuable sources. He was an active member of the Cambrian Archaeological Association, serving as president in 1850, and contributed around forty articles to *Archaeologia Cambrensis* including a catalogue of his manuscripts. He also contributed numerous articles to *Montgomeryshire Collections*, *Y Cymmrodor*, and *Bye-Gones* and published several books.[40]

---

[40] Ibid., s.v. 'Wynne family, of Peniarth, Mer.'.

THE following is a list of some of the notable people mentioned in the letters collected in this volume. Some of the people listed here also corresponded with Stephens themselves, although their letters have not been selected for this anthology.

John R. Bartlett (1805–1886) was an American ethnologist, philologist, and historian, perhaps best-known today for his *Dictionary of Americanisms* (1848). From 1850 he was the United States commissioner of the Mexican Boundary Survey tasked with negotiating the U.S. Boundary with Mexico following the Treaty of Guadalupe Hidalgo (1848), causing great controversy with his decision to concede the Mesilla Valley to Mexico. He published his *Personal Narrative* of his experience working on the commission in 1854. In 1855 he was elected Secretary of State for Rhode Island, during which time he published *Records of the Colony of Rhode Island and the Providence Plantations* (ten vols, 1856–65). He also compiled several volumes on the literature of the American Civil War and produced a catalogue of colonial Americana housed at the John Carter Brown Library.[1]

Christian Carl Josias von Bunsen (1791–1860) was a notable Prussian diplomat and scholar who served as Prussian diplomat to Rome before becoming the Prussian Ambassador to the Court of St James (1841–1854). The husband of Francis Waddington Bunsen, the sister of Lady Augusta Hall of Llanover, Bunsen was a prominent member of the Abergavenny Cymreigiddion Society and contributed greatly to facilitating continental European involvement in that society. In addition to being an important diplomat, Bunsen was also a highly capable

---

[1] *American National Biography*, s.v. 'Bartlett, John Russell'.

linguist and religious scholar, publishing many works throughout his life.[2]

Henry Octavius Coxe (1811–1881) was an English librarian and cleric who served as sub-librarian at the Bodleian from 1839 and librarian from 1860. Coxe also edited and published editions of several manuscripts and investigated manuscripts in Greece at the Government's behest in 1857. He was a curator of Oxford University's galleries, a delegate of Oxford University Press, and a chaplain of Corpus Christi College.[3]

Evan Davies (Myfyr Morganwg, previously Ieuan ap Dafydd, Ioan Morganwg, Ieuan Morganwg, and Ieuan Myfyr Uwch Celli) (1801–1888) was a Welsh bard and archdruid. Although he claimed to have received no formal education, Myfyr Morganwg took a keen interest in the study of bardic poetry, astronomy, mathematics, religion, history, and antiquities. In 1845 he settled in Pontypridd as a watchmaker and after the death of Taliesin ab Iolo in 1847 declared himself ab Iolo's successor as 'Archdruid of the Bards of the Isle of Britain'. From 1849 he began holding Gorseddau on equinoxes and solstices at the 'Maen Chwyf' (Rocking Stone), near Pontypridd, which he had worked to expand and 'restore' since the previous June. These ceremonies continued to be held until 1878. Myfyr became a notable figure in Wales, publishing several books on Druidism and participating in eisteddfodau, including the 1858 Llangollen Eisteddfod where he served as one of the adjudicators for the prize essay on the discovery of America by Madoc.[4]

---

[2] See Frances Baroness Bunsen, *A Memoir of Baron Bunsen: Late Minister Plenipotentiary and Envoy Extraordinary of His Majesty Fredric William IV. at the Court of St. James*, two vols (London: Longmans, Green, and Co. 1868). For his involvement with the Abergavenny Cymreigyddion Society see David Thorne, 'Cymreigyddion Y Fenni a Dechreuadau Ieitheg Cymharol yng Nghymru', *Cylchgrawn Llyfrgell Genedlaethol Cymru*, 27: 1 (Haf 1991), 97–107; Marion Löffler, 'Bunsen, Müller a Meyer: Tri Almaenwr, y Gymraeg, y Frenhines a'r Ymerodraeth', *Y Traethodydd* (Ionawr 2018), 19–32.

[3] *Oxford Dictionary of National Biography*, s.v. 'Coxe, Henry Octavius'.

[4] *Dictionary of Welsh Biography*, s.v. Davies, Evan (Myfyr Morganwg)'; Dillwyn

Evan Evans (Ieuan Fardd or Ieuan Brydydd Hir) (1731–1788) was a Welsh scholar, poet, and cleric. Regarded as one of the greatest scholars of eighteenth-century Wales, he was involved with the circle of scholars and patrons surrounding the Morris Brothers of Anglesey, especially Lewis Morris, as well as notable English poets such as Thomas Gray and Thomas Percy. In 1764 he published his most notable work, *Some Specimens of the Poetry of the Antient Welsh Bards*, which contained valuable transcriptions and translations of Welsh poetry, as well as essays (in English, Latin, and Welsh) by Evans on Welsh literature and bardism. From 1771 to 1778 he was patronized by Sir Watkin Williams Wynn II in order to utilize the library at Wynnstay as well as conduct further extensive research on Welsh manuscripts, compiling extensive notes and transcriptions for publication, although this never came to fruition.[5]

Theophilus Evans (1693–1767) was a Welsh cleric and historian, best known for his extremely popular Welsh-language history *Drych y Prif Oesoedd* (1716, second edn 1740) in which he glorified the antiquity and nobility of Wales, and his *A History of Modern Enthusiasm* (1752, second edn 1757) in which he championed the Protestantism of the Church of England as the true Christian religion.[6]

Thomas Gee (1815–1898) was a Welsh, printer, journalist and Calvinistic Methodist preacher. The son of the printer Thomas Gee, he was apprenticed to his father at the age of fourteen and took over after his death in 1845. His press printed several important works and periodicals including the

---

Miles, *The Secrets of the Bards of the Isle of Britain* (Llandybie, Dinefwr Press, 1992), pp. 71–73; Marion Löffler, *The Literary and Historical Legacy of Iolo Morganwg*, pp. 51–53. See also Huw Walters, 'Myfyr Morganwg and the Rocking-Stone Gorsedd', in Geraint H. Jenkins (ed.), *A Rattleskull Genius: The Many Faces of Iolo Morganwg* (Cardiff: University of Wales Press, 2005), 481–500.
[5] *Dictionary of Welsh Biography*, s.v. 'Evans, Evan (Ieuan Fardd or Ieuan Brydydd Hir)'.
[6] *Dictionary of Welsh Biography*, s.v. 'Evans, Theophilus'.

Traethodydd (from 1845), and *Y Gwyddoniadur*, the Welsh encyclopaedia (1854–1878, 1896). From 1857 he published the newspaper *Baner Cymru* (after 1859, *Baner ac Amserau Cymru*), soon taking full control of it, through which he popularized his political, educational, and religious views.[7]

John Griffith (*c*.1818–1885) was appointed as vicar of Aberdare by the Marquis of Bute in 1846, where he served until he became rector of Merthyr Tydfil in 1859. He was embroiled in several major controversies during his career, notably through his support of the 1847 Commission on Education in Wales and criticism of the Church for the appointment of monoglot English speakers to positions in Welsh-speaking areas. He knew Stephens, and wrote to him in 1861 praising Stephens's work which was noted in Charles Knight's *English Cyclopaedia* (1854–62) as well as working with him to raise financial assistance for the victims of the Gethin Colliery disaster in 1862.[8]

Jakob Grimm (1785–1863) was a German folklorist, mythologist, and philologist. He is best-known for compiling (with his brother Wilhelm) *Kinder und Hausmärchen* (1812–1815) as well as his *Deutsche Sagen* (1816–1818), *Deutsche Grammatik* (1819), *Deutsche Mythologie* (1835) and *Deutsches Wörterbuch* (1854).[9]

Edwin Guest (1800–1880) was an English historian philologist and master of Caius College, Cambridge. He was elected Fellow of the Royal Society in 1839 and honorary Fellow of the Society of Antiquaries in 1852. He contributed several articles and essays on medieval literature, history and philology. His *History of English Rhythms* was published in 1838 while his *Origines Celticae* was published posthumously in 1883.[10]

---

[7] *Dictionary of Welsh Biography*, s.v. 'Gee, Thomas'.

[8] Ibid., s.v. 'Griffith, John'; Wilkins, *History of Merthyr Tydfil*, pp. 291–2; John Griffith to Thomas Stephens, Swansea, 2 September 1861, NLW, MS. 964E, Letter 97c; 'The Gethin Accident Relief Fund', *Merthyr Telegraph, and General Advertiser for the Iron Districts of South Wales*, 5 April 1862, Accessed via *Welsh Newspapers Online*.

[9] *Allgemeine Deutsche Biographie*, s.v. 'Grimm, Jakob'.

[10] *Oxford Dictionary of National Biography*, s.v. 'Guest, Edwin'.

Joseph Hughes (Carn Ingli) (1803–1863) was a Welsh cleric, poet, and translator. Although based in Yorkshire for most of his life, he returned to Wales each year to attend eisteddfodau, at which he was highly regarded. He was also the secretary and official bard of the Association of Welsh Clergy in the West Riding. Along with John Williams ab Ithel, he was one of principal promoters of the 1858 Llangollen Eisteddfod.[11]

George Petrie (1790–1866) was an Irish painter, folksong collector, and antiquarian. He was elected an associate member of the Royal Hiberian Academy in 1826, became a full member in 1828, was appointed the librarian of the Academy in 1829, and served as president 1857–1859.[12] From 1833 to 1842, he worked on the topographical portion of the Irish Ordinance Survey, assisting in the work of establishing the English orthography of Irish place names, alongside other Irish scholars, notably John O'Donovan and Eugene O'Curry. In 1828, he was elected to the Royal Irish Academy and he served as vice president of that body 1844–1847. He was an active member, founding the Academy museum and library and assisting in purchasing manuscripts for the Academy. He competed for several Academy prizes, most notably in 1833 when he controversially argued that Irish round towers were Christian structures. The essay was expanded and finally published, after much controversy, in 1845 as *The Ecclesiastical Architecture of Ireland, Anterior to the Anglo-Norman Invasion, Comprising an Essay on the Origin and Uses of the Round Towers of Ireland*.[13]

John Peter (Ioan Pedr) (1833–1877) was Welsh scholar and pastor of the Independent churches of Bala and Tŷ'n-y-bont, and a subscriber and contributor to *Revue Celtique*. He was a capable scholar on several subjects, including science and Welsh

---

[11] *Dictionary of Welsh Biography*, s.v. 'Hughes, Joseph (Carn Ingli).'
[12] He was elected president in 1856 by part of the membership, with Martin Cregan serving as a rival president.
[13] *Dictionary of Irish Biography*, s.v. 'Petrie, George'.

language and literature, and was particularly known for his work on Welsh philology.[14]

Thomas Phillipps (1792–1872) of Middle Hill, Worcestershire, was an antiquarian, bibliophile, and book and manuscript collector, whose collection, the largest of its time in Britain and, possibly, western Europe, included several notable Welsh manuscripts such as the 'Book of Aneirin' which had formerly been in the possession of Carnhuanawc. He also established a private press for the purpose of printing the contents of some of his manuscripts.[15]

Robert Plot (c.1640–1696) was an English naturalist and antiquarian, whose works included *The Natural History of Oxford-shire* (1677), *De Origine Fontium* (1684), and *The Natural History of Stafford-shire* (1686). He was elected to the Royal Society of London in 1677 and served as second secretary to that body from 1682 to1684, during which time he edited the *Philosophical Transactions*. He was the first Professor of Chemistry at the University of Oxford, as well as the first Keeper of the Ashmolean Museum, appointed to both positions in 1679.[16]

Robert John Prys (Gweirydd ap Rhys) (1807–1889) was a self-educated Welsh writer, editor, and man of letters. Prys was a weaver by trade, until, in 1857, he went to work in the office of the publisher Thomas Gee, mainly on the Welsh encyclopaedia, *Gwyddoniadur*, and dictionaries. He contributed extensively to the *Gwyddoniadur*, furnishing almost a volume's worth of entries on his own, produced five dictionaries, and edited various works, including a reprint of the *Myvyrian Archaiology* (1870). He also produced two notable works on *Hanes y Brytaniaid a'r Cymry* (1872–74) and *Hanes Llenyddiaeth Gymreig, 1300–1650* (1855). In 1858, he worked with Stephens to reform Welsh orthography.[17]

---

[14] *Dictionary of Welsh Biography*, s.v. 'Peter, John'.

[15] Ibid., s.v. 'Phillips, Sir Thomas'.

[16] *Oxford Dictionary of National Biography*, s.v. 'Plot, Robert'.

[17] *Dictionary of Welsh Biography*, s.v. 'Prys, Robert John'; See also the letters from Prys to Stephens at NLW, MS. 965E, letters 244–259.

Leopold von Ranke (1795–1886) was a German historian, often considered to be the father of modern history. He was appointed professor at the University of Berlin in 1824 as well as the Prussian Historiographer Royal from 1841. Ranke's groundbreaking historical approach advocated historical study based on primary sources with an emphasis on objectivity. He advocated viewing historical periods and events within their own contexts (*'wie es eigentlich gwesen'*), rejecting a teleological view of history.[18]

Samuel Smiles (1812–1904) was a Scottish writer, radical, and biographer. He wrote several industrial biographies in addition to his biography of George Stephenson (1857), mentioned in a letter from W. Walker Wilkins to Thomas Stephens dated 30 December 1862, such as *Lives of the Engineers* (3 vols, 1861–2), *Industrial Biography: Iron Workers and Tool Makers* (1863), and *Lives of Boulton and Watt* (1865) as well as work on *Physical Education, or the Nurture and Management of Children* (1837), *A History of Ireland and the Irish People under the Government of England* (1844), and *The Huguenots in France after the revocation of the edict of Nantes; with a visit to the Vandois* (1874). He was an advocate of Individualism, especially in education, and published *Self-Help, with Illustrations of Character and Conduct* in 1859.[19]

William Smith (1813–1893) was an English classical and biblical scholar, who excelled at popularizing classical and biblical scholarship through contributing to and editing dictionaries and encyclopaedias. Among his prolific edited works were the *Dictionary of Greek and Roman Antiquities* (1842), *Dictionary of Greek and Roman Biography, Mythology and Geography* (1844–49), *Dictionary of Greek and Roman Geography* (1857), *Dictionary*

[18] *Neue Deutsche Biographie*, s.v. 'Ranke, Franz Leopold von'. See also, Robert Harrison, Aled Jones, and Peter Lambert, 'Methodology: "Scientific" History and the Problem of Objectivity', in Peter Lambert and Phillip Schofield (eds), *Making History: An Introduction to the History and Practices of a Discipline* (London: Routledge Taylor and Francis, 2004), pp. 26–37 (pp. 27–29).
[19] *Oxford Dictionary of National Biography*, s.v. 'Smiles, Samuel'.

of the Bible Comprising its Antiquities, Biography, Geography and Natural History (1860–63), and *Dictionary on Christian Antiquities* (1875–80). Smith received honorary doctorates from Oxford, Dublin, Glasgow, and Leipzig, and was knighted in 1892.[20]

William Thomas (Gwilym Mai) (1807–1872) was a Welsh poet and printer who frequently competed in eisteddfodau. He worked as a compositor in the office of David Rice Rees and William Rees in Llandovery before working in the offices of the *Carmarthen Journal* and eventually establishing his own business at Carmarthen. He was a member of the Oddfellows for thirty-five years and wrote a treatise on the Oddfellows as well as an awdl to the same subject.[21]

Charles Vallancey (*c.*1725–1812) was a soldier, military engineer and surveyor, and Irish antiquarian. He was an active member of the Dublin Society's Committee on Antiquities and the Hibernian Society of Antiquarians and was a co-founder of the Royal Irish Academy in 1785. He published several works on Irish history, antiquities, and language. For much of the mid-nineteenth century he was known for his unorthodox and largely disproven theory that the Gaelic language, as well as much of Irish culture, derived from the Phoenicians.[22]

John Williams (Ab Ithel) (1811–1862) was a notable Welsh cleric and antiquary. In 1846, he co-founded, with Harry Longueville Jones, the Cambrian Archaeological Association and its organ *Archaeologia Cambrensis*, which he edited until 1853 when, owing to intellectual disagreement with Jones, he began the Cambrian Institute and its organ the *Cambrian Journal* which he edited until his death. In 1852 he published an edition of the early Welsh poem *Y Gododdin*. Ab Ithel believed strongly in the theories, forgeries, and institutions of the Welsh cultural inventor Iolo Morganwg and the *Cambrian Journal* became a forum for many of these views.[23] In 1862, Ab Ithel edited a section

---

[20] Ibid., s.v. 'Smith, Sir William'.

[21] *Dictionary of Welsh Biography*, s.v. 'Thomas William'.

[22] *Oxford Dictionary of National Biography*, s.v. 'Vallancey, Charles'.

[23] Notably, much of Stephens's criticism of this material also appeared in its

of Iolo's manuscripts concerning supposed Druidic theology entitled *Barddas*. Ab Ithel was also one of the organizers of the 1858 Llangollen Eisteddfod at which Stephens competed unsuccessfully for the best prize essay on the discovery of America by Madog ap Owain Gwynedd.[24]

Robert Williams (1810–1881) was a Welsh antiquary and Celtic scholar and the vicar of Llangadwaladr from 1837–1877. In 1835 he published *The History and Antiquities of the Town of Aberconwy*, followed in 1852 by his *Enwogion Cymru: A Biographical Dictionary of Eminent Welshmen*, which was based on his prize winning essay for the Cymmrodorion Society in 1831. He also made a major contribution to the study of Cornish in 1865 with his *Lexicon Cornu-Britannicum* as well as his discovery of the Cornish drama *Beunans Meriask*. In 1876 he completed the first volume of his *Selection from the Hengwrt* Manuscripts. The second volume was published in parts in 1878 and 1880, and was completed by G. Hartwell Jones in 1892. Williams was also on the editorial board of the Cambrian Archaeological Association and contributed articles to *Archaeologia Cambrensis* and the *Cambrian Journal*.[25]

Rowland Williams (1817–1870) was a Welsh cleric and scholar who was appointed vice-principal and professor of Hebrew at St Davids College, Lampeter, in 1850. In 1862 he settled at Broad Chalke near Salisbury, to which living he had been appointed in 1858.[26]

Taliesin Williams (Taliesin ab Iolo) (1787–1847) was a Welsh schoolmaster, poet, and antiquarian, and the son of the Welsh poet, antiquarian, hymnist, stonemason, and cultural inventor, Edward Williams (Iolo Morganwg). Like both his father and Thomas Stephens, Taliesin was an Unitarian, and both he and Stephens attended the same chapel in Merthyr Tydfil. Around 1813, Taliesin was appointed an assistant at Rev. David Davis's

---

pages, see section 5, 'Revolutionising Welsh Scholarship'.
[24] *Dictionary of Welsh Biography*, s.v. 'Williams, John'.
[25] Ibid., s.v. 'Williams, Robert'.
[26] Ibid., s.v. 'Williams, Rowland'.

school in Neath, but left in 1815. In 1816 he began his own school in Merthyr Tydfil, and through his school and wider activities Taliesin became a major figure in the cultural and social life of Merthyr and wider Wales. He was active in eisteddfodau and, a firm believer in Iolo's bardic vision and lore, was to a great degree responsible for the cultural transmission, survival, and importance of his father's ideas in nineteenth-century Wales, serving as custodian and interpreter of his father's manuscripts. He assisted Iolo in publishing *Cyfrinach Beirdd Ynys Prydain* (1829), won a prize at the 1838 Abergavenny Cymreigyddion Society Eisteddfod for his essay on 'Hynafiaeth ac Awdurdodaeth Coelbren y Beirdd', which was published in 1840, and selected and edited a selection of his father's manuscripts for the Welsh MSS. Society, which was published posthumously as *Iolo Manuscripts* (1848).[27]

John Windele (1801–1865) was a Cork-based antiquarian, archaeologist and collector, particularly of Irish manuscripts and ogham stones and inscriptions. After his death, the Royal Irish Academy set up a fund and succeeded in purchasing the majority of his collection, although he was not a member. Windele was a member of the South Munster Antiquarian Society, the Anchorites Club in Cork, and a founding member of of the Cork Cuvierian Society in 1836, which led excursions and even excavations around Cork. His publications included *Historical and Descriptive Notices of the City of Cork* (1839) and *A Guide to Killarney* as well as articles and papers in various journals, notably the *Journal of the Kilkenny Archaeological Society*.[28]

---

[27] Ibid., s.v. 'Williams, Taliesin'. See also Brynley F. Roberts, 'Mab ei Dad: Taliesin ab Iolo Morganwg', in Hywel Teifi Edwards (gol.), *Merthyr a Thaf* (Llandysul: Gwasg Gomer, 2001), pp. 57; Idem., '"The Age of Restitution"'.

[28] *Dictionary of Irish Biography*, s.v.'Windele, John ("Trismagistus MacSlatt", Seághan Bhindele)'. See also Anon., 'Three memorable Cork Archaeologists', 35–39.

Bernard Bolingbroke Woodward (1816–1869) was an English librarian and writer with interests in botany and antiquities. He was elected a fellow of the Society of Antiquaries in 1857 and was appointed librarian in ordinary to Queen Victoria at Windsor Castle in 1860. He founded and edited the *Fine Arts Quarterly Review* in 1863 (it lasted until 1867), and published histories of Hampshire, the United States, and Wales as well as other works on English history and the artistic collections at Windsor Castle.[29]

Johann Kaspar Zeuss (1806–1856) was a German philologist and Celticist. He is best-known for his groundbreaking *Grammatica Celtica* (1853), which established the Celtic languages within the Indo-European linguistic family, providing a scientific basis for Celtic philology.[30]

---

[29] *Oxford Dictionary of National Biography*, s.v. 'Woodward, Bernard Bolingbroke'.
[30] See *Allgemeine Deutsche Biographie*, s.v. 'Zeuß, Johann Kaspar'.

BIBLIOGRAPHY

BIBLIOGRAPHY

Manuscripts

Bibliotèque de Genève, Geneva. MS fr 4229 f. 151–52. Letter. Thomas Stephens to Adolphe Pictet. Merthyr Tydfil. 27 May 1869.

Cardiff Central Library, Cardiff. MS. 4.208. Letters sent to John and Rees Jenkin Jones, Aberdare.

Glamorgan Archives, Cardiff. MS. DG/A/1/283. Dowlais letter book, 1853, S–W.

National Library of Ireland, Dublin. MS 2252. Letters sent to James Henthorn Todd.

National Library of Wales, Aberystwyth (hereafter, NLW). MS. Minor Deposit 151 A. Thomas Stephens's personal copy of Thomas Stephens, *The Literature of the Kymry: Being a Critical Essay on the History of the Language and Literature of Wales*, (Llandovery: William Rees. 1849), with various notes, cuttings, and letters.

NLW. MS. 916 E. Thomas Stephens, 'The Evils Arising from Killing Salmon, out of Season, and, when full of Spawn'.

NLW. MS. 922 C. Thomas Stephens's notes on J. C. Zeuss, *Grammatica Celtica* (Leipzig: Weidmannos. 1853).

NLW. MS. 942 C. Various letters sent to Thomas Stephens.

NLW. MS. 961 C. The manuscript of Thomas Stephens's 'Madoc: An Essay on the Discovery of Amercia by Madoc ap Owen Gwynedd in the Twelfth Century'.

NLW. MSS 962–3 C. Various letters to Thomas Stephens and press cuttings related to his essay disproving the discovery of America by Prince Madoc ap Owain Gwynedd.

NLW. MSS 964–5 E. Four volumes of various letters sent to Thomas Stephens, with various other personal papers. Full PDF transcriptions of these manuscripts are available on the *National Library of Wales Archives and Manuscripts* website.

NLW. MS. 966 C. 'A few notes for the biography of Thomas Stephens, by Mr E. J.'.

NLW. MS. 1808 E. Various letters written to Walter Davies (Gwallter

Mechain).

NLW. MS. 5175 C. G. T. Clark. 'Contributions towards a History of Glamorgan', containing printed articles, manuscript notes, and letters.

NLW. MS. Cwrtmawr 412B. Miscellaneous nineteenth- and early twentieth-century letters.

NLW. MS. Cwrtmawr 900B. Letters to D. Silvan Evans from Henri Gaidoz.

NLW. MS. Cwrtmawr 919 B. Letters written to D. Silvan Evans.

NLW. MS. Tredegar 1310. Letter. Thomas Stephens to Thomas Wakeman. Merthyr Tydfil. 16 December 1856.

Royal Irish Academy, Dublin (hereafter, RIA). MS. 12 N 23/1/52. Letter. Thomas Stephens to William Wilde. Merthyr Tydfil. 26 June 1855

RIA. MS. 24 O 39/JOD/354. Letter. Thomas Stephens to John O'Donovan. Merthyr Tydfil. 2 November 1855

Printed Sources

Anon. 'Topography of Merionethshire'. *The Cambrian Register, for the Year 1795*. London: E. and T. Williams. 1796. pp. 287–315.

—. 'Topography of Anglesey'. *The Cambrian Register, for the Year 1796*. London: E. and T. Williams. 1799. pp. 390–415.

—. *Dictionarium Scoto-Celticum: A Dictionary of the Gaelic Language*, two vols (Edinburgh: William Blackwood under the direction of The Highland Society of Scotland. 1828).

—. 'Cambrian Archaeological Association, Third Annual Meeting, Cardiff, August 27th to September 1st, 1849'. *Archaeologia Cambrensis*. 16 (October 1849). 294–320.

—. 'Cambrian Archaeological Association. Fifth Annual Meeting, Tenby, August 20th to 26th, 1851'. *Archaeologica Cambrensis*, New Series, 8 (October 1851), 309–340.

—. 'Bards of the Sixth Century — Stonehenge'. *The Quarterly Review*. 92 (September 1852). 273–315.

—. 'Cambrian Archaeological Association, Seventh Annual Meeting, Brecon'. *Archaeologia Cambrensis*. New Series. 16 (October 1853). 307–38.

—. 'The Cambrian Institute'. *Archaeologia Cambrensis*. New Series. 16 (October 1853). 338.

—. 'Stephens *versus* Stephens', *Cambrian Journal*. 2 (Alban Hevin 1855). 143.

—. Review of 'Notices des Principaux Manuscrits des Anciens Bretons, avec fac-simile, lues a l'Institut (séances des 2 et 30 Novembre, 1855). Par Th. Hersart de la Villemarqué, M.C. de l'Academie de Berlin. Paris: Imprimerie Impériale. 1856'. *The Cambrian Journal*. 13 (March 1857). 79–80.

—. Review of 'Le Mystere des Bardes de l'Ile de Bretagne on la Doctrine des Bardes Gaules du Moyen Age sur Dieu, la vie future et la Transmigration des Maes Text original, Traduction et Commentaire par Adolphe Pictet. Geneve: Joel Cherbuliez, Libraire-Editeur. Paris. Même Maison, Rue de la Monnaie, 10. 1856'. *Cambrian Journal*. 14 (June 1857). 158–60.

—. 'William Owen Esq. of Tan y Gyrt'. *Cambrian Journal*. (Alban Eilir 1859). 62.

—. Review of 'Druidism. Second Article in the *Gwyddionadur; or Encyclopedia Cambrensis*. 32. Denbigh: T. Gee'. *Cambrian Journal*. (Alban Elved 1860). 231–232, 333–40 [Typesetting error in original pagination].

—. 'Cambrian Archaeological Association. Swansea Meeting, 1861'. *Archaeologia Cambrensis*. Third Series. 28 (October 1861). 333–372.

—. 'Gower'. *Saturday Review*. 311: 12 (12 October 1861), 375–76.

—. 'Obituary'. *Archaeologia Cambrensis*. Third Series. 55 (July 1868), 340–41.

—. 'Three Memorable Cork Archaeologists'. *Journal of the Cork Historical and Archaeological Society*. 6: 45 (1900), 32–47.

Allibone, Samuel Austin. *Critical Dictionary of English Literature and British and American Authors*. three vols. Philadelphia: J. B. Lippencott & Co. 1854–1871.

Armistead, Winston. *James Logan; A Distinguished Scholar and Christian Legislator; Founder of the Loganian Library at Philadelphia; Secretary of the Province of Pennsylvania; Chief Justice; Commissioner of Property; and (as president of the Council) for Two Years Governor of the Province including Several of his Letters and those of his Correspondents, Many of which are Now Printed from the Original MSS. Collated and Arranged for the Purpose*. London: Charles Gilpin. 1851.

Armstrong, R. A. *A Gaelic Dictionary, in Two Parts: I. Gaelic and English.–II. English and Gaelic*. London: James Duncan. 1825.

Bascome, Edward. *A History of Epidemic Pestilences from the Earliest Ages, 1495 Years before the Birth of our Savour to 1848 with Researches into their Nature, Causes, and Prophylaxis*. London: John Churchill. 1851.

Brash, Richard Rolt. 'On an "Elegy of Corroy, the son of Dairy," An Ancient

Gaedhelic Poem Attributed to Taliesin'. *Archaeologia Cambrensis*. Fourth Series. 3 (July 1870). 234–51.

—. *The Ecclesiastical Architecture of Ireland to the Close of the Twelfth Century with Historical and Antiquarian Notices of Numerous Ancient Remains of that Period*. Dublin: W. B. Kelly. 1875.

Bromwich, Rachel. 'Trioedd Ynys Prydain', in *Welsh Literature and Scholarship*. Cardiff: University of Wales Press. 1969.

—. 'Triodd Ynys Prydain; The Myvyrian "Third Series" (II)'. *Transactions of the Honourable Society of Cymmrodorion*'. (1969) (Part 1). 127–56.

Broughton, William Robert. *A Voyage of Discovery to the North Pacific Ocean: In which the Coast of Asia, from the Lat. of 35° North to the Lat. of 52° North, the Island of Insu, (Commonly Known under the Name of the Land of Jesso) The North, South, and East Coasts of Japan, the Lieuchieux and the Adjacent Isles, as well as the Coast of Corea, have been Examined and Surveyed*. London: T Cadell and W. Davies. 1804.

Bruce, Henry A. *Gwent and Dyfed Royal Eisteddfod, 1834: The Prize Translation of the Welsh Ode on the British Druids by Taliesin Williams*. Cardiff: William Bird. 1835.

Bunsen, Frances Baroness. *A Memoir of Baron Bunsen: Late Minister Plenipotentiary and Envoy Extraordinary of His Majesty Fredric William IV. at the Court of St. James*. two vols. London: Longmans, Green, and Co. 1868.

Camden, William. *Britannia: or, a Chronographical Description of the Flourishing Kingdoms of England, Scotland, and Ireland, and the Islands Adjacent; from the Earliest Antiquity*. ed. by Richard Gough. three vols. London: John Nichols. 1789.

'Caradoc Ap Bran'. 'Dyvynwal Moelmud'. *Cambrian Journal*. 1 (Alban Elved 1854). 269–71.

—. 'Dyvynwal Moelmud', *Cambrian Journal*. 2 (Alban Hevin 1855). 141–143.

Catlin, George. *Letters and Notes on the Manners, Customs, and Condition of the North American Indians*. two vols. London: published for the author. 1842.

—. *Catlin's North American Indian Portfolio. Hunting Scenes and Amusements of the Rocky Mountains and Prairies of America. From Drawings and Notes of the Author, Made during Eight Years' Travel amongst Forty-eight of the Wildest and Most Remote Tribes of Savages in North America*. London: Geo. Catlin. 1844.

Clark, G. T. 'Contribution towards an Account of Caerphilly Castle'. *Archaeologia Cambrensis*. New Series, 4 (October 1850). 251–304.

—. 'Essay on Caerphilly Castle'. *West of England Journal of Science and Literature*. 1 (1835–6). 62–71, 101–4, 135–43, 185–99.

Clarkson, Thomas. *Memoirs of the Private and Public Life of William Penn*. two vols. Philadelphia: Richard Taylor and Co. 1813.

Cocchiara, Guiseppe. *The History of Folklore in Europe*. trans. by John N. McDaniel. Philadelphia: Institute for the Study of Human Issues. 1981.

Constantine, Mary-Ann. 'Welsh Literary History and the Making of "The Myvyrian Archaiology of Wales"'. *European Studies*. 26 (2006). 109–28.

—. '"Impertinent Structures": a Breton's Adventures in neo-Gothic Wales'. *Studies in Travel Writing*. 18: 2 (2014). 134–147.

Coward, Adam. 'English Anglers, Welsh Salmon and Social Justice: The Politics of Conservation in Mid-Nineteenth-Century Wales. *Welsh History Review*. 27: 4 (2015). 730–54.

—. 'Exiled Trojans or the Sons of Gomer: Wales's Origins in the Long Eighteenth Century' in Lotte Jensen (ed.), *The Roots of Nationalism: National Identity Formation in Early Modern Europe, 1600–1815*. Amsterdam: Amsterdam University Press. 2016. pp. 167–81.

Davies, Edward. *Celtic Researches on the Origin, Traditions & Language, of the Ancient Britons*. London: Printed for the Author. 1804.

—. *The Mythology and Rites of the British Druids*. London: J. Booth. 1809.

Davies, W. Ll. 'The Thomas Stephens Manuscripts'. *National Library of Wales Journal*. 1: 2 (Summer 1939). 96.

Dixon, William Hepworth. *William Penn: An Historical Biography. With an Extra Chapter on 'The Macaulay Charges'*. London: Chapman and Hall. 1851.

Edwards, Charles. *Y Ffydd Ddiffuant: sef, Hanes y Ffydd Gristionogol a'i Rhinwedd*. gol. gan William Edmunds. Caerfyrddin: William Spurrell. 1856.

Edwards, Huw Teifi. *The Eisteddfod*. Cardiff: University of Wales Press, 2016.

Ellis, E. L. *The University College of Wales Aberystwyth 1872–1972*. Cardiff: University of Wales Press. 1972.

Ellis, Henry. *Original Letters, Illustrative of English History; Including Numerous Royal Letters from Autographs in the British Museum and One or Two Other Collections*. three volumes. London: Harding, Triphook, and Lepard. 1824.

England, Joe. 'Unitarians, Freemasons, Chartists: The Middle Classes in Victorian Merthyr'. *Welsh History Review*. 23: 4 (2007). 35–58.

—. *Merthyr: The Crucible of Modern Wales*. Cardigan: Parthian. 2017.

Erny, Alfred. 'Voyage dans le pays de Galles'. *Le Tour de Monde*. 15: 1 (1867).

257–88.

Evans, Chris. *'The Labyrinth of Flames': Work and Social Conflict in Early Industrial Merthyr Tydfil*. Cardiff: University of Wales Press. 1993.

Evans, Evan. *Some Specimens of the Poetry of the Ancient Welsh Bards*. London: J. Dodsley. 1764.

Evans, Leslie Wynne. 'Sir John and Lady Charlotte Guest's Educational Scheme at Dowlais in the Mid-Nineteenth Century'. *National Library of Wales Journal*. 9: 3 (Summer 1956). 265–286.

Evans, Neil and Huw Pryce. 'Writing a Small Nation's Past: States, Race and Historical Culture'. in Neil Evans and Huw Pryce (eds). *Writing a Small Nation's Past: Wales in Comparative Perspective, 1850–1950*. Farnham: Ashgate. 2013. pp. 3–30.

Forester, W. E. *William Penn and Thomas B. Macaulay: Being Brief Observations on the Charges Made in Mr. Macaulay's History of England, Against the Character of William Penn*. London: Charles Gilpin. 1849.

Fraser, Maxwell. 'Sir Benjamin and Lady Hall in the 1840's (Part II: 1846–1849)'. *National Library of Wales Journal*. 14: 2 (Winter 1965). 194–213.

—. 'Lady Llanover and her Circle'. *Transactions of the Honourable Society of Cymmrodorion*. 1968. part 2. 170–96.

[Giraldus Cambrensis]. 'Stephens *versus* Stephens'. *Cambrian Journal*. Second Series, 1 (Alban Arthan 1858). 364.

Gregory, Mair. 'Cymdeithas Cymreigyddion y Fenni' *Llên Cymru* 1: 1 (Ionawr, 1950), 97–112.

—. 'Cymdeithas Cymreigyddion y Fenni' (part 2). *Llên Cymru* 3: 1 (Ionawr, 1954), 32–42

Grimm, Jakob. *Deutsche Rechtsalterthümer*. zweite Ausgabe. Göttingen: Dieterichschen Buchhandlung. 1854. (originally published 1828).

Guest, Lady Charlotte (trans). *The Mabinogion, from the Llyfr Coch o Hergest, and Other Ancient Welsh Manuscripts*. three vols. London: Longman, Brown, Green, and Longmans. 1849.

Guest, Revel and Angela V. John. *Lady Charlotte Guest: An Extraordinary Life*. Stroud: Tempus. 2007.

Hakluyt, Richard. *The Principal Navigations, Voiages and Discoveries of the English Nation, Made by Sea or Overland*. three vols. London: G. Bishop, R. Newberie & R. Barker. 1598–1600. (first, one vol. edn, 1582).

Harris, James. 'The Massacre of the Welsh Bards: An Examination of a Passage in Stephens' *Literature of the Kymry*'. *Red Dragon: The National*

Magazine of Wales. 7 (1885). 534–41.

Harrison, Robert, Aled Jones, and Peter Lambert. 'Methodology: "Scientific" History and the Problem of Objectivity'. in Peter Lambert and Phillip Schofield (eds). *Making History: An Introduction to the History and Practices of a Discipline*. London: Routledge Taylor and Francis. 2004. pp. 26–37.

Herbert, Thomas. *Some Yeares Travels into Africa & Asia the Great. Especially Describing the Famous Empires of Persia and Industan. As also Divers other Kingdoms in the Orientall Indies, and I'les Adjacent*. London: R. B. 1638.

Huws, Daniel. 'Introduction' to Maria Jane Williams. *Ancient National Airs of Gwent and Morganwg*. ed. by Daniel Huws. [N. P.]: The Welsh Folk-Song Society. 1994.

[Idrison]. 'The Mabinogi of Taliesin. (Continued from the Cambrian Quarterly for April)'. *The Cambrian and Caledonian Quarterly Magazine*. 5: 19 (July 1833). 366–382.

James, Brian Ll. *G. T. Clark: Scholar Ironmaster in the Victorian Age*. Cardiff: University of Wales Press. 1998.

James, Lemuel J. H. 'The Llanover Manuscripts'. *The Journal of the Welsh Bibliographical Society*. 1: 6 (February 1914). 180–183.

Jenkins, David. *A Refuge in Peace and War; The National Library of Wales to 1952*. Aberystwyth: National Library of Wales. 2002.

Jenkins, Geraint H., Ffion Mair Jones and David Ceri Jones. *The Correspondence of Iolo Morganwg*. three vols. Cardiff: University of Wales Press. 2007.

Jenkins, R. T. and Helen Myfanwy Ramage. *A History of the Honourable Society of Cymmrodorion and of the Gwyneddigion and Cymreigyddion Societies*. London: Honourable Cymmrodorion. 1951.

Johnson, Samuel. *The Vanity of Human Wishes: The Tenth Satire of Juvenal, Imitated*. London: R. Dodsley. 1749.

Jones, Bedwyr Lewis.'*Yr Hen Bersoniaid Llengar*'. Penarth: Gwasg yr Eglwys yng Nghymru. 1963.

Jones, E. D. 'Deposited Collections: 3. The Wynnstay Manuscripts and Documents'. *The National Library of Wales Journal*. 2: 1 (Summer 1941). 26–32.

Jones, Harry Longueville, 'Early Inscribed Stones of Wales. The Sagranus Stone at St. Dogmael's, Pembrokeshire'. *Archaeo-logia Cambrensis*. Third Series, 22 (April 1860). 128–36.

—. 'Early Inscribed Stones of Wales. Llanfechan, Cardiganshire'. *Archaeologia Cambrensis*. Third Series, 25 (January 1861). 42–45.

Adam N. Coward

Jones, Ieuan Gwynedd. 'The Merthyr of Henry Richards'. in Glanmor Williams (ed.). *Merthyr Politics: The Making of a Working-Class Tradition* (Cardiff: University of Wales Press, 1966). pp. 28–57.

Jones, Owen, Edward Williams, and William Owen, (eds.). *The Myvyrian Archaiology of Wales, Collected out of Ancient Manuscripts.* three vols. London: S. Rousseau. 1801–1807.

Jones, Rhys. *Gorchestion Beirdd Cymru: neu Flodau Godidowgrwydd Awen. Wedi eu Lloffa, a'u Dethol, allan o Waith rhai o'r Awduriaid Arddercjoccaf, a fu erioed yn yr Iaith Gymraeg.* Amwythig: Stafford Prys. 1773.

Jones, Thomas Gwynn. *Cofiant Thomas Gee.* Dinbych: Gee a'i Fab. 1913. 113–19.

Jones, William Basil. 'Vestiges of the Gael in Gwynedd'. *Archaeologia Cambrensis.* Supplement. 1850 (London: W. Pickering. 1851). 1–85.

Kenward, James. *Ab Ithel: An Account of the Life and Writings of the Rev. John Williams Ab Ithel, M.S., B.B.D., Late Rector of Llanymowddwy, Merioneth.* Tenby: R. Mason. 1871.

Kohl, J. G. *Geschichte der Entdeckung Amerika's von Columbus bis Franklin.* Bremen: Heinrich Strack. 1861.

—. *A Popular History of the Discovery of America, from Columbus to Franklin.* trans. by R. R. Noel. two vols. London: Chapman and Hall. 1862.

La Villemarqué, Hersart De. *La Légende celtique, en Irelande, en Cambrie et en Bretagne, suivie des Textes originaux Irelandais, Gallois et Bretons, rares ou inédits.* Paris : A. Durand. 1859.

—. *Myrdhinn ou l'Enchanteur Merlin son Histoire, ses Œuvres, son Influence.* Paris: Librairie Académique. 1862.

Lambert, Peter and Phillip Schofield (eds). *Making History: An Introduction to the History and Practices of a Discipline.* London: Routledge Taylor and Francis. 2004.

Lawson, John, *A New Voyage to Carolina; Containing the Exact Description and Natural History of that Country: Together with the Present State thereof. and A Journal Of a Thousand Miles, Travel'd thro' several Nations of INDIANS. Giving a Particular Account of their Customs, Manners, &c.* London: [James Knapton]. 1709.

Lewis, M. G. *Romatic Tales.* four vols. London: N. Shury. 1808.

Lhuyd, Edward. *Archæologia Britannica Giving some Account Additional to What Has Been Hitherto Publish'd of the Languages, Histories and Customs of the Original Inhabitants of Great Britain, Vol I: Glossography.*

Oxford: Printed at the Theatre for the Author. 1707.

Light, Julie. 'The Middle Class as Urban Elites in Nineteenth-Century South Wales'. *Welsh History Review.* 24: 3 (2009). 29–55.

Löffler, Marion. *The Literary and Historical Legacy of Iolo Morganwg, 1826–1926.* Cardiff: University of Wales Press. 2007.

—. 'Failed Founding Fathers and Abandoned Sources: Edward Williams, Thomas Stephens and the Young J. E. Lloyd' in Neil Evans and Huw Pryce (eds). *Writing a Small Nation's Past: Wales in Comparative Perspective, 1850–1950.* Farnham: Ashgate. 2013. pp. 67–81.

—. 'Class, Ethnicity, and Religion: The Marginalized Welsh Amateur Scholar before 1875', unpublished paper presented at the international workshop organised by The University of Wales Centre for Advanced Welsh and Celtic Studies on 'The Amateur Historian and Knowledge Exchange in Nineteenth-Century Europe' at the National Library of Wales, Aberystwyth on 24 October 2015.

—. 'Bunsen, Müller a Meyer: Tri Almaenwr, y Gymraeg, y Frenhines a'r Ymerodraeth', *Y Traethodydd* (Ionawr 2018). 19–32.

Löffler, Marion with Hywel Gethin Rhys. 'Thomas Stephens and the Abergavenny Cymreigyddion: Letters from the *Cambrian*, 1842–3'. *National Library of Wales Journal* (May 2009).

—. 'Thomas Stephens a Llythyru Cyhoeddus yng Nghymru Oes Victoria'. *Y Traethodydd* (Ionawr 2010). 35–49.

Martin, Henri. *Études D'Archéologie Celtique Notes de Voyages dans les Pays Celtiques et Scandinaves.* Paris: Librairie Académique. 1872.

Mason, Rhiannon. *Museums, Nations, Identities: Wales and its National Museums.* Cardiff: University of Wales Press. 2007.

McKenney, Thomas L. *Memoirs, Official and Personal; with Sketches of Travels among the Northern and Southern Indians; Embracing a War Excursion, and Descriptions of Scenes along the Western Borders.* two vols. New York: Paine and Burgess. 1846.

McKenney, Thomas and James Hall. *History of the Indian Tribes of North America, with Biographical Sketches and Anecdotes of the Principal Chiefs.* three vols. Vol. 1: Philadelphia: E. C. Biddle. 1836. vols 2–3: Philadelphia: D. Rice and J. G. Clark. 1842–44.

Meyer, Carl. 'An Essay on the Celtic Languages, in which they are Compared with Each Other, and Considered in their Connection with the Sanscrit [sic], and the Other Caucasian Languages'. trans. by Jane Williams

(Ysgafell). *Cambrian Journal*. 1 (Alban Eilir 1854), 1–33.

Michel, Francisque. *Charlemagne: An Anglo-Norman Poem of the Twelfth Century*. London: William Pickering. 1836.

Mitchell, G. F. 'Antiquities'. in T. Ó Raifeartaigh. *The Royal Irish Academy: A Bicentennial History, 1875–1985*. Dublin: Royal Irish Academy, 1985. pp. 93–165.

Miles, Dillwyn. *The Secrets of the Bards of the Isle of Britain*. Llandybie: Dinefwr Press. 1992.

[Moeddyn]. 'Barn Iolo Morganwg am Hu Gadarn'. *Y Brython*. 5: 39 (December 1862). 43.

Monson, William. *A True and Exact Account of the Wars with Spain, in the Reign of Q Elizabeth, (of Famous Memory.) Being the Particulars of What Happened Between the English and Spanish Fleets, from the Years 1585 to 1602. Shewing, The Expeditions, Attempts, Flights, Designs, Escapes, Successes, Errors, &c. on Both Sides. With the Names of Her Majesty's Ships and Commanders in Every Fleet. Being the Pattern and Warning to Future Ages*. London: W. Crooke. 1782.

Morgan, Prys. 'The Creation of the National Museum and National Library' in John Osmond (ed.). *Myths, Museums and Futures: The National Library and National Museum in the Story of Wales*. Cardiff: Institute of Welsh Affairs. 2007. pp. 13–22.

—. 'Lady Llanover (1802–1896), "Gwenynen Gwent"'. *Transactions of the Honourable Society of Cymmrodorion*. New Series. 13 (2007). 94–106.

Murray, Damien. *Romanticism, Nationalism and Irish Antiquarian Studies, 1840–80*. Maynooth: National University of Ireland. 2000.

Nash, D. W. *Taliesin; or, the Bards and Druids of Britain*. London: John Russell Smith. 1858.

O'Curry, Eugene. *Lectures on the Manuscript Materials of Ancient Irish History Delivered at the Catholic University of Ireland during the Sessions of 1855 and 1856*. Dublin: James Duffy. 1861.

O'Donovan, John. *Annala Rioghachta Eirann: Annals of the Kingdom of Ireland, by the Four Masters*. second edn. six vols. Dublin: Hodges, Smith, and Co. 1856.

O'Reilly, Edward. *An Irish-English Dictionary*. Dublin: J. Barlow. 1817.

Oppenheim, Michael (ed.). *The Naval Tracts of Sir W. Monson*. five vols. London: Navy Records Society. 1902–1904.

Owen, Aneurin. 'The Hengwrt MSS.'. *Cambrian Journal* (Alban Arthan 1859).

276–296.

Owen, William. *The Heroic Elegies and Other Pieces of Llywarç Hen, Prince of the Cumbrian Britons.* London: Printed for J. Owen and E. Williams. 1792.

Parry, John (gol.). *Y Gwyddoniadur Cymreig: gan Ysgrifenwyr Enwocaf y Genedl.* Dinbych: Thomas Gee. 1856–1879.

Parry, Thomas. 'Daniel Silvan Evans, 1818–1903'. *Trafodion Anrhydeddus Gymdeithas y Cymmrodorion.* (1981). 109–185.

[Peckham, Sir George]. *A Trve Reporte, of the late Discoueries, and Possession, taken in the Right of the Crowne of Englande, of the Newfound Landes: By that Valiaunt and Worthye Gentleman, Sir Humfrey Gilbert Knight.* London: I.C. for Iohn Hinde. 1583.

Phillips, D. Rhys. *A Romantic Valley in Wales: The History of the Vale of Neath.* facsimile edn. Llandybïe: Welsh Glamorgan County Archive Service and Neath Borough Council. 1994.

Pictet, Adolphe. *Le Mystère des Bardes de l'Ile de Bretagne ou la Doctrine des Bardes Gallois du Moyen Age.* Genève: Joël Cherbuliez. 1856.

Pinkerton, John. *A Dissertation on the Origin and Progress of the Scythians or Goths. Being an Introduction to the Ancient and Modern History of Europe.* London: John Nichols. 1787.

—. *A General Collection of the Best and Most Interesting Voyages and Travels in All Parts of the World.* seventeen vols. London: Hurst, Rees, and Orme. 1808–1814.

Pope, Alexander. *An Essay on Man, Being the First Book of Ethic Epistles. To Henry St John, L Bolingbroke.* London: John Wright for Lawton Gilliver. 1734

Powel, David. *The Historie of Cambria, Now Called Wales: A Part of the Most Famous Yland of Brytaine, Written in the Brytish Language about Two Hundreth Yeares Past: Translated into English by H. Lhoyd Gentleman: Corrected, Augmented, and Continued out of Records and Best Approoued Authors.* [London: Rafe Newberie and Henrie Denham. 1584]. (Reprinted London: John Harding. 1811).

Price, Thomas (Carnhuanawc). *Hanes Cymru a Chenedl y Cymry, o'r Cynoesoedd hyd at Farwolaeth Llewelyn ap Gruffydd.* Crughywel: Thomas Williams. 1842.

Prichard, James Cowles. *The Eastern Origin of the Celtic Nations Proved by a Comparison of their Dialects with the Sanscrit, Greek, Latin, and Teutonic Languages: Forming a Supplement to Researches into the Physical History of Mankind.* ed. by R. G. Latham. London: Houlston and Wright. 1857.

Purchas, Samuel. *Haklvytvs Posthumus or Pvrchas his Pilgrimes. Contayning a History of the World, in Sea Voyages & Lande Trauells, by Englishmen & Others.* London: Henrie Fetherstone [1625].

Rearick, Charles. 'Henry Martin: From Druidic Traditions to Republican Politics'. *Journal of Contemporary History.* 7: 3/4 (July–October 1972). 53–64.

[Redwood, Charles]. *The Vale of Glamorgan: Scenes and Tales among the Welsh.* London: Saunders and Otley. 1839.

Rees, Thomas. *History of Protestant Nonconformity in Wales from its Rise to the Present Time.* London: John Snow. 1861.

Rees, W. J. *Liber Landavensis, Llyfr Teilo, or the Ancient Register of the Cathedral Church of Llandaff; From MSS. in the Libraries of Hengwrt, and of Jesus College, Oxford.* Llandovery: William Rees 1840.

—. *Lives of the Cambro British Saints, of the Fifth and Immediate Succeeding Centuries, from Ancient Welsh and Latin MSS, in the British Museum and Elsewhere, with English Translations, and Explanatory Notes.* Llandovery: Welsh MSS. Society. 1853.

Reynolds, Llywarch, 'Editor's Preface' in Thomas Stephens. *Madoc: An Essay on the Discovery of America by Madoc ap Owen Gwynedd in the Twelfth Century.* ed. by Llywarch Reynolds. London: Longmans, Green, and Co. 1893. pp. v–xv.

Roberts, Brynley F. 'Welsh Scholarship at Merthyr Tydfil'. *Merthyr Historian.* 10 (1999). 51–62.

—. 'Mab ei Dad Taliesin ab Iolo Morganwg' in Hywel Teifi Edwards (ed.). *Merthyr a Thaf.* Llandysul: Gwasg Gomer. 2001. pp. 57–91.

—. '"The Age of Restitution": Taliesin ab Iolo and the Reception of Iolo Morganwg' in Geraint H. Jenkins (ed.) *A Rattleskull Genius: The Many Faces of Iolo Morganwg.* Cardiff: University of Wales Press. 2005. pp. 461–79.

—. 'Taliesin ab Iolo'. *Merthyr Historian.* 20 (2009). 47–59.

Roebuck, John Arthur. *History of the Whig Ministry of 1830, to the Passing of the Reform Bill.* two vols. London: John W. Parker and Son. 1852.

Rowlands, Henry. *Mona Antiqua Restaurata: An Archaeological Discourse on the Antiquities, Natural and Historical, of the Isle of Anglesey, the Ancient Seat of the British Druids.* Dublin: Robert Owen. 1723.

Schoolcraft, Henry R. *Travels in the Central Portions of the Mississippi Valley: Comprising Observations on its Mineral Geography, Internal Resources, and Aboriginal Population.* New York: Collins and Hannay. 1825.

Schulz, Albert (San Marte). *Die Sagen von Merlin. Mit wälschen, bretagnischen, schottischen, italienischen, und lateinischen Gedichten und Prophezeihungen Merlins, de Prophetia Merlini des Gottfried von Monmouth, und der Vita Merlini, lateinischem Gedichte aus dem driezehnten Jahrhundert.* Halle: Verlag der Buchhandlung des Waisenhauses. 1853.

—. *Gottfried's von Monmouth Historia Regum Britanniae, mit literar-historischer Einleitung und ausführlichen Anmerk-ungen, und Prut Tysylio, altwälsche Chronik in deutscher Uebersetzung.* Halle: Eduard Anton. 1854.

—. (Trans.). *Geschichte der wälschen Literatur von XII. bis zum XIV. Jahrhundert Gekrönte Preisschrift von Thomas Stephens.* Halle: Berlag der Buchhandlung des Waisenhauses. 1864.

Scott, Walter. *Marmion; A Tale of Flodden Field.* second edn. Edinburgh: J. Ballantyne and Co. 1808.

—. *The Lady of the Lake. A Poem.* Edinburgh: James Ballantyne and Co. 1810.

Shaw, William. *An Analysis of the Gaelic Language.* Edinburgh: W. and T. Ruddiman. 1788.

Skene, William F. *The Four Ancient Books of Wales: Containing the Cymric Poems Attributed to the Bards of the Sixth Century.* two vols. Edinburgh: Edmonston and Douglas. 1868.

Smirke, E. 'An Account of an Ancient Inscribed Stone Found at Fardel, near Ivybridge, in Devon'. *Royal Institution of Cornwall.* Spring 1861. 1–16.

—. 'An Account of an Ancient Inscribed Stone Found at Fardel, near Ivybridge, in Devon'. *Archaeologia Cambrensis*, Third Series, 28 (October 1861).

Smith, John. *The Generall Historie of Virginia, New-England, and the Summer Isles with the Names of the Adventurers, Planters, and Governours from their First Beginning An: 1584 to this Present 1624. With the Procedings of those Severall Colonies and the Accidents that Befell them in all their Journyes and Discoveries. Also the Maps and Descriptions of all those Countryes, their Commodities, People, Government, Customes, and Religion yet Knowne. Divided into Six Bookes.* London: I.D. and I.H. 1624.

Stephens, Thomas. *The Literature of the Kymry: Being a Critical Essay on the History of the Language and Literature of Wales.* Llandovery: William Rees. 1849.

—. 'The Poems of Taliesin. No. 1'. *Archaeologia Cambrensis.* New Series. 6 (April 1851). 149–55.

—. 'The Poems of Taliesin. No. III'. *Archaeologia Cambrensis.* New Series, 8

(October 1851). 261–74.

—. 'Studies in British Biography I: Dyvynwal Moelmud'. *Cambrian Journal.* 1 (Alban Hevin 1854). 160–72.

—. 'Studies in British Biography II: The Laws of Dyvynwal Moelmud'. *Cambrian Journal.* 6 (February 1855). 33–59.

—. 'On the Names of Cromlechau'. *Archaeologia Cambrensis.* Third Series. 6 (April 1856). 99–109.

—. Studies in British Biography III: Prydain ab Aedd Mawr'. *Cambrian Journal.* 4 (Alban Arthan 1857). 241–67.

—. 'Sefyllfa Wareiddiol y Cymry'. *Y Traethodydd.* 13 (1857). 230–40, 297–323, 385–415.

—. 'Llewarch Hen and Uriconium'. *Archaeologia Cambrensis.* Third Series, no. 37 (January 1864). 62–74.

—. 'The Chair of Glamorgan'. *Archaeology Cambrensis.* Fourth Series. 11 (July 1872). 262.

—. 'An Essay on the Bardic Alphabet Called "Coelbren y Beirdd"'. *Archaeologia Cambrensis.* Fourth Series. 11 (July 1872). 181–210.

—. *The Gododin of Aneurin Gwawdrydd: An English Translation with Copius Explanitory Notes; A Life of Aneurin; and Several Lengthy Dissertations Illustrative of the 'Gododin', and the Battle of Cattraeth.* ed. by Thomas Powel. London: The Honourable Society of Cymmrodorion. 1888.

—. *Madoc: An Essay on the Discovery of America by Madoc ap Owen Gwynedd in the Twelfth Century.* ed. by Llywarch Reynolds. London: Longmans, Green, and Co. 1893.

Taylor, Margaret S. 'Thomas Stephens of Merthyr (1821–1875)'. *Merthyr Historian.* 2 (1978). 135–41.

Thomas, Ben Bowen. 'The Cambrians and the Nineteenth-Century Crisis in Welsh Studies, 1847–1870'. *Archaeologia Cambrensis.* 127 (1978). 1–15.

Thomas, Mair Elvet. *The Welsh Spirit of Gwent.* Cardiff: University of Wales Press. 1988.

Thorne, David. 'Cymreigyddion Y Fenni a Dechreuadau Ieitheg Cymharol yng Nghymru'. *National Library of Wales Journal.* 27: 1 (Summer 1991). 97–107.

Trübner, Nicholas. *Trübner's Bibliographical Guide to American Literature.* London: Trübner and Co. 1859.

Tyler, J. Endell. *Henry of Monmouth, or Memoirs of the Life of Character of Henry the Fifth, as Prince of Wales and King of England.* two vols. London:

Richard Bentley. 1838.

Vallancey, Charles. *A Grammar of the Iberno-Celtic or Irish Language to which is Prefixed an Essay on Celtic Language.* Dublin: R. Marchbank. 1782.

—. *Prospectus of a Dictionary of the Language of the Aire Coti, or Ancient Irish.* Dublin: Graisberry and Cambell. 1802.

Van Hulle, Dirk and Joep Leerssen (eds). *Editing the Nation's Memory: Textual Scholarship and Nation-Building in Nineteenth-Century Europe.* Amsterdam: Rodopi. 2008.

Wachteri, Johannis Georgii. *Glossarivm Germanicvm Contens Origines et Antiqvitates Totius Lingvæ Germanicæ, et Omnium Pene Vocabulorum, Vigentium et Desitorum.* Leipzig: Joh. Frid. Gleditschii B. Filium. 1737.

Walter, Ferdinand. *Das alte Wales. Ein Beitrag zur Völker-, Rechts- und Kirchen-Geschichte.* Bonn: Adoph Marcus. 1859.

Walters, Huw. 'Myfyr Morganwg and the Rocking-Stone Gorsedd'. in Geraint H. Jenkins (ed.). *A Rattleskull Genius: The Many Faces of Iolo Morganwg* (Cardiff: University of Wales Press. 2005. pp. 481–500.

Watt, Robert. *Bibliotheca Britannica; or a General Index to British and Foreign Literature.* four vols. Edinburgh: Archibald Constable and Company. 1824.

Westwood, J. O. 'Ogham Characters in Glamorganshire'. *Archaeologia Cambrensis.* 2 (April 1846). 182–3.

—. 'The Turpillian Inscription, near Crickhowel, Brecknockshire, Welsh Oghams, Bardic Alphabet and Destruction of Ancient Monuments'. *Archaeologia Cambrensis.* 5 (January 1847). 25–29.

—. 'The Early Inscribed and Sculptured Stones of Wales'. *Ar-chaeologia Cambrensis.* Third Series, 23 (July 1860). 223–28.

Wheeler, John H. *Historical Sketches of North Carolina, From 1854 to 1851. Compiled from Original Records, Official Documents, and Traditional Statements,* two vols. Philadelphia: Lippencott, Grambo and Co. 1851.

Wilde, W. R. *Irish Popular Superstitions.* Dublin: William S. Orr and Co. [1852].

Wilkins, Charles. *The History of Merthyr Tydfil.* Merthyr Tydfil: Harry Wood Southey. 1867.

Williams, B. T. 'The Life of Thomas Stephens' in Thomas Stephens. *The Literature of the Kymry: Being a Critical Essay on the History of the Language and Literature of Wales During the Twelfth and Succeeding Centuries.* ed. by D. Silvan Evans. second edn. London: Longmans, Green, and Co. 1876. pp. xix–xlviii

Williams, E. I. 'Thomas Stephens and Carnhuanawc on the "Blue Books" of 1847'. *Bulletin of the Board of Celtic Studies.* 9: 3 (November 1938). 271–274.

Williams, Glanmore. 'Printers Publishers and Book-Lovers in Merthyr Tydfil'. *Merthyr Historian.* 11 (2000). 1–11.

Williams, Gwyn A. 'The Merthyr of Dic Penderyn' in Glanmor Williams (ed.). *Merthyr Politics: The Making of a Working-Class Tradition.* Cardiff: University of Wales Press. 1966, pp. 9–27.

—. *Madoc: The Making of a Myth.* London: Eyre Methuen. 1979.

—. *The Merthyr Rising.* Cardiff: University of Wales Press. 1988.

Williams, Heather. 'La construction du Moyen Âge dans les récits de voyage français portant sur le pays de Galles, ou: Alfred Erny, celtomane en Galles en 1862'. in Hélène Bouget and Magali Coumert (eds). *Enjeux épistémologiques des recherches sur les Bretagnes médiévales en histoire, langue et litérature.* Brest : CRBC-UBO. 2018. pp. 1–17.

Williams, J. Gwynn. *The University of Wales 1839–1939.* Cardiff: University of Wale Press. 1997.

Williams, Jane (ed.). *The Literary Remains of the Rev. Thomas Price, Carnhuanawc.* two vols. Llandovery. William Rees. 1854–55.

Williams, John. 'On One Source of the Non-Hellenic Portion of the Latin Language'. *Transactions of the Royal Society of Edinburgh.* 13: 2 (January 1836). 494–563.

—. 'Cyfrinach y Beirdd'. *The Cambrian Journal.* 15 (Sep 1857). 224–27.

Williams, John (Ab Ithel) (ed. and trans.). *Y Gododin. A Poem on the Battle of Cattraeth, by Aneurin with an English Translation, and Numerous Historical and Critical Annotations.* Llandovery: William Rees. 1852.

—. 'Editorial Note'. *Cambrian Journal.* 6 (February 1855). 59.

—. (ed. and trans.), *Dosparth Edeyrn Davod Aur; or The Ancient Welsh Grammar, Which Was Compiled by Royal Command in the Thirteenth Century by Edyrn the Golden Tongued, To Which is Added Y Pum Llyfr Kerddwriaeth, Or the Rules of Welsh Poetry, Originally Compiled by Davydd Ddu Athraw, in the Fourteenth, and Subsequently Enlarged by Simwnt Vychan, in the Sixteenth Century.* Llandovery: William Rees. 1856.

—. 'An Essay of the Discovery of America in the Twelfth Century by Prince Madoc ap Owen Gwynedd'. *Cambrian Journal.* (Alban Hevin and Alban Elvid 1859). 90–106, 161–193.

—. *Barddas; or a Collection of Original Documents, Illustrative of the*

Theology, Wisdom, and Usages of the Bardo-Druidic System of the Isle of Britain. Llandovery: Welsh MSS. Society. 1862.

Williams, Robert (ed.). *Enwogion Cymru, A Biographical Dictionary of Eminent Welshmen*. Llandovery: William Rees. 1852.

Williams, Taliesin (ab Iolo). *The Iolo Manuscripts: A Selection of Ancient Welsh Manuscripts, in Proze and Verse, from the Collection Made by the late Edward Williams, Iolo Morganwg, for the Purpose of Forming a Continuation of the Myfyrian Archaiology; and Subsequently Proposed as Materials for a New History of Wales*. Llandovery: William Rees. 1848.

Zeuss, J. C. *Grammatica Celtica*. Leipzig: Weidmannos. 1853.

Unpublished Theses

Gruber, Edith. 'King Arthur and the Privy Councillor: Albert Schulz as a Cultural Mediator Between the Literary Fields of Nineteenth-century Wales and Germany'. unpublished PhD thesis. Bangor University. 2013.

Newspapers

Cardiff Times

Cardiff and Merthyr Guardian, Glamorgan, Monmouth, and Brecon Gazette

Merthyr Telegraph, and General Advertiser for the Iron Districts of South Wales

Monmouthshire Merlin

North Wales Chronicle and Advertiser for the Principality

Star of Gwent

The Western Mail

Reference Works and Online Resources

Allgemeine Deutsche Biographie

American National Biography

Dictionary of Irish Biography

Dictionary of Welsh Biography Online

European Travellers to Wales Database

Lexikon der Schweiz

Oxford Dictionary of National Biography

Welsh Journals Online

Welsh Newspapers Online

Stephens, Meic. *The New Companion to the Literature of Wales*. Cardiff: University of Wales Press. 1998.

INDEX

INDEX

IN THIS index, page numbers in **bold** refer to pages on which a letter to or from an individual appears. With the exception of works by Thomas Stephens, references to printed works appear under their author's name.

Also available from Celtic Studies Press:

THE ADVENTURES AND VAGARIES OF
TWM SHON CATTI
DESCRIPTIVE OF LIFE IN WALES
INTERSPERSED WITH POEMS

T. J. LLEWELYN PRICHARD
Edited with an Introduction by Rita Singer

For further information and a view of the full catalogue of
CSP-Cymru Cyf, please visit our website:
https://celticstudies.wales